AF526425

DAMPIER VII

GUYNES
PRINTING COMPANY OF NEW MEXICO, INC.
2709 GIRARD N.E. • ALBUQUERQUE, NEW MEXICO 87107 • (505) 884-8882

IN THE WAKE OF THE BUCCANEERS

IN THE WAKE OF THE BUCCANEERS

BY

A. HYATT VERRILL

AUTHOR OF "PANAMA, PAST AND PRESENT," "ISLES OF SPICE AND PALM," "THE BOOK OF THE WEST INDIES," "THE REAL STORY OF THE PIRATE," ETC.

ILLUSTRATED WITH DRAWINGS AND PHOTOGRAPHS BY THE AUTHOR AND RARE OLD ENGRAVINGS

The Rio Grande Press, Inc.

GLORIETA, NEW MEXICO · 87535

First edition from which this edition was reproduced was
supplied by
INTERNATIONAL BOOKFINDERS, Inc.,
P. O. Box 1
Pacific Palisades, Calif. 90272

A RIO GRANDE CLASSIC

First published in 1923.

ISBN 0-87380-168-7

First Printing
1990

IN THE WAKE OF THE BUCCANEERS

THE DANGEROUS VOYAGE

IN THE WAKE OF THE BUCCANEERS

BY

A. HYATT VERRILL

AUTHOR OF "PANAMA, PAST AND PRESENT," "ISLES OF SPICE AND PALM," "THE BOOK OF THE WEST INDIES," "THE REAL STORY OF THE PIRATE," ETC.

ILLUSTRATED WITH DRAWINGS AND PHOTOGRAPHS BY THE AUTHOR AND RARE OLD ENGRAVINGS

PUBLISHED BY THE CENTURY CO.

NEW YORK AND LONDON MCMXXIII

Copyright, 1923, by
THE CENTURY CO.

PRINTED IN U. S. A.

INTRODUCTION

There is no more entrancing body of water in either the Western or the Eastern Hemisphere—than the Caribbean Sea, with a fringe of lovely tropical islands on the one side and on the other the Spanish Main and its picturesque centuries-old towns and fascinating sights. Aside from its beauty, its delightful climate, and its ever-shifting scenes, the Caribbean and its shores are redolent of romance. It was the starting-point of those brave though ruthless adventurers who carved a new world for Castile and Leon. For centuries it was the treasure-house of the world and the battle-ground of the mightiest European powers. Across this sapphire sea sailed the caravels of Columbus, the *Golden Hind* of Drake, and the stately, plate-laden galleons of Spain.

And across this same sea coursed those fierce sea-rovers the buccaneers.

Of all the dare-devil spirits who sailed the Caribbean and ravaged the Spanish Main, the buccaneers were the most picturesque and romantic.

Villains though they were; reddened with the blood of the innocent and helpless though their hands; black-hearted cutthroats beyond denial—yet there is something about them that appeals to all, and that, despite their ill deeds, fills one with admiration.

Perchance it is the fact that we all appreciate bravery—and, notwithstanding their multitude of sins, the buccaneers were brave beyond compare. Again, it may be that in all of us lurks a little of the gambling spirit and we admire those who can take a chance, even though we do not, and no greater gamblers ever lived than the buccaneers. They staked their lives at every turn, they gambled with death, and the greater the odds the more readily did they throw themselves into the game. And it was this gambling spirit, this recklessness that enabled them to defy the world of their day.

We hear much of the bold, wild ways of these adventurers; we have been taught by history and tradition to consider them devoid of redeeming qualities, and few of us realize that the buccaneers were far from being true pirates, that they were not alike, that many were corsairs through force of circumstances rather than by choice, that they had their own laws and code of honor, and that they were a most important factor in shaping the destiny of the New World. To them, incredible as it may seem, we owe an immense debt of gratitude. Had it not been for them the British never would have retained their foothold in the Caribbean, and we, to-day, might be under Spanish rule. Many of them, too, were educated men and left us records which are of incalculable scientific or historic value; for example, Dampier, who was a keenly observant field naturalist and devoted far more of his time to penning descriptions of fauna and flora than to slitting Spanish throats; [1] and Esquemelling,[2] the erstwhile accountant, who

1 Dampier was the son of a Somerset farmer, but at seventeen years of age was apprenticed to a sea captain sailing from Weymouth. Deserting in the West Indies, he took to the occupation of a logwood cutter for a time, and later joined the buccaneers. He wrote several books, working at his manuscripts between battles, and keeping his notes in a joint of bamboo which, to use his own words, he "kept stopt at the ends with wax to keep out water. In this I preserved my Journal and other Writings tho' I was often forced to swim." His descriptions of fauna and flora, his maps, and his detailed accounts of the Indians and their customs and languages are of great scientific value, though his conclusions are often erroneous.

2 Esquemelling was a Hollander who went to Hispaniola in the capacity of clerk for the French West India Company. When the latter withdrew their business from Tortuga and sold off all their possessions, the clerk went to the auction block with the other chattels and was purchased for three hundred pieces of eight (approximately $300.00) by a cruel master. Under the treatment accorded him Esquemelling became dangerously ill, and his owner, fearing to lose his slave and his money at the same time, disposed of the sick man, for seventy pieces of eight, to a surgeon who treated Esquemelling kindly, nursed him to health, and granted him his freedom on condition that the penniless ex-clerk should pay him one

left us a classic as a result of his years as a ship's supercargo among the buccaneers.

Yearly, Americans by the thousands flock southward to tour or to stop for a time in the West Indies or about the shores of the Caribbean, but few of these are aware of the intimate associations with the buccaneers which all these places hold. Yet we may dwell in the very hostelry wherein pirate chieftains reveled and spent their ill-gotten gold; we stroll through little towns which have echoed to the ribald songs and lusty shouts of roistering pirate crews; we sail, in palatial steamships, above the long-forgotten hulks of burned and scuttled galleons, and we haggle with shopkeepers or native boatmen in whose veins may flow the blood of Morgan, Hawkins, or Montbars.

Bereft of the buccaneers, the Caribbean and its shores lose their greatest fascination, and as the most desirable localities are those intimately associated with the sea-rovers and their deeds or misdeeds, it seems fitting to travel about the Spanish Main and the West Indies in the wake of the buccaneers.

It is to point out the romantic associations of

hundred pieces of eight when able to do so. He promptly joined the buccaneers and took part in most of their notable exploits for nearly seven years. His records, especially his "Buccaneers of America," are the best histories of these men extant.

these waters and islands and make a visit to them more interesting, to weave a little of the lives and deeds of the buccaneers into the story of the locality, and to give brief sketches of the most noteworthy, while at the same time describing the places, their attractions, and their present condition, that this book has been prepared.

So much of a purely fictional nature has been related of these sea-rovers that many of the statements contained herein will come as a distinct surprise, for time and tales have woven a glamour and a deal of misconception about them. But even stripped of all romance, with their histories before us, the "Brethren of the Main" retain enough and to spare of adventure, deeds of daring, and picturesque villainy, and many of the true stories of these men are more thrilling, more astounding than any the imagination could invent.

When such stories are made more vivid by a setting of actual present-day scenes, or are read in the very places and in the same surroundings in which the buccaneers held forth, their interest is enhanced, while the whole neighborhood is given an added attraction.

The author, who has lived and traveled in the West Indies and about the shores of the Caribbean for nearly thirty years, knows every island and town intimately. Being deeply interested in the history of the vicinity and particularly in the reckless freebooters who frequented it, he has written this narrative of a most novel cruise. A cruise taken in a real pirate ship manned by a native West Indian crew some of whom were lineal descendants of notorious buccaneers; and while not all the Caribbean islands or the lands and towns of the Spanish Main were visited, those places are included which are of particular interest from an historical point of view and their associations with the freebooters.

The volume is not intended as a guide-book, but rather as a colorful account of the places visited on this unusual cruise; a description of many little-known, out-of-the-way corners; with mention of their most interesting features, the customs of the people, a bit of their turbulent past and their somnolent present, and their existing relics of buccaneer days.

TABLE OF CONTENTS

LIST OF ILLUSTRATIONS

IN THE WAKE OF THE BUCCANEERS

The Cruise in the Wake of the Buccaneers

IN THE WAKE OF THE BUCCANEERS

CHAPTER I

AMONG THE CARIBBEES

I HAD started forth on a novel journey, a trip I had long wanted to take—a cruise in the wake of the buccaneers. Many a time I had traversed the Caribbean, steaming from port to port of those island gems, the Lesser Antilles, that are strung, like emeralds and sapphires, in a great curving chain stretching from our own St. Thomas, five days south of New York, to Trinidad at the mouth of the Orinoco. Many a time, too, I had skirted the coasts, climbed the mountains, and explored the bush of Cuba, Porto Rico, Santo Domingo, and Jamaica. And whenever I had stood upon a liner's deck and watched the huge-sailed island sloops and schooners courtesying to the sparkling waves and, with lee rails awash, surging through the blue sea toward some distant isle, I had envied those aboard.

I had vowed that sooner or later I too would stand upon the heaving deck of a nimble sailing-craft and cruise hither and thither among the islands, going and coming as humor willed, seeing the out-of-the-way places, the little-known islets, the hidden, quiet bays and coves which no churning screws had disturbed and no smoke-belching funnels had besmirched.

No locality is more filled with romance, more remindful of adventurous deeds of the past, more closely associated with the early history of our country than the Caribbean. Here is the islet first sighted by Columbus after his long and thrilling voyage into the west. Here dwelt the conquistadors, the explorers, the voyagers who with fire and blood blazed their trails across the continents of North and South America. Here one may still see the crumbling houses in which such noted old dons as Ponce de Leon, De Soto, Pizarro, Cortez, and others dwelt when Hispaniola (Santo Domingo) was the center of wealth and fashion in New Spain. Here was established the first university of the New World wherein Las Casas taught his pupils a century and more before the *Mayflower* sailed into Plymouth harbor. Here the great nations of Europe contended for control of the new-found lands, and here cruised the buccaneers, ever seeking their prizes. But to sail these waters and visit these isles in a modern steamship robs them of their greatest charm. Who can visualize gilded, purple-sailed galleons swinging to anchor when buff steel masts, huge funnels, and wireless aërials fill the foreground? Who can picture swashbuckling, roistering pirates when the streets they once trod swarm with jitneys? Who can imagine mail-clad men about to embark on some great adventure when the jetty bears a creaking, wheezing crane, and sweating negro stevedores bustle and crowd and swear? No, to find the romance of these islands, to visualize their past and appreciate their present, one must forego luxuries and leave the beaten path, and, like the voyagers of old, seek new scenes in a white-sailed craft whose motive power is the humming trade wind and whose crew is made up of natives who, in appearance at least, might well have stepped out of the past.

And at last Fate—in the guise of good-natured and sympathetic friends in the islands—had made possible my dream and I was cruising one-time pirate waters in a pirate ship. Yes, a real pirate ship, the *Vigilant,* whose solid teak keel was laid well over a century ago; the oldest boat plying the Caribbean, but still as stanch, seaworthy, and fast as when, manned by sea-rovers, she had swept under her cloud of canvas upon some lumbering merchantman or had showed her fleet heels to British corvettes, as, laden with a cargo of "black ivory," she had crept forth from the fetid mouth of some African river, bound with her human freight for the slave marts of the Antilles. Privateer, pirate, slaver, and man-o'-war she had been in turn through the long years she had sailed the seas. Within her hold were still visible the ring-bolts to which the groaning blacks had been chained. In her timbers were still the wounds of round shot and bullets, and despite her peaceful present-day employment as a packet between the islands, she was yet the typical pirate craft—the "long, low, black schooner with raking masts" so dear to writers of lurid fiction.[1] And we were bound to that erstwhile haunt of the sea-rovers, the Virgin Islands.

[1] According to the most reliable records, the *Vigilant* was built in Baltimore in the latter part of the eighteenth century. Originally named the *Nonesuch,* she was intended for a privateer, but, the Revolution being virtually over before she was launched, she was sold and won an unsavory reputation as a pirate. She later turned privateer, during the War of 1812, and afterward engaged in the slave-trade until England's anti-slavery crusade made this work too dangerous. She was then sold again, and became a notorious smuggler. Still later she changed hands once more, and under her new owner, a Danish West Indian merchant, resumed privateering with letters of marque from the Danish Government. In 1825 the *Vigilant* became a man-of-war. A Spanish privateer had been harassing the Danish shipping, and, all available Danish warships being too large to follow through the shallow channels where she sought refuge, the *Vigilant* was chartered and a company of soldiers

When Columbus, cruising westward on his second voyage, sighted these green-clad islets rising above the blue Caribbean, he despaired of finding saint's names for all of them, and so called them collectively "The Virgins," in honor of the eleven thousand companions of St. Ursula. The name was not inappropriate, for while there were not eleven thousand of the isles, they were far too numerous to be counted. The history of these bits of wave-washed coral and volcanic rock, since their discovery by the great navigator, has been anything but happy and peaceful. The Spaniards, finding neither gold nor precious stones upon them, contented themselves with kidnapping the primitive inhabitants and then, having depopulated the islands, left them severely alone. Later, after a period of varying fortunes and misfortunes, they were parceled off among the European powers, changed hands over and over again, were sold, bartered, and fought for,

concealed upon her. As she cruised within sight of the privateer the latter swept down upon her, thinking her a helpless merchantman, only to be surprised and completely overwhelmed by the hidden troops. After this episode the old schooner became a peaceful mail-packet among the Virgin Islands. She has been repeatedly sunk and raised again. In the hurricane of 1876 she went on a reef off Christiansted, St. Croix, and again, in 1916, a hurricane sent her to the bottom in almost the same spot. Her rig originally was that of a topsail schooner, but this was later changed to that of a fore-and-aft schooner with gaff topsails. Probably very little besides the keel and timbers of the original craft remains, as she has been repaired from time to time during her long career.

and at last, with the exception of St. Thomas, St. Croix, and one or two others, were dubbed worthless and were virtually forgotten by the nations which had battled so long and bloodily to retain them.

Here in close proximity, often but two or three miles apart, were islands belonging to half a dozen powers,—British, French, Danish, Swedish, Dutch,—with one owned jointly by Holland and France, while close at hand, conveniently and temptingly near, in fact, were rich Spanish possessions. And here, to the eleven thousand Virgins, came the pirates and the buccaneers. So it was fitting that my cruise in the ancient but rejuvenated *Vigilant* should begin with the Virgin Isles.

Presently, above the impossibly blue sea loomed a bit of land, a tiny, gray-green, barren cay, rimmed with ragged, weather-beaten rocks in whose coves and hollows coral beaches gleamed, white as the beating surf, beyond the turquoise water. Leaning upon the schooner's rail, I gazed idly and curiously at the little isle, the one break upon the shimmering sea, a lonely spot whose only signs of life were the circling sea-birds hovering over it in clouds.

I turned to the fellow at the wheel—a giant of a man, black as ebony and muscled like a Hercules, naked to the waist, his dungaree trousers rolled to his knees and supported by a wisp of scarlet sash, his huge flat feet wide-spread, and a flapping jipi-japa hat upon his huge head. His lusterless eyes, bloodshot from constant diving (for he was a sponger by profession), and the huge hoops in his ears, gave him a fierce, wild look, and, glancing at him, one might well have imagined him a member of a pirate crew, a corsair steering toward some doomed prize.

"Sam," I asked, "what 's that island over there to port?"

The big negro slowly turned his head and gazed at the speck of rock and sand.

"Tha' 's Dead Man's Chest, Chief," he replied in the soft drawl of the Bahaman.

Dead Man's Chest! Instantly, at his words, the song made famous by Stevenson flashed through my mind: "Fifteen men on the Dead Man's Chest —Yo-ho-ho, and a bottle of rum!"

Dead Man's Chest! The little cay at once took on a new interest. Now I could almost picture them yonder,—those shipwrecked men, fifteen of them,—gaunt, fierce-visaged, unshorn; sprawled on the sand in the scanty shade of the twisted sea-grape trees above the surf. Marooned, cast away, but reckless daredevils to the last; gambling in the face of death, tossing a gleaming golden doubloon in their final game of chance—the stake, their lives against that one bottle of rum! And then drink and the devil would have done for them as for the rest, and only their whitening bones over which the sea-birds fought and screamed would remain to tell their grim tale.

Dead Man's Chest! What more fitting than that this bit of ocean-girt land should have been the first of the isles made famous by the buccaneers to greet my eyes, and what more appropriate than that I should have sighted it from the deck of a real pirate craft! Fortunate indeed had I been when her owners delivered the *Vigilant* into my hands for my cruise, and I pondered, as we sped past wave-beaten Dead Man's Chest, on the story the *Vigilant* might tell could she but speak. Then my thoughts were brought back to the present as Sam spoke:

"The' says as how the' 's plenty o' tr'asure yonder, on Dead Man's Chest," he remarked, "but Ah can' say as how true 't is, Chief. Plenty folks has s'arched for it, but Ah can' say as the' 's foun' it. I 'spec' the' 's tr'asure a plenty on th' cays here 'bout. The' says as how th' pirates was num'rous roun' here."

"Yes, it was a great place for pirates," I replied.

"You know these islands well, Sam. Have you ever run across any old guns or forts or wrecks on any of them? By the way, what 's your last name?"

Sam grinned.

"Ah got a right funny name, Chief," he responded. "Ah don' 'spec' you ever hear it. It 's Lithgow, Chief."

Lithgow! What a name to conjure with, in the old buccaneer days! Red Lithgow, the bold, unprincipled pirate chieftain who hailed from Louisiana and met death at the end of a rope from his own yard-arm! Perchance—nay, in all probability—some of the old rascal's blood still flowed in Sam's veins; for all through the islands one finds lineal descendants (though they may be brown, black, or yellow) of the buccaneers, whose progeny was legion.

But Sam was again speaking, replying to my first question and telling me that hidden among the brush and weeds on St. John, St. Martin, and others of the Virgins, were numerous old walls, ruins, and cannon which, rumor had it, were relics of the pirates who once made the islands their stronghold.

My itinerary included all of these in turn, and so the *Vigilant's* course remained unaltered and with the wind humming through the taut rigging and filling the great straining sails, we rushed on toward St. Thomas, looming like a cloud upon the horizon far ahead.

And now, as the schooner races onward toward the quaint port of Charlotte Amalie, a word about the crew that manned the *Vigilant;* for Sam was not by any means the only or the most important personage besides myself. A mixed lot they were, but most valuable factors in my cruise and an entertaining lot as well. Originally they were all Virgin Islanders, save Sam, the Bahaman pilot and "captain," and Joseph, the long-legged, solemn-faced cook, who, notwithstanding his ebony skin and kinky head, dubbed all of his race "stupid niggers," who found everything not to his liking "pure corruption," and who proudly boasted of being a Turks Island boy.

With the Chesterfieldian manners of a duke, painstakingly perfect English, and the dignity of a Spanish grandee, Joseph looked down upon the "stupid niggers" of the crew as from an impregnable height, and fraternized with Sam only, the others being merely tolerated. A right good cook and a faithful boy was Joe, and a never-ending source of amusement because of his assumption of a sort of guardianship over me.

But ere the cruise was over he and Sam and one other were the only remaining members of my original crew. Never did the *Vigilant's* mud-hook seek bottom in the limpid waters of some lovely isle that one or more of my sailors did not desert. Not that they had aught of which to complain, or found their duties on the ship irksome, but good American dollars in their pockets, a rich green shore, and chocolate-colored sirens were temptations beyond the black man's power to resist. Yet never were we short-handed. For every man who left, a score clamored to be taken on, and had the *Vigilant* been on a pirating adventure I could have filled her to the hatches with as varicolored and vari-charactered a crew as ever swarmed over the bulwarks of a stricken prize.

To the West Indians, every American is a millionaire and a philanthropist, and in their eyes, apparently, he is morally bound to carry each, all, and sundry to that dreamed-of-land the States, the Mecca of every inhabitant of the islands. Wherever the *Vigilant* folded her white wings and came to rest, we were besieged by a small army of black, brown, yellow, and every intermediate shade, all begging to be allowed to accompany us. For the West Indian is a restless soul, never content unless on the move and caring not a jot where day or night may find him, albeit he is intensely patriotic, and thinks his island preferable to all others and his people the salt of the earth.

Thus it came about that, what with deserters and new-comers, the crew was a sort of kaleidoscopic aggregation, shifting from yellow to brown, from black to tan, from soft-voiced, slurring-tongued "patois men" to h-dropping 'Badians and brogue-speaking Montserratans. And a happy family they were at that—good-naturedly chaffing one another, having long-winded arguments over the respective merits of their various island homes, using preposterous, meaningless words of their own invention. And all and each making life miserable for the hapless natives of that "right little, tight little island" designated on the maps as Barbados, affectionately dubbed "Little England" by its sons and daughters, and also known as "Bimshire Land," [1] whose natives seem for some strange reason ever to be the butt and the jest of the other

[1] The origin of the colloquial name of "Bimshire Land" for Barbados and of "Bims" for its natives appears to puzzle many people. One writer in a well-known magazine went so far as to suggest that it was a corruption of "bam"! In reality it was applied to the island owing to the fact that Robert Bims (who was one of the earliest colonizers of St. Kitts), hearing of Barbados, went there with a party of settlers and took possession. Half-humorously and half-sarcastically (for it was generally believed the island was worthless) it was referred to as "Bim's Shire," a nickname which has always stuck.

islanders, and who are the pariahs of their race, if we are to believe their fellow negroes of the Caribbees.

Never did my men tire of taunting some poor 'Badian with the doggerel verse

A ha'penny loaf an' a bit o' salt fish,
Da' 's wha' de 'Badian call' a dish.
A bottle o' soda divided 'twix' t'ree,
Da' 's wha' de 'Badian call' a spree.

If the 'Badians happened to be in the minority, they bore it as best they might or retorted that "You men awnt civ'lized. You don' know better 'n to wear alpargats to a church of a Sunday," a response which usually brought on a loud cracking of tough skulls, as, like enraged goats, the men butted one another's wool-covered craniums—a contest in which the 'Badian always emerged victorious. For to accuse an islander of wearing alpargatas (the sandal-like footgear brought from Venezuela) to church, is an insult not lightly to be suffered. Indeed, if ever there was a being who outshone Solomon in all his glory, it is the West Indian negro on the Sabbath; and his highest ambition is, in order to draw greater attention to his gorgeous raiment, to possess a pair of brilliant, pumpkin-colored shoes which, to quote his own words, "goes queek, queek when Ah walks in de charch."

As might be expected, in the constant change and interchange of multicolored flotsam and jetsam, we picked up many a strange and interesting, not to say downright weird, character.

There, for example, was Trouble. He appeared one glorious golden morn as we lay at anchor off St. John, like Aphrodite rising from the sea, his scanty garments dripping with brine; for, being both boatless and penniless, he had used nature's gifts to win his way from shore to ship like the amphibious creature he proved to be. But, aside from the unexpected manner of his appearance, nothing could have resembled the goddess of the sea less. In fact, he was unquestionably the ugliest and most repulsive representative of the genus *Homo* and the species *Sapiens* that I have ever gazed upon—bony and big, with gorilla-like arms and a face so broad and forehead so low that his head appeared to have been forced out of shape by hydraulic pressure, while his natural absence of human-like features had been enhanced by some accident which had deprived him of even the semblance of a nose. There, above his immense mouth, were two huge round holes which, when he grinned,—as he constantly did,—stretched into slits that seemed ever on the point of meeting his ears and literally severing his black face into upper and lower hemispheres.

Like a prize bull-pup, he was so extravagantly ugly that he actually was fascinating, and not until he spoke could I take my eyes from him. And his first words were almost as astounding and unexpected as his appearance:

"Ah 'm beggin' o' yo' pawdon, Boss, for mah audacity an' assumption o' de manner o' mah absence o' dignification for precip'tately discommodin' yo', but Ah 'd like for to propoun' de interrogation ef yo' can absorbinate mah sarvices for a member o' de crew, sir, for to circumnavigate de islan's, sir."

Was I dreaming, or had the climate affected my brain? I literally gasped.

But the next instant I had recovered myself, for I knew that this noseless apparition with his wide mouth filled with long words could have originated in but one locality in all the islands, Antigua, whose dusky inhabitants seem to pride themselves upon the amplitude of the words they can command, regardless of their meaning or aptness.

"What 's your name, and what can you do?" I

asked, more as a formality than anything else, for I never dreamed of taking this creature on.

The noseless negro scratched his head and wiggled his bare toes.

"Ah was christened wi' de cognomen o' Henry Francis William Nelson Wellington Shand, sir," he replied; and then, as an afterthought, "but Ah 'm most usually designated by de name o' Trouble, sir."

"Trouble!" I exclaimed.

"Yaas, sir," responded the grinning negro, instantly. "Thank yo' sir, for mekkin' acceptance o' mah sarvices, sir. Ah 'll endeavor for to conduc' mahself wif circumspection an' implicitness. Ah 's a sailor, sir, an' Ah 'm not expandulatin' buncomb when Ah takes upon mahself de assumptiveness o' de assertion, sir."

I was speechless,—so astounded at the man's "assumptiveness" that he had been hired that I could not find words to inform him of his mistake,—and by the time I recovered from my astonishment he had disappeared in the forecastle.

Sam stood by, chuckling to himself.

"Ah 'spec's he may be a good sailor, Chief," he vouchsafed. "An' we 're in need o' two han's, Chief."

"All right, Sam," I replied. "I suppose he

does n't need a nose to run aloft or tail onto a rope."

And so Trouble came unto us, but if ever a man belied his name it was "Henry Francis William Nelson Wellington Shand, sir," for Trouble was a very treasure of a hand. He was as much at home in the water as on land or deck, and when, later, our anchor fouled one day, in fifteen fathoms, Trouble made nothing of diving down and releasing the fluke from its lodgment under a mass of coral and rock, while the height of his enjoyment was to challenge Sam to dive overboard and kill a big shark in a single-handed duel beneath the sea. And Sam, though a diver by profession, who had killed many a man-eater with a blow of his long, keen-bladed knife, freely admitted Trouble's amphibious superiority.

Aloft he was a very monkey; he was ever scouring decks or polishing brass; he was as good-natured as he was ugly, and even dignified Joseph unbent and passed many a half-hour chinning with this weird waif of the sea. As for the other members of the crew, after one or two tests and trials they abandoned all attempts to out-talk or out-argue him, for his ready flow of multisyllabled words left them floundering in a vocabulary totally inadequate to cope with Trouble's "expandulations" and "supercil'ous methodictions." On one occasion I overheard a bit of argument between our Antiguan find and a recent addition to the crew—for the older members invariably egged on new recruits to argue with Trouble.

I do not know what the argument had been about nor what the new man had said, but as he was a French mulatto from Dominica,—or, as the other islanders have it, a "patois man,"—I presume he had been referring in no complimentary terms to Henry Francis et cetera's native heath.

"Yo' worthless specimen o' misguided humanity yo'!" exclaimed Trouble. "Yo' insignificant an' fragment'ry yaller element! For wherefo' yo' have de audacity to let yo' imagination direc' yo' to dat assumption? Who yo' t'ink yo' addressin' in dat highfalutin', presumptious, dictatious manner? Ah desire yo' to distinc'ly an' def'nitely absorbinate de eminen'ly interestin' an' important info'mation Ah's propoundin', an' if yo' declinates to precip'tately reconsider de sentiments yo' jus' expressed an' at once an' immediately an' hereby and in witness whereof retrac' yo' asservations once, forever, an' henceforth, der' 's boun' for to occur a casulty an' a deceased patois nigger, an' de gentleman is goin' for to be compulsified for to discommode hisself to acquire another incumbent for to fill de work what yo' lack o' intellec' don' fit yo' for."

Needless to say, in the face of this dire threat—which to the fear-stricken recipient savored of an incantation by a witch doctor or "obeah man"—the French islander promptly and "precip'tately" reconsidered and retracted whatever it was that had inadvertently brought on Trouble's outburst.

To the last day of the voyage Trouble was with us in name if not in spirit, and never did I regret that he had hired himself, so to speak.

Aside from him and Sam and Joe, the only fixture was a red-haired, freckle-faced Montserratan boy whom I could not resist employing on account of his rich brogue and who served as cabin-boy, laundryman, and clown, and with the ready wit of his wild Irish ancestors kept us all in good humor throughout the cruise.

CHAPTER II

ST. THOMAS AND ITS PAST

ST. THOMAS is very beautiful when seen from a distance, with its gray-green mountains rising above the sea, mottled with soft mauves of shadow and dazzling silvery sunlight—a mass of opalescent tints, as though the hills were carven from a giant pearl shell. And as the harbor opens to view, and the little town of Charlotte Amalie is seen spreading fanwise up its three hillsides in triangles of soft buff, creamy white, and red, it seems a bit of the Mediterranean detached and transplanted here in the Caribbean.

But it must be confessed that the enchantment is mainly loaned by distance, for St. Thomas is a barren, arid island. Charlotte Amalie—shut in by the hills—is unbearably hot; there is but one level street, and while steep lanes, often ascending in stairways, lend picturesqueness to the place, they are most discouraging thoroughfares on a sweltering tropical day. Moreover, St. Thomas, having ever been a world's mart, a free port depending entirely upon commerce, has not the foreign, fascinating atmosphere we find in many of the islands.

Its people, a marvelous potpourri of nationalities, of necessity have become remarkable linguists, with a smattering of virtually every civilized tongue, but they are neither picturesque nor interesting.

On such a cruise as ours, however, this Virgin Island possession of Uncle Sam's could not well be passed by, although, truth to tell, its piratical associations are somewhat meager and of questionable authenticity.

I had seen this famed source of bay-rum under both Danish and American rule, in rain and in shine, in war and in peace; in prosperity with a forest of masts in its snug harbor, and, again, devastated by hurricanes, its shores strewn with tangled wrecks of countless vessels. But never before had St. Thomas appeared to me just as it did when, passing Sail Rock in the lee of the land, we entered the harbor and dropped the *Vigilant's* anchor before Charlotte Amalie.

I was looking at it now from a new point of view. I was blind to the great coaling-piers, to the gaunt dry-dock, to the fact that gray-painted cruisers and big liners rode upon the glassy surface of the harbor, that the Stars and Stripes flew from the mastheads and flagstaffs, that motor-cars scurried along the waterfront street. I was trying to visualize St. Thomas as it had been two centuries and more before, when ships with lateen yards, high poops, and wall-sided hulls pierced with cannon ports had swung to anchor before the town; when roistering crowds of fierce-whiskered, besashed sea-rovers with cutlasses at their belts and bandanas on their heads had swaggered through the steep and crooked streets; when the little pink "Christian's" fort beside the quay had been looked upon as a real fortification, and the Danes had not been above receiving the corsairs with open arms.

It is not a difficult matter to imagine Charlotte Amalie's streets filled with buccaneers, for after a few encounters with boatmen, beggars, guides, and gamins the average visitor will be convinced that the pirates still haunt the place in spirit if not in body. Maybe the freebooters' traits have been passed down in their blood that flows to some extent in the veins of a large proportion of the Virgin Islanders; but, however that may be, the present inhabitants of St. Thomas know little and care less about piratical history or relics.

And an investigation of the contents of the shops in Charlotte Amalie will lead one to think that much of the buccaneers' loot still remains in stock after a lapse of two centuries or more. Such juxtaposition of odds and ends from all quarters of the world, it would be hard to duplicate in any other port upon the planet.

Predominant, and everywhere in evidence, are the two items inseparably associated with St. Thomas,—jipijapa hats and bay-rum,—although I understand that since my last visit to the island the Volstead law has shown its effects even on bay-rum. But formerly—at any rate, until its acquisition by Uncle Samuel—St. Thomas was more famous for its bay-rum than for anything else; bayrum and St. Thomas were synonymous around the world. Charlotte Amalie reeked of bay-rum: every ragged negro one met upon the streets besought one to purchase it, and from mysterious pockets or other receptacles produced a bottle or two; every shop was filled with it, and the bumboats that flocked about every incoming and departing ship were laden with it. And, strangely enough, very little bay-rum is or was made in St. Thomas. To be sure, it was adulterated, bottled, and labeled there, but the oil itself, the distilled extract of the aromatic bay-tree, was largely produced in St. John. Not one person in a million has ever heard of St. John, perhaps the most charming island of the Virgins, and yet it is really the home of the bay-rum which made St. Thomas famous. Such are fate and the effects of publicity; and as the St. Johnians ultimately reaped a goodly portion of the profits, I do not suppose they ever complained.

If the visitor to St. Thomas could not be cajoled or nagged into purchasing bay-rum, then the islanders at once pressed upon him their next most famous commodity, the jipijapa or Panama hats. Somehow the visiting public was imbued with the idea that Panama hats could be purchased more cheaply in St. Thomas than elsewhere, and despite the fact that very few of the St. Thomas head-coverings ever saw the Isthmus of Panama, and still fewer ever were made in far-off Ecuador (the home of the bona-fide Panama), tourists, seamen, and other visitors to St. Thomas invariably stocked up. It made no difference, apparently, whether the hats were made in the neighboring Virgins or in Porto Rico; as long as they were bought in St. Thomas the purchasers reasoned that they must be genuine and cheap. Even the braided paper affairs made by the Japanese were often passed off on the unsuspecting and gullible tourists as real Panamas—whatever that may mean. Of course, St. Thomas being formerly under Danish rule and a free port, many articles which were subject to high duties in the United States were to be had in the island at bargain prices, but Monte Cristi Panama hats were not among them.

In the good old days before our country and all its colonies became Saharas, St. Thomas was noted up and down and roundabout the islands for its liquid refreshments. Not only was there the justly famed St. Croix rum, but countless other beverages were procurable there, brought from every liquor-producing country on the globe, in addition to several native concoctions that were not to be laughed at, especially after a few glasses with the jovial Danes on a holiday. Oddly enough, inhabitants of tropical lands, especially the West Indies, consume incredible quantities of alcoholic drinks and seem to thrive upon them. Indeed, it is a source of pride among the islanders that their native islets consume more alcohol per capita than any other lands, and there is always a keen rivalry between Barbados, Bermuda, and Demerara in this respect. But I had never heard that St. Thomas strove for first honors and when, on one occasion, I inquired of a huge blond-bearded St. Thomas Dane why this was so, he informed me in all seriousness that as the St. Thomas people consumed more than all the others combined, it was beneath them even to mention the question. Surely it must make the old buccaneers squirm in their graves to think of St. Thomas, of all places, being dry, dry as old Dead Man's Chest with its one bottle of rum to fifteen men, at least on the surface, though I know there is many a cask, bottle, and keg stored safely away in private stocks for the proper drinking of a skoal when occasion arises.

But to return to the shops of Charlotte Amalie and their strange and motley contents. Here, with the bay-rum, jipijapa hats, and dried corals and starfish, are French perfumes, picture post-cards, and seed necklaces. Miscellaneous hardware, groceries, tinned goods, cloth, and bric-à-brac are inextricably mixed. A salesman searches among piles of cordage and bundles of rowlocks to find a pair of shoes or a package of patent medicine, for every shop in Charlotte Amalie, save the drug stores, is a little of everything with nothing in its place. I remember seeing a pair of very old-fashioned skates dangling rusty and forlorn outside a shop one blistering December day. Curious to know how such things happened to be in the island, or to whom the proprietor expected to sell them I entered and inquired. Imagine my amusement and surprise when I was solemnly informed that they had been there for years, that no one knew exactly what they were used for, but, in the words of the chocolate-colored shopkeeper:

"I am aware that they are significant of the holiday season, and so I hang them outside regularly each year as an indication to passers-by that my Christmas stock of merchandise is on sale." Truly, an original method of advertising!

In another shop a pair of strange slipper-like objects, unlike anything I had ever seen, were displayed. The owner of the shop, without appearing to think it at all curious, told me they were from Lapland, and, perhaps with a faint hope of making a sale, thereupon rummaged among his stock of countless years' standing and proudly produced a pair of moth-eaten Eskimo boots! Had he brought forth a full suit of armor or the skeleton of a buccaneer, I could scarcely have been more astonished. But after all, when we come to think of it, it is not so remarkable, for both Greenland and St. Thomas were Danish colonies, and no doubt some far-cruising Dane brought the reindeer-skin foot-coverings here on one of his trading voyages. We may laugh at the Dane for not realizing that such things were hardly suitable for everyday wear in the Virgin Islands, but is his mistake any more ridiculous than that of our own countryman who shipped a cargo of warming-pans to St. Kitts, or our own United States Senator who, when about to start on a mission to Porto Rico, asked a friend if the people there had means of heating their houses in winter?

Far more interesting than the shops, however, and a spot which every visitor who is interested in maritime matters should see, is the "ships' graveyard" at Krum Bay, near the harbor entrance.

Here, for countless years, have been towed the disabled, storm-beaten ships condemned as unworthy of repair, and here they have found their last port, their final resting-place. Stripped of rigging and other fittings, they have been burned for the copper they contained; but though they are lost forever, though history makes no mention of them, though their very names have long since been forgotten, yet they still live on, perpetuated in their figure-heads which have been saved and, while sadly neglected, are prized as relics.

There is something pathetic, almost tragic, in these dumb and lifeless figures lying there exposed to the elements, their once-gay paint and gilt tarnished, faded, and flaked off by storm and wind and sun. They seem almost like tombstones, as indeed they are—monuments to dead and gone ships that once proudly plowed the seven seas and the five broad oceans. Only carven effigies, perhaps, but all that remain to tell of stately hulls and towering pyramids of canvas, of lofty trucks and clipper bows, of craft that, disabled, maimed, battered, and wrecked, have left their bones here in St. Thomas at Krum Bay.

Looking at these reminders of a bygone day, one can visualize the ships of which they formed a part, can almost identify the craft beneath whose soaring bowsprits these figures once gazed forth across the tumbling, foam-flecked brine. Here, leaning against a cocoanut palm, is a Roman legionary, his short sword broken at the hilt as though in some hard-fought battle, his shield dented and bruised, and his wooden face seamed and scarred. Faded, weather-beaten, and forlorn, he is still a martial figure. He has fought more battles, has seen victory in more hard-won fights than ever soldier of Cæsar,—battles against the elements, struggles between lashing, storm-flung waves and puny man,—and while in the end the sea was victorious, yet we know that the stern-visaged warrior fought a good fight and bore the brunt of battle always in the foremost rank, ever there with threatening falchion at the bows. Massive, heroic he is, and we feel sure that in years gone he looked proudly, defiantly upon the sea from some ship of war or privateer with grinning ports along her sides.

Close by, coquettishly peeping from behind a pile of junk, is a very different figure, a female form with doll-like, simpering face, long, flowing hair, and clinging draperies. Upon her cheeks are still patches of pink, as though she had but freshly rouged; her skirts and low-cut bodice still are gaudy with red and yellow, and we can see that once her wooden tresses were of raven hue. Looking at her, we can reconstruct the ship she graced, we can see the bluff-bowed, wallowing, honest merchantman, and we feel sure, could we but look upon the stern, we should see, painted across her counter, "Polly" or "Betsy" or perchance even "Mary Ann."

Near this lady, with her fixed wooden smile that has withstood the tempests of centuries, a sailor lad in glazed hat lurches drunkenly, propped up by an iron post just as his living counterpart no doubt was supported many a time after a glorious night ashore. Now his eyes are fixed in an unwinking stare upon raven-haired Polly, while behind him, with outflung arm, one shapely foot spurning a carven shield, poises a Victory. A masterpiece she, albeit her wings are sadly clipped and disrespectful insects have pitted her classic features with their borings until she looks as though she had suffered from smallpox. But the finely chiseled draperies, the perfectly proportioned, softly rounded limbs speak eloquently of beauty long since faded, of expert craftsmanship. All who love ships must pause before her in reverence, for once she flew gracefully at the sharp prow of some famous clipper-ship, a grayhound of the sea, a fabric such as never will be seen again,—the very acme of Yankee shipbuilding skill. A craft with sky-piercing masts, vast tapering yards, and acres of billowing canvas, the clipper was the queen of transatlantic liners, and proudly she flaunted the Stars and Stripes for all the world to see.

And something of an epitome of St. Thomas's history and St. Thomas's trade is this graveyard of the ships. As each old sailing-craft was towed to its funeral pyre at Krum Bay the island took a step nearer its doom, for with the passing of the old West India trade, with the discarding of crossed yards and square sails, St. Thomas's greatness departed. Never again will her harbor be filled with a forest of masts flying the flags of every maritime nation.

Perchance under the United States Government she may be more stable than heretofore: she may suffer less from lack of cash and a mother country's interest. Coaling-docks and grimy colliers will attract a certain number of hideous tramps and spotless liners to her harbor; tourists may spend a few hours and a few dollars in quaint Charlotte Amalie, but never again will this port be world-famed as of yore.

But even so,—even though the island's romantic past is little more than tradition, with the old days gone forever; even with the omnipresent marines and Fords upon the streets and the American flag flying over the old pink fort,—St. Thomas is still a charming resort with its three hills rising like pyramids of multicolored, red-roofed buildings, its gray-green mountains over all, its blue sky and bluer waters and its brown, black, and yellow good-natured, care-free inhabitants, who, though the blood of pirate chieftain or old Viking may run in their veins, one and all proudly proclaim themselves "Americans."

Of all things in St. Thomas, the most cherished, even sacred, to the natives, and invariably the first to be pointed out to the visitor, is the famous "Blackbeard's Castle" at the apex of the hillside town of Charlotte Amalie.

Perhaps old Blackbeard never dwelt in the tower that bears his name, any more than Bluebeard of the inquisitive wives built or occupied the neighboring structure which bears his name. Indeed, there is no denying that Blackbeard's Castle bears a striking resemblance to an old stone windmill tower. But the skeptics who have pointed this out and have scoffed at the beloved legend of the St. Thomians have overlooked the fact that even if the tower was originally only an unromantic cane-mill, there is no valid reason why Teach should not have made use of it. Dutch windmills were built, used, and abandoned years before the famous pirate saw the light of day, and a cylindrical tower of massive stone, whether designed for a windmill or otherwise, was an ideal structure for a freebooter's dwelling and fortress, and was admirably adapted to defensive tactics.

In fact, between the two, I would far rather have been within that tower on the hill than in the squat pink fort, in case of attack in the days when muzzle-loading guns and round shot were in vogue, and the fact that Blackbeard's Castle bears a family likeness to a windmill proves or disproves nothing. Everywhere in the West Indies one finds Spanish, French, Dutch, and even English towers built for forts and as much like that upon this St. Thomas hilltop as peas in the same pod. Right on the splendid Malecon in Havana there is one; several are scattered about Puerto Plata, Macoris, and other towns in Santo Domingo. They may be seen in a more or less ruined state all up and down the Antilles and the Main, and yet no one has the temerity to suggest that they were once windmills!

Why, then, should any one try to destroy this almost sacred tradition of St. Thomas? Why try to rob the islanders of that one reminder of the buccaneers? No, let us not be doubting Thomases, but rather be thankful that this old-time haven of the pirates still retains at least one landmark that links it with the past.

And there is no reason why Blackbeard should not have dwelt in St. Thomas in those days of his prosperity. All the Virgin Isles—Danish, Dutch, and British—were safe refuges for the pirates, retreats wherein they could lie in peace, where they could refit and careen their craft, could secure supplies, could exchange their loot for gold and silver currency, and could gamble and carouse to their hearts' content.

Very canny were the thrifty islanders in thus opening their doors to the freebooters. It protected them from attack, and it insured a lively trade. And they well knew that whatever they paid in good pieces of eight and golden onzas for plundered goods would eventually return to their own pockets over bars and gaming-tables, for the pirates were free spenders and money ever burned holes in their pockets. So we may feel sure that St. Thomas has sheltered many a pirate ship and many a famous or infamous buccaneer, especially in the great harp-shaped bay to the west of Charlotte Amalie, and separated from the harbor by a rocky peninsula. Here the pirates were wont to lie in wait for unsuspecting merchantmen bound through the Virgin Passage between the island and neighboring Porto Rico, until, to save their faces, the Danish authorities were compelled to request their welcome but disreputable guests to confine themselves to more peaceful pursuits while in Danish waters or else betake themselves elsewhere.

CHAPTER III

THE BUCCANEERS IN THE VIRGIN ISLES

IT WAS due to peculiar circumstances that the Virgin Islands and their harbors became neutral ground—or, rather, neutral waters—wherein the corsairs could be sure of safety, and where they never harmed the inhabitants or such peaceful craft as might come to trade or to seek refuge.

With the European countries constantly at one another's throats, the men without a country, flying no flag but the Jolly Roger, could always find safety among these disputed isles, and were always sure of a welcome. The hated Spaniards were the chief sufferers from the pirates' attacks, and while they might virtually be at peace with Spain, yet the other powers saw no real reason to interfere with the pirates' activities merely to aid an hereditary enemy who might at any moment see fit to start another war. England, as ever, desired the supremacy of the seas, and, hard put to it to maintain her grip in the Antilles, she was quite willing that the Dons should be kept in check by fair means or foul. France was too busy with more serious matters to bother about the freebooters in the far-off Caribbean. The thrifty Dutch found it more profitable to trade with the pirates than to fight them, and the Danes,—with the adventurous blood of the Vikings in their veins,—no doubt had more or less of a fellow-feeling for the sea-robbers.

And so, although the governments of Europe sent forth royal decrees, bearing most impressive seals, gay with colored ribbons and engrossed with lengthy words and involved sentences, and on parchment frowned upon the corsairs, yet no real effort was made to enforce the law. So the buccaneers laughed at the "scraps of paper" and went merrily and virtually unchecked upon their way.

It may be well here to call attention to the fact that we should not confuse the buccaneers with ordinary pirates, for while buccaneers were pirates, yet pirates were not necessarily buccaneers; and even in their piracy the buccaneers or "Brethren of the Main," as they called themselves, were by no means the conventional pirates of fiction.

Nearly all of them started on their careers as privateers with royal warrant to prey upon the enemy's ships. Then, having found the game to their liking and with no other means of earning a livelihood when peace was declared, they kept it up, regardless of such trifling matters as treaties of peace between kings and emperors several thousands of miles distant. With a few exceptions, they continued their depredations in much the same manner and along the same lines as they had conducted their privateering ventures.

The British buccaneers—and the majority were of that nationality—never attacked a vessel flying the thrice-crossed flag of England; they did not molest the Dutch, who were ever friendly, for as long as there were plenty of Spaniards, Portuguese, and Frenchmen for the plucking they were quite content to pick and choose. The French buccaneers were perhaps a little less squeamish, while the Dutch and the Spanish apparently preyed on friend and foe alike.

But, no matter what their nationality or origin, all left certain places free from molestation, and among these the favorites were the Virgin Isles, the island of Tortuga off Haiti, the islets about Santo Domingo, Aves Island off Venezuela, the Caymans south of Jamaica, Jamaica itself, and the Bay Islands off Honduras. These islands, especially the Virgins, became known far and wide as lairs of the reckless sea-rovers, whither none dared to follow and where they could, for a space, cast aside all fear of shipwreck, murder, and sudden death and live in peace.

Callous, case-hardened, and ruffianly as they were, yet they knew well which side their bread was buttered on, and they made and enforced strict laws and discipline in their retreats. The natives' lives and property were sacred, the towns were patrolled by armed men selected by the buccaneer chiefs, and death, swift and sure, was the punishment for any infringement of rules, or a violation of the hospitality accorded. Many a drunken pirate was pistoled out of hand by his own comrades for taking, or attempting to take, liberties with some Virgin Island maid. Many a buccaneer has kicked and writhed as he swung to his ship's yard arm as a penalty for picking a quarrel with some citizen of St. John or St. Barts, and more than one corsair has been cut down without mercy and his body thrown to the waiting sharks because he refused to pay for drinks or commodities purchased in the island shops or bar-rooms.

Strange, incomprehensible, quixotic men, these reckless buccaneers. Cruel, relentless, unprincipled, and yet with their own inexorable laws, their own code of honor, their streak of gallantry and their bravery which, despite their sins and their wickedness, we cannot but admire.

We cannot understand them; it would baffle the most expert psychoanalyist to fathom the workings of their brains; but we must not judge them by modern standards. In their day piracy was a profession rather than a crime and, while openly frowned upon by the powers, privately abetted and encouraged. Indeed, it was looked upon rather as a gentleman's profession, and not a few gentlemen were engaged in it. To us these men appear bloodthirsty monsters, but we must bear in mind that in their day life was cheap and torture was legalized as a punishment for the most trivial crimes.

Such pleasantries as burning holes through liars' tongues, cutting off eavesdroppers' ears, branding the palms of thieves' hands, or putting out eyes were in the same category as ten days' imprisonment or ten dollars' fine to-day. And death in fiendish forms was meted out for violations of the law which in our day we should think severely punished with six months in a modern jail with such accessories as motion pictures, baseball games, and musical concerts in lieu of rack, wheel, and thumb-screw.

In the days when the Virgins were a haven for pirates the bodies of men hanging in chains and surrounded by carrion crows were almost an essential part of the waterside landscape in all seaports, and attracted no more attention than an illuminated advertisement on Broadway does at the present time.

No doubt the country people who came to town for a holiday or to do their marketing, stared with bulging eyes at the rotting corpses swaying in the wind and pointed them out to their young hopefuls as awful examples of the end they would come to if they ran away to become sea-rovers, just as to-day our country cousins stare and gape at the sights of the metropolis. And unquestionably the denizens of the ports snickered and made rude jokes about the "rubes" and "bumpkins" who were such "jays" as to stare at a pirate's body in chains.

But such a fate overtook the buccaneers only when, by some mischance, they forgot themselves and overstepped the bounds of propriety; for as a rule they had a peculiar sense of patriotism—although men without a country, legally—and seldom troubled persons or ships of the land of their birth. And as long as they confined their activities to harassing hereditary enemies, even though official peace might have been established, their countrymen put tongues in cheeks, figuratively speaking, and let well enough alone.

Indeed, from a diplomatic and economic point of view it was not a bad plan to have a score or two of corsairs preying on a competitor nation's commerce, or within call in case of war. No small proportion of the buccaneer ships were fitted out and partly owned by law-abiding and highly respectable gentlemen and merchants who would have become apoplectic with righteous indignation if any one had dared assume that they were even morally in sympathy with piracy.

Many of the buccaneers were exceedingly interesting characters, and the pity is that, aside from Esquemelling and one or two others, they had no chroniclers, no biographers to leave us a true account of their lives, to give us a real insight into their natures, their ideals, and their aims, and to thrill us with their adventures. A few have become famous, have lived on in history and legend; but doubtless many more, whose careers were far more thrilling and whose characters were far more interesting, have been completely forgotten. Now and then some bit of tradition, some fragment of story makes us wish we knew more of them.

It is hard to imagine a swashbuckling, blood-spilling pirate, spending his leisure hours in writing poetry, but it was no other than Foster, a pirate who served under Morgan and whom the famous Sir Harry one time rebuked for his ruthlessness, that penned "Sonnyettes of Love," which, although they may not be good verse, are certainly more intelligible than much of our modern poetry, and express delightful and tender sentiments.

No doubt the screams of captive Spanish wives and daughters maltreated by his ruffianly crew furnished the author with inspiration and turned his mind to thoughts of shady Devon lanes or ivy-clad Surrey cottages and buxom, fair-haired, red-cheeked English lassies. But this is mere speculation; all we know is that he was a romantic soul and preferred writing tender effusions of love, in

(From an old print)

BLACKBEARD'S CASTLE (ST. THOMAS)

his cramped, painstaking hand, to carousing ashore and making merry with negro wenches.

Old Teach, the Blackbeard associated with the castle in St. Thomas, was a most interesting type, a man such as even Poe or Stevenson could not have created out of whole cloth or vivid imagination. Born as Edward Teach, in Bristol, England,—a port, by the way, where many a redoubtable freebooter was recruited,—the youngster in due course of time became a sailor and voyaged, among other places, to the West Indies. To be sure, the heyday of buccaneering was then over, but still, in 1716, there were many freebooters afloat upon the Caribbean. Having heard, in Port Royal and other notorious resorts, glowing tales of the pirate's life, Edward decided that life aboard a merchantman was a very unattractive and unprofitable one and that piracy was the most promising get-rich-quick scheme.

Regardless of his failings, we must admit that young Teach would have won the highest esteem of an efficiency expert (had such beings existed in his day), for he believed implicitly that a thing worth doing at all was worth doing well and bent all his energies to practising his profession in a thorough manner. As an example of the rewards or successes attendant upon application to an idea, Teach was a model, for within a space of two years from the time he announced his intention of turning corsair he could lay undisputed claim to being the world's greatest pirate.

Moreover, the amiable Edward was a firm believer in publicity and in the spectacular. Indeed, he very evidently was far in advance of his time, and to-day he would have brought untold joy to the heart of a film director and would be drawing a far larger income than he ever enjoyed through his chosen career. If ever there was an original of the buccaneer of melodrama and lurid fiction, it must have been Teach; only, no author or playwright would ever dare draw a character as bizarre, repulsive, and hideously ferocious as this Prince of Pirates.

Of immense size and coarse and brutal aspect, Teach nurtured a huge black beard which covered his ugly face to his eyes, and which, falling to his waist, was braided into innumerable small pigtails, the ends being tied together over his ears. His hair, also of inky hue, fell to his shoulders and almost met his beetling, bushy black eyebrows over his forehead. As though not ferocious-looking enough naturally, he was accustomed, when making an attack, to stick burning slow-matches in hair and beard, which surrounded his fierce face and gleaming eyes with a ring of fire and smoke and, according to a contemporaneous description, "glowed most horribly." Unlike many of his notorious predecessors and compeers, Blackbeard was no dandy. His favorite costume was a long-skirted, deep-cuffed coat, much the worse for wear and dribbled liquor; a rough shirt open to the waist and exposing a chest as hairy as a gorilla's; short, wide breeches, and low seaman's shoes. Stockings he usually dispensed with, and a battered felt hat of the type made familiar by stage robbers crowned his ebon mane, while, to complete his get-up, a pair of cutlasses and a knife or two hung at his belt and half a dozen pistols were stuck through his sash.

And, in truth, Blackbeard's character was as ferocious as his looks, and his soul as black as his whiskers. There was not a single redeeming feature about him, unless it was his sheer courage, and altogether he was a despicable scoundrel. On more than one occasion he robbed and murdered his own men, and he cared not a whit whether prizes he took were flying the flag of his mother country or of another. To him, torture and butchery were mere pastimes, and one day, just as a joke, he placed seventeen of his own crew on a tiny desert island, promising to return at intervals

BLACKBEARD

THE *VIGILANT* AS ORIGINALLY RIGGED

to see how long they could survive without food or water. Fortunately for the castaways, Teach was unable to carry out this, to him, interesting experiment in human endurance, for another corsair,—and a rank amateur, at that,—Major Stede Bonnet, rescued the marooned pirates.

No doubt time hung heavy on the pirates' hands at times as they sailed aimlessly about waiting for a prize, but those upon Blackbeard's ship could always be sure that tedium would not be their lot. As an entertainer Teach was a marvel, albeit his ideas of amusement were not always appreciated by others and he must have devoted a considerable portion of his spare time to inventing new schemes to relieve the monotony between fights.

Once, when his ship was becalmed on a blistering hot day and no sail broke the scintillating horizon, the resourceful Blackbeard appeared on deck hatless, coatless, and in his bare feet, and proposed that his shipmates should make a little "hell of their own," adding that, as they were all bound for the lower regions eventually, it would be interesting to learn in advance who would be able to bear it the longest. As his crew well knew that any imitation devised would be nothing to the inferno their captain would raise if they declined his invitation, they rather hesitatingly and half-heartedly fell in with his plan. Thereupon Teach and his men—some of whom had to be urged by sundry well-aimed kicks and blows—descended into the ship's hold and, having securely fastened the hatches, set fire to several kegs of sulphur and seated themselves upon the stone ballast.

We can well imagine that in the ill-smelling, unventilated hold a very creditable imitation of the infernal regions soon resulted, while Blackbeard might well have served as a model for the Evil One himself. At any rate, the officers and crew soon decided that even if they were on the straight road to perdition they had no desire to arrive ahead of time, and, choking and gasping, they broke through the hatches and climbed on deck. But not so with old Teach. Long after the last of his men had deserted the hold, he remained, seated on the stones, breathing the brimstone fumes, and throughout the rest of his days it was his greatest pride that he had been the last to give in.

Indeed, when one of his officers informed him that he had looked like a half-hanged man as he emerged, Teach seemed greatly pleased and declared that at some future time he was going to make a test to see who could dangle the longest from a noose without being wholly hanged.

Blackbeard believed in keeping himself before the

public and in not allowing even his friends to forget who he was or what his character, as illustrated by an incident in his career when he was entertaining his own sailing-master and a pilot in the cabin of his sloop, which was at anchor in one of the Virgin Island harbors.

After a time conversation lagged and Teach, blowing out the solitary candle, cocked his pistols, and, crossing his arms, fired point-blank toward his companions. The unfortunate sailing-master was shot through the knee and permanently crippled, but in the darkness of the cabin the other shot went wild and the pilot escaped with nothing worse than a fright. When, after this pleasantry, the candle was re-lit and the two indignant seamen demanded an explanation, Teach cursed them fluently and at length, and finished by cxplaining that they would forget who he was if he did n't shoot one of them now and then.

Strangely enough, Blackbeard, despite his unattractive face and still more unattractive personality, appears to have been a good deal of a lady-killer, figuratively if not literally, for he managed to win the hearts and hands of fourteen maidens whom he married. History fails to record their subsequent fate or whether Teach devised some speedy form of divorce to suit himself. The fourteenth wife was a "most charming young creature of sixteen," if we are to believe those who wrote of her at first hand.

Blackbeard's courtships would have made entertaining reading had they been recorded, and it would be interesting to know what there was about him that appealed so strongly to feminine tastes, but chroniclers evidently considered such matters too trivial to record.

Of course it would be expected that a man of Edward Teach's character and attainments would die with his boots on and fighting to the last, and he was not one to disappoint the lover of lurid adventure. In the end he completely fulfilled everything expected of him. So great a menace had he become to shipping, especially to the merchant marine of the British colonies in America, that the powers that were demanded that his activities be brought to a speedy end. Accordingly, the Governor of Virginia, in 1718, posted divers and sundry notices to the effect that forty pounds sterling would be paid as a reward for the capture of any pirate captain, and that Edward Teach, otherwise known as "Blackbeard," was worth one hundred pounds to the authorities, whether he be brought in dead or alive. In those days such a sum was a small fortune, enough to tempt any brave and hardy soul to have a try for it, but the first to camp on Blackbeard's trail was Lieutenant Maynard of H. M. S. *Pearl.* By some means never fully revealed, Maynard learned that the redoubtable pirate was enjoying a brief vacation in a secluded cove near Ocracoke Inlet (North Carolina). Gossip had it that the Governor of Carolina was on far too friendly terms with Teach, and that no small portion of that worthy gentleman's wealth had found its way into the governor's pockets, owing to the pirate's appreciation of being left undisturbed in his chosen haven on the Carolina coast.

Whatever the truth may be, the young naval officer started forth in a sloop he had fitted out and manned, intent on Blackbeard's capture or death. Although the pirate was apprised of the lieutenant's approach, he scorned to move from his retreat, but spent the night before the expected visit in striving to outdrink a friendly merchant skipper who had dropped in for a call. Toward daylight, however, Teach's men saw Maynard approaching, and the pirate, realizing that the officer really meant business, cut his cables, hoisted the Jolly Roger, and let his vessel drift ashore. Here, in the shoal water, he felt sure the sloop could not follow, and as, oddly enough, neither vessel carried cannon and it would be a hand-to-hand conflict, Blackbeard's ruse was worthy of him.

But the one hundred pounds still glittered before the lieutenant's eyes, and, determined to do or die, he cast everything possible overboard, including the water-casks, set his sails, and headed directly for the pirate vessel. Thereupon Blackbeard, with his slow-matches smoking and sputtering in hair and beard, "hailed him in a most rude manner," cursed him, defied him, and, to show his utter contempt, stood in plain view upon his ship's rails and drank a goblet of liquor to Maynard's damnation. Finding that, even with everything movable jettisoned, his sloop still drew too much water to grapple with the pirate, the lieutenant manned small boats and attempted to board Blackbeard's craft. He was met with so hot a welcome of musketry and pistols that twenty-nine men were killed and wounded, and the boats retreated to the sloop.

Meanwhile the tide was rising, and Maynard's sloop was constantly drifting closer to the pirate. Still confident of success, the lieutenant ordered all his men below, he alone remaining on deck with the helmsman. Presently, the sloop grated and bumped against the other vessel, and immediately the pirates began to pelt her with fire-grenades. Then, drawing cutlasses and pistols, they sprang over the bulwarks and swarmed upon the sloop's decks in true melodramatic piratical style. Up from the hold poured Maynard's men, and hot and furious was the battle. Teach and the lieutenant were face to face. Both fired at the same instant, at point-blank range, but while the officer dodged, Teach was less fortunate, and Maynard's bullet buried itself in the pirate's face.

With blood streaming from the wound and dripping from the braided ends of his beard, the maddened pirate flung down his pistol, whipped out his cutlass, and, swearing horribly, leaped at the officer, who also had drawn his sword. Then followed a duel, a hand-to-hand struggle to the death between the gigantic, cursing, horrible-featured pirate and the young officer—a contest between brute strength and trained swordsmanship. Chasing each other back and forth across the blood-covered deck, stumbling and tripping over dead and wounded men, they hacked and parried and thrust. Again and again the officer's sword went home, more than once the pirate's cutlass found its mark, until at last a terrific blow of Blackbeard's heavy blade snapped his opponent's light sword at the hilt and the lieutenant was at the pirate's mercy.

With a blood-curdling yell and a terrible oath, Teach swung his cutlass and struck with all his failing strength, expecting to cut his enemy down with a single blow. But Maynard, leaping back, escaped, the stroke falling short and merely slicing off several fingers from the officer's hand. Before Teach could strike again, ere he could raise his arm, one of Maynard's men leaped forward, his naval hanger flashed, and the pirate chief staggered back, his head lolling on one side, his neck half severed. But even then, with his life-blood spouting like a crimson fountain from the gaping wound, with his head rolling horribly on his shoulders, Blackbeard swung his cutlass and with a mighty blow cut the brave sailor down.

Knowing his doom was sealed, realizing his death was but a matter of moments, the pirate was still game. Kicking off his shoes, that his feet might not slip upon the bloody planks, he backed to the bulwarks, fighting off a half-dozen men who fell upon him. Dripping with blood from a score of wounds, holding his all but decapitated head in place with one hand, he roared like a maddened bull, drew a pistol from his sash, cocked it, and with a last superhuman effort aimed at the oncoming men. But the piece was never fired; before his finger could pull the trigger, before a swinging blade could reach him, his hands fell at his sides, his head dropped forward in ghastly fashion on his blood-drenched beard, and he slumped to the deck, dead.

Those of the pirate crew still alive had leaped into the water; the fight was over, the battle won, the notorious, inhuman Blackbeard was no more. Cutting the sinews and muscles that still kept Teach's head and body together, the victorious Maynard suspended the gruesome trophy at his sloop's bowsprit end, and with thirteen captured pirates under hatches, sailed into Bath Town, North Carolina, where the unlucky thirteen were promptly hanged and Lieutenant Maynard received his well-merited and hard-won reward.

Oddly enough, the one man of Blackbeard's crew who escaped unscathed was his sailing-master, Israel Hands, the selfsame man whom Teach had wounded in the knee a short time previously, and who, owing to his late captain's practical joke, was ashore nursing his injured leg at the time of Maynard's attack.

CHAPTER IV

ON THE WAY TO ST. JOHN

SAM had assured me that there were many relics of buccaneer days on St. John, and in St. Thomas his statements had been confirmed by several persons. Moreover, the names of many a bay and cove that broke the coast-line of this near-by neighbor of St. Thomas were associated with the buccaneers, and so, although I had originally planned to pass it by and set sail direct for Anegada, I changed my itinerary to include this neglected Eden of the Virgins.

Sam had rounded up the crew—who, considering that St. Thomas is supposedly "dry," were, with the exception of Joe, extremely hilarious—and had them safe aboard and under his watchful eye the evening preceding our departure; for the Bahaman, unlike the majority of his race, never believed in putting off until the morrow what could be done the night before.

Many an old-time friend of pre-American days had I met in Charlotte Amalie, and many a toast to the success of my cruise had been drunk in delectable guava-berry cordial and other beverages dear to the Danish West Indians,—a fine, hospitable, easygoing lot,—and it was with real regret that I bade them farewell.

Hardly had the first rosy tints of approaching dawn lightened the eastern sky when Sam routed out his men. The creak and purr of tackle and sheave broke the silence of the sleeping harbor, the capstan clanked and clattered to the rhythm of shuffling black feet upon the deck, and the *Vigilant* glided slowly from the land as the sun rose above the gently swaying cocoanut-palms and transformed the ancient schooner's sails to cloth of gold.

To the west as we cleared the land, and looming sharply in the morning light, rose Sail Rock, more than ever the very semblance of a ship. And, my mind filled with thoughts of pirate and of buccaneer, I could picture the solitary pinnacle as a great galleon sailing majestically southward through the narrow channel. There, shimmering in the sun, was the high, ornate stern; along the low, dark waist the creamy foam sparkled brightly; upward in towering pyramids soared the huge, square sails; and toward her—like a falcon after a helpless gull—the *Vigilant* swept.

How often, I wondered, had the little schooner's bowsprit swung toward some distant gleam of sail?

How many times had her dark-skinned, fierce-faced crew run out the long guns and sent round shot hurtling through the hull and rigging of a prize?

And then Sam spoke:

"Tha' Sail Rock mos' cert'n'y do have th' aspec' o' a ship, Chief. Did y' ever hear o' th' 'casion when one o' th' 'Merican battle-ships fired on th' rock for a target, an' th' Danes made plenty o' rumpus an' humbuggin' 'bout it?"

The spell was broken. The galleon vanished in thin air. I saw only a curiously formed rock surrounded by screaming sea-birds, and as a smoke-belching, grimy tramp appeared from behind it I turned away and looked toward the soft, deliciously green hills to the eastward—the hills of St. John. And as though she too were suddenly disillusioned and had bethought herself that she was no pirate ship running down a prize, but a law-abiding and peaceful packet carrying an American on an innocent mission, the *Vigilant* swung about and headed for St. John.

But, as Sam said, the rock did certainly have the "aspec'" of a ship, and I could not blame the bellicose captain of a French frigate who, a century and more ago, sighted the rock one night and, mistaking it for a privateer, ran close and hailed the supposed enemy. No response being forthcoming, he blazed a broadside at the shadowy mass. Back came an echoing thunder of the cannonade, and the rebounding shot, falling on the frigate's deck, convinced the Frenchman that the privateer was returning his fire.

For hours the battle raged, the French gunners pouring broadside after broadside at the massive cliffs, and not until day dawned did the deluded commander of the frigate discover his mistake and, crestfallen and mortified, creep away, leaving Sail Rock unscathed and triumphant.

Sailing in a fresh breeze, with a buoyant, well-built, easily handled ship under one's feet, is a never-ending delight to one fond of the water, regardless of what portion of the seven seas one's craft may be spurning from her bow. But to me no other water is so sparkling, no other wind so free, balmy, and life-giving, as that of the Caribbean; no other sea is so delightful for sailing.

Never, I am sure, should I tire of voyaging this sea in a speedy vessel, of watching the streaming, far-flung wake of verdigris, turquoise, and veridian; of standing in the very eyes of the plunging craft and, with the rushing wind whipping the salt spray in my face, gazing at the hissing, prismatic curling bow wave and the skittering flying-fish like miniature hydroplanes. Never should I weary of watching those wondrous masses of a thousand shades of green rising above the rim of the sea, of seeing the hazy, opalescent forms develop into mile-high mountains, stupendous gorges, and vast, forest-clad hills. Glorious are the saffron-and-pink-hued dawns when the sea seems swept and scoured, so scintillating it is. And equally wonderful are the flaming orange-and-crimson sunsets, with the water mauve, lavender, and royal purple in the fading light of day. Then, when night comes, suddenly and like a black curtain dropped from the zenith, and the myriad gleaming stars spangle the velvety dome of the sky and the Southern Cross glows low in the heavens,—then is the world filled with romance and peace as the gentle rise and fall of the vessel lulls to rest, the creaking tackle and rigging and the soft lapping of the waves whisper a lullaby, and the balmy night wind touches one's cheek with a caress. If I could have my heart's desire, I should, I think, choose to spend my declining years sailing the Spanish Main in a swift and handy ship, cruising aimlessly, touching where fancy willed, free as one of the swift-winged frigate-birds, untrammeled as the leaping porpoises.

Being possessed of a passion for the sea and for the ships that sail thereon, and with an even greater fondness for my familiar and beloved Caribbean, I can well understand why the buccaneers loved their wild life.

It was not simply gain, murder, debauchery, or lawlessness that lured them, that kept them ceaselessly reaching, scudding, tacking, and beating back and forth, round and about the Spanish Main. Most of them had more treasure than they could ever need—more than they could ever spend—cached here and there. No, it was largely sheer love of the sea, a resistless desire to feel the heaving decks under their feet, the pure fascination of adventure.

So let us not judge them too harshly. In their day, loot in time of war was legitimate and included the females of the vanquished; slavery flourished; debtors were sold as slaves. Taken all in all, the buccaneers were gentlemanly in their treatment of prisoners according to the customs of their times, while, compared with other forms of death then in vogue, walking the plank was a merciful end.

Besides, men's tastes, ideas, constitutions, feelings, and sensitiveness vary. Many a man would have found the blazing sun and the spray-sprinkled deck of the *Vigilant* a most uncomfortable and unpleasant spot, and would have gone mad had he been obliged to sail hither and yon on the old packet. To straddle a yard, soaring back and forth sixty feet above the sea, as must those of my crew, would have been a physical impossibility to thousands. To climb mountains is pure enjoyment to many, and yet I can imagine nothing more irksome. Big Sam, standing there on his firm flat feet, and deftly twirling the wheel, would have found it far harder and more of a strain to write a dozen misspelled lines than to dive for sponges in shark-infested waters day after day. And so we cannot hope to fathom the depths of others' thoughts, to realize their sensations, or to understand their points of view, and we might just as well give up trying to analyze the buccaneers and, forgetting their shortcomings, enjoy the romance of their lives.

Thus musing, I glanced at Sam; and, remembering that in his veins flowed a bit of the wild blood of Red Lithgow, I asked:

"Sam, how would you like to be a pirate?"

For a brief instant the huge negro looked puzzled,—perhaps thinking the sun had affected my head,—and then a broad, tooth-filled grin spread over his shining black face.

"Lordy, Chief!" he rumbled. "Ah' spec' yo' 's jus' tryin' for to spoof me. The' ain't pirates now-'days; th' parsed on years agone."

"Are n't there!" I exclaimed. "You 've never

ridden in a New York taxi, Sam, or dined in an American restaurant, or traveled in a Pullman."

The Bahaman's eyes widened.

"Lordy!" he ejaculated. "You don' is tellin' me true, Chief?"

Sam's childlike simplicity and his utter innocence were irresistible, and I burst into a roar of laughter.

"I was just speaking figuratively," I explained. "But honestly, Sam, would n't you like to sail up alongside a ship, leap over her rails with a pistol in one hand and a sword in the other, and murder her crew and take her treasure?"

Sam shook his broad-hatted, kinky head decidedly.

"No-o, sir, Chief!" he declared. "Ah 's a man o' peace, Ah is, an' Ah 's no desire for to do nothin' that 's like what yo' says. An' ah 's tellin' yo' true, Chief, if Ah sees a man wif a gun or pistol approachin' me, Ah don' mek to remain to argify. No, sir! Ah jus' says to mah feet, 'The Lord put you on mah laigs for to run, an' now you obey the Lord.' "

Truly, Red Lithgow's blood had turned to water in his descendant's veins!

But now St. John was close aboard, and there were other matters to engage attention besides jollying good-natured, harmless old Sam. Rugged and bold the coast-line loomed above the beating surf. Behind the beetling cliffs and ragged, needle-pointed rocks of the shore rose the rich green hills and mountains, and, like glimpses of fairyland between the outjutting fangs of rock, were cream-white beaches rimmed with turquoise, shaded with nodding palms, and backed by luscious green.

Almost like a continuation of St. Thomas seemed the island, with only the narrow sound three miles in width separating its western tip from its sister isle; while, beyond, Mingo, Grass, Lovango, and Congo cays looked from the distance like low-lying connecting land.

But if the two islands were separated by a thousand miles of sea, there could not be a greater difference in their appearance. St. Thomas—dry, barren, denuded of trees—reminds one of a gray-haired man oppressed with the weight of years; it is as though sere autumn made its abode there. But St. John—fresh, green, forest-clad—is perpetual youth, everlasting summer epitomized in sunshine, sparkling streams, and luxuriant verdure.

Swiftly the *Vigilant* drew near the island gem, heading in for Rendezvous Bay, once the favorite meeting-place of privateer and freebooter, and off the beach the schooner's anchor splashed over and dropped swiftly through the crystalline water to the floor of coral sand. Here, in the neighboring bush, I had been told, was to be found many a relic of buccaneer days; but so wild and untouched did the shore appear that it was hard to believe even the buccaneers ever had set foot upon it.

But then, St. John is almost deserted throughout its length and breadth. Yet it was once a prosperous and well-inhabited spot, a land of broad fields, great plantations, and rich estates. Its shores were fortified, its sheltered bays were filled with shipping, and it was a source of envy, dispute, and even bloodshed among the powers. To-day it is all but unknown; its landlocked harbors are bare of ship or sail; its plantations are overgrown with bush; great forest trees have sprung from gardens and have hidden the crumbling remains of once stately residences; its forts are ruins.

St. John is one of the most fertile of the islands, the best by far of all the Virgins, incomparably superior to St. Thomas in point of scenery, climate, and resources, and worth more intrinsically than St. Thomas and St. Croix rolled into one, while Coral Bay is probably the safest and most commodious harbor in the Lesser Antilles. Unlike St. Thomas, it is well watered, with an abundance of streams; it is the source of nearly all the bay-oil which goes to make the famed St. Thomas bay-rum, its waters teem with fish, and as a winter resort it would be ideal. Why, we may ask, is the most attractive of Uncle Sam's three Virgin Isles in so lamentable a state? It is difficult to say, but present conditions are due largely to its past; for, like human beings with a shady record, the West Indies find it hard to live down a reputation acquired in years gone by, and lands, like individuals, seldom "come back."

And so, while Sam and his black and brown shipmates are furling the old *Vigilant's* sails, a brief outline of St. John's turbulent history may not come amiss.

Although the Spaniards saw little in the Virgin Isles to attract their cupidity and insatiable lust for gold, and, with so many far richer and more promising lands to loot and ravage, left them alone, yet other Europeans saw promise in them and took possession in the names of their respective sovereigns.

Just when St. John was first settled, or by whom, is not recorded; but in 1687 the papers appointing the governor of the Danish islands included St. John as a Danish possession. Two years previously Barbadians had attempted to settle on the island, but the jealous governor of the Leeward Islands promptly ejected the forty colonists who had established their homes on St. John. From that time on, the little island was a bone of contention between England and Denmark, and although the Danes were anxious to settle and to cultivate St. John they hestitated because of the dog-in-the-manger attitude of the governor of the neighboring British island of Tortola.

It was not until 1717 that, acting under instructions from the Danish West Indian Company, Governor Erik Bredal—arriving in an armed vessel carrying five soldiers with an officer, sixteen negro slaves, and twenty planters—set the flag of Denmark on St. John's soil and, having duly fired a salute and drunk the king's health, erected a fort overlooking Coral Bay. But while the little garrison remained loyally to guard this addition to the Danish possessions, the faint-hearted planters withdrew to the more secure shores of St. Thomas until it might be seen how the dreaded British would take the move. And they had not long to wait. No sooner was word carried to the Leeward Islands that the Danes had had the temerity to place their flag upon a fort on St. John than a man-of-war was despatched to St. Thomas, demanding, with dire threats, that the Danes at once withdraw their claims and abandon the fort. But, apparently, stout old Governor Bredal had inherited some of the Viking spirit as well as blood, and instead of meekly acceding to the British demands he promptly sent to Denmark a request for one hundred soldiers to augment his little garrison on St. John. With this reinforcement the Danes felt quite secure, and by 1720 thirty-nine planters were established on the island.

From this nucleus the colony rapidly grew, for the land was fertile and the grants given the settlers were larger than in St. Thomas. By 1733, or only thirteen years after the first real settlement was established, St. John had a population of nearly thirteen hundred, of whom two hundred were whites and the other one thousand and eighty-seven negro slaves. Oddly enough, these settlers were not Danes but Dutch, and to-day the majority of local names and the family names of the few remaining inhabitants are largely Dutch.

But in that same year, 1733, other and more serious troubles than the British beset the islanders, for in November the inhuman treatment accorded the slaves resulted in a bloody revolt. And if we look at the old records we can scarcely blame the negroes, and can almost forgive the fiendish savagery with which they carried on their hopeless struggle for freedom.

Gardelin, who was then governor, was an unusually brutal man even for his time, and in order to prevent the slaves from running away to Porto

Rico an inhuman assortment of punishments were decreed. A leader of runaway slaves was to be hanged after having been pinched three times with red-hot irons. Any runaway slave was to forfeit an ear or a leg, or receive one hundred and fifty lashes, according to his owner's preference. A slave who was cognizant of a plot and did not betray his fellows was branded on the forehead and received one hundred lashes as well, and any black who raised his hand against a white was hanged, or had his right hand cut off, as his accuser chose. To attempt to poison a white man meant to be pinched three times with red-hot irons and then broken on the wheel. Any slave giving information of a conspiracy received a reward of money equal to about ten dollars for every negro named as participating in the plot.

These terrible measures—which every four months were publicly proclaimed to the beat of drums—did not in the least repress the slaves, but, if anything, made matters worse, and the negroes secretly planned to surprise the garrison of the fort, which then consisted of only eight men and two officers. Knowing that an open attack would be fruitless, the slaves resorted to strategy. On the morning of November 23d a small band of them, carrying bundles of firewood, approached the fort, and in reply to the sentry's challenge stated that they had been ordered to bring the fuel for the use of the soldiers. Not suspecting the smoldering revolt, the sentry allowed them to enter, whereupon the negroes, casting the fagots aside and whipping cane-knives from their bundles, massacred all but one man who had secreted himself under a bed.

Once in possession of the fort, the slaves fired three guns as a signal, and instantly a general slaughter of the whites began. The first place to fall was the Caroline Estate, where the presiding judge of St. John was murdered together with his daughter and twenty-five men, women, and children. But as was ever the case in negro revolts in the West Indies, a few slaves who had been fortunate enough to have kind and humane masters remained faithful, and as a result many of the planters were warned in time to escape. Accompanied by their faithful blacks, these people sought refuge at Peter Duerloo's plantation at Little Cinnamon Bay, known nowadays as K. C. Bay, on the northwestern coast. This estate was in effect a fortification, as it was situated on a height and was armed with two cannon; and, moreover, it was within easy distance of St. Thomas. Reaching the place in safety, the women and children were despatched to outlying cays, and messages were sent to Charlotte Amalie telling of the revolt and beseeching assistance.

Hardly had the appeal been sent and the defenses strengthened when the horde of blood-crazed negroes arrived; but instead of finding easy victims they were met with a fusillade which wrought havoc among them, and, demoralized and frightened, they drew off. Before they could summon enough courage to attack the estate again, eighteen soldiers arrived by boat from St. Thomas and a larger body landed at Coral Bay. But although the troops relieved the refugees at Little Cinnamon Bay, they could not suppress the revolt nor capture the negroes, who held the entire island with the exception of the estate of Peter Duerloo. Having disposed of the few remaining planters, the slaves burned and pillaged, firing cane-fields, wrecking and destroying buildings and machinery, and doing everything in their power to transform the fair and fertile land into a desolated wilderness. Unable to cope with the situation, the Danes called on their one-time enemies for aid, and a British frigate, which happened to be at Tortola, sent her boats' crews of bluejackets to the island. But even these allies were unsuccessful, and, being ambushed, were forced to retreat with heavy loss.

A second attempt on the part of the British to aid the Danes, resulted in an ignominious defeat when in 1734 volunteers from Nevis sought to conquer the victorious negroes. With a loss of several killed and more wounded ere they had really set foot on St. John the English beat a hasty retreat and left the Danes to their own devices. By now the Danes, deserted by the British, had become desperate and sought to induce the French in Martinique to help them, offering to the French four fifths of all negroes taken prisoners. This was a strong temptation, and two Martinique barks sailed for the stricken island, carrying a force of two hundred and twenty men. Forcing a landing at Coral Bay, this large company,—who had had much experience in putting down uprisings in the French possessions,—augmented by the Danish and local forces numbering nearly two hundred men, began a systematic guerrilla warfare, hunting down and killing the revolting slaves wherever these were found. As an island less than ten miles in length and but four miles wide is easily covered by four hundred determined men, the negroes were very soon put to death or captured. A few, rather than surrender and suffer the tortures which they knew would be their lot, committed suicide, and one band of twenty-five were found all of whom had taken their own lives.

By May 24th the revolt was over. Only fourteen slaves were still at liberty, and these soon gave themselves up, relying on a promise of pardon. But, as usual, a promise to a negro was not looked upon as binding, and the fourteen were promptly executed. What the French gained is hard to see, for from the records it appears there were no living negroes to be turned over to the Martinicans as their share, the twenty-seven rebels who had been captured during the fighting having been tortured and put to death as a grim warning to others.

During the insurrection many of the St. John planters moved bag and baggage to Tortola. But, despite these desertions and the almost complete loss of everything on the island, the place rapidly recovered, and by 1789 had a population of over twenty-four hundred, consisting of about one hundred and seventy whites and over twenty-two hundred slaves. Indeed, this was the period of St. John's greatest prosperity. From that time on the island's fortunes slowly declined, until, to-day, it is doubtful if a complete census of the island would show eight hundred human beings, including the Moravian missionaries at Emmaus. There are no towns, the only settlements being at Cruz Bay, where there are fewer than two hundred people, East End with fewer than one hundred, and Emmaus with about fifty.

By burning charcoal, making baskets, fishing, gathering and distilling bay-leaves, and raising a few cattle and some garden truck, the natives make an easy if not very luxurious living, while all that remains to testify to the island's former prosperity are the crumbling ruins of the mills, the overgrown walls and courtyards of the estate buildings, and the remains of the forts upon the hills.

CHAPTER V

ST. JOHN AND SOME DISCOVERIES

NO one can say when the buccaneers first selected St. John as a refuge, but no doubt it was long before the Danes or the Dutch first settled there. Pirates haunted the Virgin Islands previous to 1687, and it would not be surprising if honor for the first buildings erected on St. John and for the first settlements should be accorded them. Many of its bays and coves bear names which associate them with the corsairs,—as, for instance, Rendezvouz Bay and Privateers' Bay,—and undoubtedly these names wcrc already in use when the first Dutch and Danes arrived on St. John. There are also ruins of forts and buildings covered with brush and jungle which unquestionably antedate the first peaceful settlement; but history took no cognizance of the freebooters, and the story of their occupancy of St. John probably will never be known. At any rate, for many a year, the Virgin Isles were notorious as a resort of buccaneers, and in Coral Bay, Privateers' Bay, and Rendezvouz Bay they beached and careened their ships and romped and skylarked on the coral sands, while the woods and cliffs rang to the echoes of their lusty songs and shouts and the smoke of barbecue fires rose in blue wisps against the greenery, just as a column of lilac smoke from a negro hut was rising upward in the clear morning air as the *Vigilant's* anchor splashed overboard and the big sails came rattling down within the sheltered bay that had harbored many a pirate craft.

We know too, from historical records, that the Danish authorities were friendly to the pirates and buccaneers before St. John was settled, for in 1682 Jean Hamlin made his headquarters in St. Thomas and was well received by the governor, who no doubt shared the corsair's loot in return for the refuge accorded.

In the year mentioned, Hamlin made a prize of the French ship *La Trompeuse* and, finding her a better craft than his own, fitted her out with guns, shipped a pirate crew, and proceeded to ravage the Caribbean, making Charlotte Amalie his headquarters. Hamlin was by no means an ideal buccaneer. He attacked any merchantman he sighted, regardless of flag or nationality, and in 1683 a number of British ships fell to his cannon. Not content with the pickings to be had among the islands, he sailed for the African coast and there had a joyous and profitable time, taking seventeen Dutch and English vessels. But the fever-ridden, jungle-covered coasts of the Dark Continent did not appeal to the romantic soul of the merry sea-rover; and so, feeling he had accomplished quite enough to have earned a vacation, he hoisted sail and headed westward for St. Thomas.

Here he was warmly welcomed by his old crony the governor, who willingly gave him permission to bring the loot of the cruise ashore for safekeeping —and probably division as well—and entertained the piratical chieftain in right good style. Three days after Hamlin's arrival, however, another ship sailed into Charlotte Amalie's snug harbor and came to anchor before the picturesque town. And, to the discomfiture of some and the delight of others, this new arrival proved to be no other than H. M. S. *Francis* under command of Captain Carlile of His Britannic Majesty's navy, who had been sent forth by Governor Stapleton of the Leeward Islands to hunt for all pirates in general and one known as Jean Hamlin in particular.

We may imagine the satisfaction with which the scarlet-faced old sea-dog noted the long-sought *La Trompeuse* snugly moored within easy reach. With the British seaman's usual disregard for red tape and diplomatic correspondence, he took matters into his own hands and promptly disposed of the pirate craft by blowing her up. To be sure, the buccaneer captain and some of his crew were on board, but Hamlin was no such fool as to attempt to resist when under the broadsides of a frigate half a gunshot distant; and, after firing a few shots merely as a protest or to ease his conscience, he decided discretion to be the better part of valor, and sought the shore and his Danish friends.

No doubt, over their cups, the governor and the corsair gazed forth with mingled sorrow and resentment as the glare of the blazing ship illuminated the harbor and the red-roofed town, for *La Trompeuse* had proved a lucky and profitable craft. As the two discussed the matter and damned the British, the governor waxed exceeding wroth, and he forthwith penned a note to Captain Carlile, vigorously denouncing his actions in having brazenly and unwarrantedly destroyed a frigate which had been confiscated in the name of the King of Denmark. But the governor was a mortal who believed in never letting his left hand know what his right was doing, and as he scribbled his note to the Englishman he sent Hamlin and his men to a safe refuge in another part of the island and, providing the captain with a speedy sloop,

ST. JOHN The careenage, Rendezvous Bay

STATIA Along the waterfront

ST JOHN A vista on the Peter Duerloo estate

wished him God-speed on his way to join the French buccaneers in Tortuga.

Indeed, this worthy governor, who bore the name of Adolf Esmit, had the reputation of being an all-round bad egg. Privateering had been his former occupation, and while buccaneers and their ilk were looked upon, even by law-abiding citizens, as something of gentlemen and good fellows, and no one greatly blamed Adolf for protecting these soldiers of fortune—for a consideration, of course—still, the islanders did not like the idea of his harboring riffraff from far and near and gathering under his hospitable wing a crowd of runaway slaves and servants, deserting seamen, and debtors. Moreover, he was a usurper. He had driven away his brother Nickolas, who was the rightful governor, and then, having acquired what we should nowadays dub a case of "swelled head," had seen fit to declare himself governor of all the Virgin Isles and snapped his fingers, figuratively if not literally, at the British claimants and the Danish authorities as well. In the meantime he piled up a goodly sum for a rainy day by outfitting pirate ships and refusing to restore to their rightful owners prizes brought to his island.

But even Adolf realized that there was a limit

to effrontery, and when protests became too numerous for comfort he hinted to his associates that St. John was far more attractive than St. Thomas, that its harbors were safer and more commodious, and that, it being uninhabited, his corsair friends could be sure that no one would object to their presence there. And as the place was but three miles distant from St. Thomas, it was quite feasible for him and his cronies to spend jolly evenings together and none the wiser.

Of course, in time, tales of Esmit's activities reached Denmark; and, whatever his private opinions may have been, the Danish sovereign was in no mind to have serious difficulties with Great Britain. Therefore he promptly despatched a new man, named Iversen, to take charge of St. Thomas's fortunes, and, foreseeing difficulties in getting rid of Esmit, suggested that Governor Stapleton should aid the new executive with force of arms. The British, nothing loath, gladly agreed, and, reinforced with an armed sloop from the British islands, Iversen arrived at St. Thomas in October, 1684, and without resistance took possession not only of the islands but of Adolf as well.

Possibly Iversen had no ill-will against the buccaneers; or possibly he followed his orders to the letter and, not being quite certain in his mind as to whether St. John was under his jurisdiction or not, left the freebooters in the neighboring isle unmolested and diplomatically informed the British that if they wished St. John rid of pirates they could do the job themselves. Whether they attempted it or not, history fails to record, but if they did they must have been unsuccessful, for English history seldom fails to call attention to every victory, no matter how small, although British historians are often remarkably absent-minded regarding the other side of the ledger.

Moreover, as the islands then under the British flag were not above harboring well-disposed pirate craft, it is exceedingly doubtful if even peppery old Governor Stapleton bestirred himself greatly, with his meager forces, against the buccaneers. He well knew that he could not hope to destroy or capture them all and that too much hostility would merely result in reprisals on British merchant ships which the struggling English colonies could ill afford.

My quest for buccaneer relics or remains on St. John was not very successful. Sam and my St. Thomas friends had, as I have already mentioned, assured me that the place possessed many remains such as buildings and forts; that pirate cannon were scattered in the brush, and that weapons, pieces of eight, doubloons, and onzas had often been found by the natives. It was even hinted that somewhere about Rendezvouz Bay there was a vast pirate treasure hidden. But as there is no bit of land upon this planet whereon pirates actually or traditionally ever set foot that does not boast of its treasure-trove, I took the last-mentioned report for what it was worth and no more. Even on matter-of-fact St. Thomas—or, rather, on the outlying cays—there is supposed to be vast treasure concealed; and many a St. Thomian has spent much time and no little energy in industriously digging the soil in the vain hopes of unearthing this pirate gold.

However, I did place credence in the tales of pirates' ruins and pirates' guns, and did not think it either impossible or improbable that an occasional ancient coin had been found. Indeed, when one old man vowed that there were even pirate wrecks to be seen, coral-incrusted, upon the sandy bottom of Privateers' Bay, I judged it within the bounds of possibility that this might be so, for buccaneers' ships sometimes sank, like other craft, and wood—especially stout oak and teak—will endure for many centuries under salt water.

But, while I found St. John charming; although

I enjoyed my tramps and rambles through its bay-filled forests and along its beautiful coast; while I found many an overgrown, deserted plantation and crumbling ruin of great house and mill bearing mute testimony to the negro uprising of two centuries ago; while I stood upon the height whereon that sturdy little company of Dutch and Danes had gathered at old Peter Duerloo's barricaded and cannon-guarded home and driven back the savage black hordes; while near at hand I tripped over a rusty, ancient carronade which I saw fit to believe was one of the "two small guns" which according to history had hurled their death-dealing grapeshot among the blood-crazed negroes, still, of buccaneers I found no indisputable trace. There are some ancient crumbling walls near the landing-places at both Privateers' and Rendezvous Bay,—ruins of man's handiwork evidently antedating the oldest Danish or Dutch masonry upon St. John,—but there is nothing to prove that these were buildings erected by pirates.

Once, to be sure, I was greatly elated when a white-headed, tottering old negro with lackluster eyes and toothless mouth hobbled to our camp on the beach and, carefully unwrapping several layers of dried banana leaves, produced a corroded sword blade with the cross hilt of a design dating back to buccaneer days. He had found it, he mumbled in almost unintelligible words, while clearing away the brush preparatory to making a charcoal-pit, and I gladly paid him thrice the fifty cents he asked for it.

But my hopes were shattered and my romantic notions dispersed to the four winds when, in cleaning the dirt and rust from the blade, I uncovered the unmistakable imprint of the Broad Arrow near the hilt, with the half-obliterated arms of England near it. To be sure, that did not prove it was *not* a buccaneer's sword, but it seemed far more probably a trusty blade dropped from the lifeless hand of one of those Britons who had sought to help the Danes suppress the revolting blacks. Though I preferred a pirate weapon for a souvenir, there were plenty of romantic and historical associations connected with this silent, long-lost witness of the bloody days of St. John's past, whether wielded by sea-rover or by British soldier, and I was satisfied that I at least would not sail empty-handed from this half-deserted, drowsy little Virgin isle.

I must confess that I had grown very fond of the half-forgotten, sadly neglected place, and when at last the time came when we must up anchor and away from St. John, I felt really sorry to leave.

I had seen the island thoroughly. We had cast anchor in many a lovely bay and for the last night we were moored in the snug "Hurricane Hole" in Coral Bay, perhaps the finest natural harbor in all the West Indies.

Close at hand upon the headland were the scarcely distinguishable ruins of that first fort erected by old Governor Bredal, wherein the unsuspecting garrison had been butchered by the fagot-bearing slaves. Seated under the shadow of the big mainsail as the *Vigilant* rode to her anchor and the soft lapping of the waves along the beach and the chirp of crickets and the grunt of land frogs were borne to me on the soft night breeze, my mind harked back to those long-past days when these isles literally were steeped in blood.

Like a ghostly silhouette upon the hilltop I could see the ruined fort about which battle red and furious had raged. Up that green-clad slope had charged the soldiers of three, or perchance four, nations, first one then another winning the day and holding, for a brief space, the hard-won battlements, until another enemy, by greater prowess or more reckless sacrifice of life, wrested it from their grasp. Perchance, in later years, the buccaneers had also hurled themselves, through mimosa scrub and aloes, upon the stout stone walls, shouting and cursing, falling and dying, but heedless of loss, still carrying on in face of blazing musket and thundering cannon.

Within those selfsame walls the frightened women and children and the white-faced, determined men from the little town and outlying estates had huddled, while, to their eyes, the pillars of smoke rising from blazing cane-fields and smoldering mansions told of the destructive savagery of revolting slaves; and from the wrecked town beside the harbor had come fiendish cries, revolting voodoo chants, and the terrifying boom of the savage tom-tom.

But now it was silent, deserted, weed-grown, and forgotten; the home of soft-winged bats, jewel-eyed lizards, and other creeping things. Gone were the ancient bronze pieces that once filled the embrasures; gone the tramping sentries; gone the staff that once upheld the flag. And I wondered if at dead of night the spirits of these long-gone and forgotten men and women, to whom the fort had meant so much, did not haunt that crumbling, picturesque old ruin. Perhaps, even now, they were looking down upon the starlit harbor, at the black tracery of the *Vigilant's* rigging, and in her altered spars and renovated hull recognizing a craft which had been a familiar sight in the days when they walked the earth, and loved and fought and suffered and were gay in turn.

Then the spell of the night was broken. From forward came the half-barbaric music of a "sand-box" rattle, a squeaky fiddle, and a mouth organ, and echoing over the harbor came Sam's full-throated voice in a weird, garbled version of "Sally Brown":

"Oh, Sally Brown she are so pretty—
Way-ee Sally, Sally Brown!
Oh, Sally Brown o' Noo York City—
Way-ee 'll spen' mah money for Sally Brown.

"Oh, Sally Brown she fall 'n th' water—
Way-ee Sally, Sally Brown!
Oh, Ah drug her out an' had n' oughter—
Way-ee 'll spen' mah money for Sally Brown.

"Oh, Sally Brown she say she love me—
Way-ee Sally, Sally Brown!
Oh, Sally Brown to th' sea she druv me—
Way-ee 'll spen' mah money for Sally Brown.

"Oh, Sally Brown, would you b'lieve me—
Way-ee Sally, Sally Brown!
For a 'Badoes nigger she do leave me—
Way-ee 'll spen' mah money for Sally Brown."

And as the echoes of the applause that followed died away I wondered if the buccaneers themselves had sung this ancient chantey. To every sailor-man, from time immemorial, it has been known, in one version or another. In the spicy isles of the South Seas the Kanakas chant it as they labor. Its tune and words ring through the forest-hemmed lumber-camps of the Northern woods. Many a tired, footsore, struggling musher in far-off Alaska has found new courage and inspiration in the song. In the frigid Antarctic wastes it has aroused the drowsing sea-elephants on desolate isles. And up and down the Antilles the sweating negroes work in unison to the tune as they pull their huge drougher boats or snake the great logs of hardwood timbers from the mountain jungles. Up and down and round the world it has traveled, from pole to pole, and if buccaneer and pirate did not bellow it, then they were no true sailormen.

But now another voice is singing—not Sam's this time, but a higher if no less mellow voice which I recognize as Joe's. And though the air is familiar, the words with which the West Indians have fitted it are astounding, for, according to my cook's version, "John Brown's donkey had a red Morocco tail"! With all the seriousness of a great artist Joseph sings his ridiculous ditty to the end, to be rewarded with deafening applause but no laughter, for the West Indian can see nothing comical in a red Morocco tail on John Brown's donkey; he believes firmly that donkeys of the United States do possess such colorful caudal appendages, for does the verse not say so? To his mind, anything is possible in "New York," as the West Indian invariably calls the States.

This belief of the West Indian negroes that New York and the United States are synonymous is very amusing. Even Joe, who was far above his fellows, in education and intelligence, seriously confided to me on one occasion that he had seen New York. Expressing surprise at this revelation, I asked for further particulars, and was told that when he was serving as cook on a schooner bound for Matamoras, Mexico, the mate had pointed out a low-lying coast-line and had told Joe it was New York. My explanations were absolutely futile. To Joe, New York embodied all of our country. With his own eyes he had gazed upon the promised land, and to his dying day—unless by some chance he visits the States—he will boast to his less fortunate fellows that he has seen New York.

Following our cook's rendition of "John Brown" there was silence for a space and then, in place of sand-box, raucous fiddle, and discordant harmonica, the soft, liquid tinkle of a guitar rippled through the tropic night and a wonderfully rich voice began to sing:

"Vuelvo dormir,
Vuelvo sonar,
Y siempre estoy."

I was all attention; surprised, curious. I was unaware that we had a Spanish West Indian in our crew, and while I knew that Sam, Joe, and one or two others spoke a smattering of Spanish and had visited Cuba, Porto Rico, Santo Domingo, or Panama, their accent was atrocious. Never, I was sure, could they have mastered a Spanish song. And now the singer had changed his tune. There was a plaintive wail in the silvery notes of his guitar that tugged at one's heart-strings, and, filled with pathos and yearning, his voice came drifting to me, filling the night with the melody of "La Paloma."

Scores—yes, hundreds—of times, I had listened to that dreamy, haunting air. I had heard it sung by shadowy vaqueros watching their herds on broad, black llanos under twinkling stars. I had heard it borne on the night breeze, as, resting under waving palms, I had watched a lateen-sailed craft creep across the moon's silvery "Path to Spain." I had heard it hummed by the carmine lips of black-eyed, full-throated señoritas leaning from the grilled railings of their windows in many a Latin-American town, and I had heard it issuing from garish dance-halls heavy with the scent of musk and the smoke from brown cigarettes. But never had I heard it sung as on that last night that the old *Vigilant* swung to her anchor off St. John.

Rising, I strolled forward, filled with curiosity as to the identity of the singer. As I reached the galley and from its shadows glanced at the little group about the fore hatch I could scarcely believe my eyes. Seated upon the anchor winch, across his knees a battered guitar which belonged to Joseph, the final words of "La Paloma" issuing from his huge mouth, was—Trouble!

CHAPTER VI

ANEGADA AND A BIT OF TREASURE-TROVE

NORTH of St. John and so close to it as to appear, from a short distance, but a continuation, lies Tortola, the British isle which played so prominent a part in St. John's early history. In beauty rivaling its once Danish neighbor, Tortola (or "the island of the turtle dove") is even more forsaken,—an island of the blest given over to the blacks, the only white men being the resident magistrate and a half-dozen representatives of his Britannic Majesty,—while Roadtown, its capital, is but a tumble-down village of scarcely five hundred souls.

And yet in times gone by Tortola was a prosperous and wealthy island. In Roadtown's harbor scores of great square-rigged ships rode to their moorings; along the quay, drays, trucks, and carts groaned and squeaked from morn till night. Long lines of black stevedores and porters passed like a procession of restless ants from drougher boats to warehouses and marts. Sloops and long-oared boats manned by toiling slaves came from outlying plantations, laden with hogsheads of molasses, rum, and sugar; with pimento, bay-leaves, and spices; with bales of tobacco and cargoes of fruit. And the waterside taverns echoed to the shouts and songs, the boisterous laughter, and the deep-sea oaths of pigtailed sailormen in glazed hats. And here, too, the sea-rovers gathered, for Tortola, largest of the Virgins, was, like its sisters, a retreat of the buccaneers.

To-day, from time to time, ancient cannon and equally ancient coins are found here and there upon the island and, by common consent, are invariably credited to buccaneer origin. But it is very doubtful that the pirates ever had works or guns ashore at Tortola. As there was nothing to lead me to believe that they had, and as there were so many isles where they did certainly foregather and where associations that link them with the present still remain, I passed Tortola by and told Sam to shape the *Vigilant's* course for Anegada, most northerly of the Virgins, and once the buccaneers' favorite retreat among these little isles.

Close at hand rose the Fat Virgin, or, as it is more commonly and more euphoniously called, Virgin Gorda, a rather barren spot like St. Thomas in miniature with its central peaks thirteen hundred feet above the breaking surf.

Low down and nestling in the lee of Tortola is Norman Island, a tiny speck, like Dead Man's Chest, notable for its traditions and not for its size or importance; for on Norman Island is said to be buried that huge and entirely mythical treasure of the most widely known pirate of song and story, Captain Kidd.

I doubt if there is a stretch of coast ten miles in length between the Bay of Fundy and the Gulf of Mexico, or an island or wave-washed rock in the Atlantic or the Caribbean whereon Captain Kidd's treasure-trove is not supposedly buried. How many thousands of men have searched and dug and toiled to unearth that will-o'-the-wisp hoard no one can say. How much real money has been expended in that same vain quest, it is impossible to estimate, but beyond the shadow of a doubt the money spent in digging for this treasure is greatly in excess of all the gold and other riches William Kidd ever saw or hoped to see. And, oddly enough, there is no proof, no reason even to think that the notorious captain ever buried a cent's worth of loot on any spot other than Gardiner's Island, in Long Island Sound, whence it was recovered by those for whom Kidd had placed it in safety there. Strange indeed is the reputation, the fame that has been reared and built about the name of Captain Kidd. It shows what advertising and publicity will do, and how very little the public cares for facts, provided the fiction appeals to the imagination, for Captain Kidd—whose name is a synonym of piracy—was neither a pirate nor a buccaneer.

That he was hanged as a pirate is true, but many a man has been hanged for a murderer who was afterward proved innocent, and the unfortunate Kidd was a victim of circumstances, of avarice, jealousy, and revenge; the victim of what we to-day should call a "frame-up." Not a particle of evidence worthy of consideration was ever brought forward to show that he was a pirate. Indeed, Captain Kidd, instead of being a pirate, was commissioned to catch pirates, his authority being granted by King William III of Great Britain and addressed to "our trusty and dearly beloved Captain William Kidd, of the ship *Adventure*, gally."

Long before this, however, Kidd, who was a native of Greenock, Scotland, was a well-known and highly respected mariner with a reputation, along the American seaboard, for fair and honest dealing. Meeting with various influential and wealthy men who saw in the suppression of pirates and robbing of robbers a handsome profit, the worthy seaman was prevailed upon to set forth under royal warrant to deal summarily with "divers wicked and ill-disposed persons who were committing many and grievous pyraces to the hurt and danger of our loving subjects."

Setting sail from the port of Plymouth, England, in May, 1696, Kidd and his company of one hundred and fifty-five men proceeded to scour the seas in search of the "pyrates." Either the "wicked and ill-disposed persons" had heard of his mission or else luck was against him: for the pirate-exterminator failed to find pirates to exterminate. Sailors then, as ever, were a disgruntled lot, and Kidd's crew, growing weary of finding no corsairs with whom to match arms, evidently decided that the next best thing was to emulate them and do a little pirating on their own account. Consequently, the *Adventure* bore down upon a Moorish ship, the *Queda Merchant,* which was in command of an English captain, and took possession of her. Whether Kidd, finding his crew had made up their minds to turn pirates, gave in to superior numbers and consented to this temporary lapse from honesty; whether he was actually overpowered and held captive while the capture of the *Queda Merchant* was taking place, or whether the captain himself was so sorely tempted that he fell, may never be known. At his trial he contended

—and very probably with truth—that his crew mutinied, threatened his life, and confined him to his cabin while the piratical venture was being carried out. Whatever the facts were, word of the *Adventure's* seizure of the *Queda* reached the authorities, and Kidd was forthwith declared a pirate.

In the meantime, the *Adventure* had become unseaworthy, and, transferring his more valuable possessions to his prize, Captain Kidd sailed for Santo Domingo, then known as Hispaniola, with—so he stated—the intention of notifying the authorities. But at Hispaniola the "dearly beloved" William heard that he was "wanted," and, hastily purchasing a small sloop, he set sail for New England. There, being somewhat doubtful about the reception he might receive, he got into communication with his backers, and secreted what valuables he had, on Gardiner's Island.

To recount the lengthy proceedings which ensued would avail nothing and would add no interest to Kidd's story. Suffice it to say that eventually he gave himself up to the authorities in Boston, relying upon promises of a fair trial. From there he was taken as a prisoner to England, and, after innumerable delays, rank perversions of justice, and the breaking of many promises, the unfortunate captain was placed on trial at Old Bailey in May, 1701.

The trial was from first to last a travesty of justice. Instead of confining themselves to the case in hand, Kidd's accusers charged him with the murder of one of his own men (a gunner named Moore), and the charge of piracy was made secondary. Kidd freely admitted that he had killed Moore, but asserted that the man was mutinous—in fact, the ringleader of those who favored piracy—and that as a master of the ship he had a perfect right to kill a mutineer. As for the charges that he had piratically captured the *Queda,* Kidd explained as aforementioned that the prize had been taken despite him and not because of him, and that he was on the way to report the unfortunate affair when he touched at Santo Domingo. Throughout the trial, proofs and evidence requested by Kidd and promised him were withheld and only theories were admitted, and such damning evidence as the words of his own men. As a result of this farcical trial, Kidd and six of his men who had remained faithful to their captain were condemned to be hanged at Execution Dock, on May 23d. Protesting his innocence to the very last,—even when the rope gave way and, half-strangled, he was lifted up to be rehanged,—Kidd met his death.

Later his body and those of his men were hung in chains down the river, and for many years the rattling skeletons, with clinging shreds of garments and skin, swung in the wind on the dreary mud flats of the Thames, the most disgraceful witnesses to perverted justice that ever passing mariners gazed upon.

But though he died an ignominious death for crimes which he probably never committed, Kidd's martyrdom resulted in his becoming the most famous character of piratical lore, who left a name which will never die. And this is all the more remarkable because, even if we assumed that all the charges against him were true, he would have been a mediocre pirate, having but one rich prize to his score—a small matter indeed to have been the foundation for such fame and a reputation as the master of them all.

Far more romantic and picturesque than "Bold Captain Kidd" was that other sea-rover whose name is associated with the Virgin Islands, but never heard outside the chronicles of the buccaneers and by those who have delved into the story of the corsairs of the Carribbean.

Perhaps no one who has ever lived is more worthy of the title of Don Quixote of the Deep than this man—the wild, romantic, restless, tireless, and ambitious Prince Rupert of the Rhine, who in his ship *Swallow* experienced more adventures and met with more romances than any score of other corsairs. Impetuous, high-strung, nervous, the royal pirate could never be idle for a moment; and it was his terror of doing nothing that drove him from privateering to pirating.

Originally sailing forth to aid his king's cause against Spain, Prince Rupert departed from Ireland in 1648, with a fleet of seven ships and accompanied by his brother, Prince Maurice, who captained the *Defiance*. To paraphrase Longfellow, wild was the life they led, many the souls that sped, for the next five years, and the handsome, brilliant prince, whose "sparkish" dress was ever the envy and admiration of all beholders, mingled piracy and knight errantry in an inextricable manner. Indeed, this wilful scion of royalty was ever a champion of the ladies and an irresistible lover, and even when—long before he took to the sea—he was a prisoner at Linz, he managed to win the heart of the governor's daughter.

But even this musketeer of the sea was fated for the buccaneer's usual short life and merry one. Being caught in a storm among the Virgin Islands one September night, his fleet was driven ashore on low-lying, reef-guarded Anegada, and of all that company few remained to tell the tale. While the *Swallow* escaped and Prince Rupert survived, Prince Maurice was lost, and, heartbroken, the pirate prince set sail for home, in his crippled ship, and landed in France in 1653. But the blow had saddened him, the sea no longer called, and quietly and obscurely he lived in his home at Spring Gardens, England, until in 1682 he succumbed to a fever and passed away, almost unknown and unnoticed.

What a contrast was his life to that of Captain Kidd! The one a romantic, reckless, chivalrous, venturesome pirate, never content save in the thick of battle, and yet dying in his bed, his deeds forgotten, his name dying with him. The other a meek, timid, vacillating seaman, lacking the courage to keep his crew in check and dying a felon's death on the gibbet, and yet living on through the centuries, his name woven into countless tales and verses, and by a single deed—which it is doubtful that he ever performed—making himself immortal as the greatest pirate of them all! And as desolate Anegada rose like some sinister sea-monster upon the horizon, I thought of how unjust is fame and how little men's real deeds count in the reputation they gain.

Ringed round with jagged coral reefs marked by the angry surf, the island is guarded more efficiently than with a battery of guns. So low it is that often it is called the "Drowned" or "Overflowed" Island, for in heavy weather the waves actually sweep across it in places. Nearly twelve miles it stretches in length, with a breadth of barely two miles, and its only inhabitants are blacks; while on its great landlocked lagoons or ponds the grotesque rose-and-scarlet flamingos still find sanctuary.

As we approached this bit of sodden land which meant so much to the buccaneers of old, there seemed to be no entrance through the churning, seething cauldron of foam that stretched away in a stupendous semicircle. But Sam never faltered. Shading his reddened eyes with a huge black hand, he peered intently shoreward, and then, with a twirl of the wheel and a bellowed order to the crew, headed the plunging *Vigilant* straight for the white water. Breathlessly I waited, and great was my trust in Sam or I most certainly should have hastily donned a life-preserver and said my prayers, for to all appearances the Bahaman had decided that this was a fitting spot on which to pile the ancient *Vigilant's* bones.

Nearer and nearer we swept, until the roaring,

boiling surf was almost under our jib-boom. Then, when I expected to feel the crashing shock and the sickening lurch of a speeding hull pierced by fangs of coral, Sam shouted an order, the great sails were close hauled, and, luffing sharply, the schooner slid through a fifty-foot gut in the thundering breakers and a moment later was floating safely on the glassy waters of the lagoon.

No wonder that here the pirates gathered and laughed at their pursuers. Knowing the reef, familiar with its narrow passages, the pursued could sail in safety to their anchorage while their disgruntled enemies, confronted by the deadly ring of coral, and usually in vessels far too large to pass through even had they known the way, turned back utterly baffled.

Throughout the days of buccaneering—yes, even in the days of that first of all sea-rovers who was neither buccaneer nor pirate, but who paved the way for the buccaneers, Sir Francis Drake—Anegada and its surrounding reef-filled waters was a favorite resort of freebooters. Whether Sir Francis ever visited the Drowned Island or not, no one knows. In his memoirs he makes no mention of it, but his name is perpetuated in the Virgin Isles by Sir Francis Drake Bay, while such names as Gallows Bay, Careenage Bay, Galleon Cove, Hawkins's Point, and Cutlass Reef were beyond question bestowed upon these localities in Anegada by the buccaneers themselves.

Aside from having been a haunt of the buccaneers, Anegada is famed for its innumerable shipwrecks. For many years, in the old sailing-ship days, the Anegadans lived mainly upon the wreckage from vessels that left their bones upon the treacherous reefs about the island. In other words, they were notorious wreckers, and they did not hesitate to murder the shipwrecked crews in order to loot the ill-fated ships. Even to-day the natives spend a deal of time—which, it must be confessed, hangs heavily on their hands—on the lookout for luckless vessels. While no open hostility or violence is shown castaway mariners, the inherited instincts of the inhabitants of the island cannot be controlled, and they look upon every wreck as legitimate loot. All about, in every stage of decay and destruction, are to be seen the gaunt skeletons of ships which have found their final resting-place on Anegada's reefs, and the native houses are built very largely of odds and ends of wreckage. Here, a hut fashioned from a ship's galley; there, another made of a partly shattered deck-house; one built of battered hatches or weatherbeaten ships' planking, another roofed with a vessel's rudder, still others with timbers of spars—such are seen on every hand; while every article of any value, such as old metal, cordage, or junk, is collected and saved to be ultimately carried to St. Thomas and disposed of for a few dollars.

As an island, Anegada can boast of no attractions whatsoever. It is quite lacking in scenic beauty, and its inhabitants are miserable folk who win a precarious existence, although there are deposits of copper, silver, and manganese which perchance, in years to come, may be worked and cause this almost forgotten corner of the world to become even more famous than of old.

Anegada also is supposed to hold a pirate treasure of vast size, though why the pirates should have hidden their loot in a haunt of their fellows, whose proclivities they well knew, is a mystery which those who tell of the hidden wealth never attempt to explain. But, unlike so many of the other traditional hiding-places of loot, Anegada furnishes a slight excuse for belief in the tale, for, from time to time, ancient Spanish, French, Dutch, and English coins of gold and silver have been picked up on the beaches and among the coarse grass on the island, while rusty cannon are not infrequently found in the rank underbrush.

As Anegada was never fortified, was never

of sufficent importance to its owners to warrant a garrison, these mute old guns were no doubt used by the buccaneers. It is quite possible that the freebooters built some manner of stockades or forts and mounted guns; but, even if they did not, they unquestionably carried their artillery and other fittings ashore when refitting and careening their craft, and no doubt kept a reserve supply here on Anegada for emergencies.

Moreover, we know from historical records that the buccaneers did not give up this favorite refuge of theirs without demur when Sir Henry Morgan saw fit to turn his recently knighted back on his old shipmates and sent an expedition from Jamaica to drive the "Brethren" from Anegada. On the contrary, they put up a stiff and lively fight, and while neither side can be said to have been victorious,—for the battle resulted in a draw, and the expedition sent by Sir Henry retired,—yet the corsairs soon drifted away to more secure and less conspicuous retreats. So, for aught we know, the ancient cannon lying forgotten in Anegada may be the very ones that belched forth death and defiance at the men despatched to the Drowned Island by the ex-pirate governor of Jamaica.

The coins, too, may well have been the spoils of piracy and pillage, though by no means necessarily a part of buried treasure, as the natives would have us think and—to do them justice—themselves implicitly believe. Far more likely they were dropped from some careless seaman's pocket or lost in a drunken brawl or gambling quarrel.

In Anegada I was more fortunate than in St. John, for I was shown the rusting, corroded cannon that once had pointed—or so I convinced myself, at least—from the open ports of some swift buccaneering craft and many a time had roared out doom to the terror-stricken men and women on some galleon returning from the mines of Darien to Spain. What tales of adventure and of blood, of desperate fight and swarming, ruthless pirates these old guns might tell could they but speak! But, like the pirates, they are silenced forever, their yawning muzzles snug homes for scuttling soldier-crabs and striped lizards, their ornate decorations all but obliterated by the years of calm and storm, of drenching rain and salt sea-spray. And here they will lie, perhaps, for centuries more, until but a streak of rust upon the earth marks their resting-place.

To me, scarcely an hour after first I set foot upon the island, came an extraordinary-looking individual. Tightly drawn across his bony cheeks was his yellow parchment-like skin, bristling with stubble as black as jet and as coarse as wire. Below his great hooked nose sprouted a huge, unkempt mustachio of raven hue, and deep within its shadow gleamed yellow fangs as long and sharp as those of a wolf. Almost like bare and browned bone his forehead shone under lank black hair, and below lowering, bushy brows his reddened eyes gleamed with the unnatural fire of fever, so deep within their sockets that they seemed mere pin points of glowing light. A huge ring of tortoise-shell hung in one long-lobed, pointed ear; tattered rags of many hues draped his bony frame, and a stained and battered hat covered his disheveled locks. A veritable apparition he seemed—the ghost of some long-dead pirate. An involuntary shudder, an uncontrollable chill of repugnance, ran through me as, shaking as with the palsy—or craven fear of the hangman's noose—he fixed those fierce eyes upon me and in a dry, cracked voice, such as one might expect from the dead, asked in broken English if I cared to purchase old coins. At my affirmative reply he fumbled in his rags, drew forth a dirty bit of bunting that had once been part of the scarlet banner of England, and, untying its many knots, dumped a dozen bits of metal into his unsteady, claw-like hand.

Rusty, corroded, dirt-covered, and utterly impossible of identification were the coins, if coins they were. As I examined them the fellow stood silent but shaking, and moving his long, unshaven lower jaw about as though chewing an imaginary quid of tobacco. To my questions as to where he had obtained the things, he waved a taloned hand in an indefinite arc and replied that he had picked them up about the island, and asked in a plaintive voice if they were worth a shilling to me.

To him, no doubt, a single silver coin bearing his Britannic Majesty's head and the stamp of the British mint was a miniature fortune, for despite his savage, piratical looks, he was, I found, a bit of flotsam literally cast up by the sea, the sole survivor of a Portuguese whaling-schooner which had foundered on the reefs a dozen years before, and who, for some incomprehensible reason, refused to leave this barren, half-inundated bit of land whereon Fate had so inconsiderately placed him. How he lived no one knew, for he toiled not and neither did he spin, but wandered about aimlessly, gathering shell-fish and sea-birds' eggs, begging tobacco and cast-off garments from the negroes, and spending long hours and days by himself, poking about with a stick and seeking for chance relics such as he now had brought to me. I doubt if ever in those ten years since he first found himself the one survivor of his ship he had ever jingled as much silver in his pockets as I handed him in exchange for his little treasure-trove. And for good measure I added a plug of tobacco and a supply of quinine pills, while Sam presented him with a shirt—which was so much too large for his skeleton frame that had he but sewed the tails together it would have served him for a complete one-piece suit—and Joseph fed him until he could eat no more.

Then, as though he had accomplished a mission he had sworn to fulfil, he expressed his intention of forsaking Anegada and implored me to carry him to some port whence he could work or beg a passage to Fayal. Eventually we left him at St. Kitts, a far more human-looking creature than when first I gazed upon him on the beach at Anegada; and no doubt in time he once more basked in the sun and trod the picturesque streets of his Azores home.

When in due course of time and at my leisure I scraped the incrustation of limestone soil and the corrosion of centuries from the disks which he had brought to me, I gazed in amazement at what my efforts disclosed. Truly, Manuel had earned all we did for him and more, for in that handful of coins he had patiently and aimlessly gathered were two Spanish doubloons, three pieces of eight, a castellano, and two spade-guineas! What a collection

ANEGADA The guardian reef

ANEGADA The forbidding coast

ST. MARTIN Salt ponds

ST. MARTIN A street in Gustavia

to weave story and romance about! What relics of those wild days to lure one's imagination and conjectures!

As Anegada sank below the horizon, and the tossing manes of the white horses on the reef mingled with the white-caps and were lost, I felt that my visit had been well rewarded; for did I not possess coins with which pirates had gambled, bits of gold and silver won by murder, torture, and bloodshed! Yes, perhaps the very ones with which the ill-fated fifteen gambled life against a bottle of rum on Dead Man's Chest. For who can say aught of the travels of these coins? Who can trace their multitude of owners as they passed from hand to hand, from pocket to pocket, from ship to ship, from land to land through the centuries, to come to rest for a time in Anegada's sands and at last to be treasured and guarded and admired in a land which was but a howling wilderness when the rude bits of metal were first struck from the dies?

CHAPTER VII

LONELY ISLES

FROM Anegada to St. Martin is, in the vernacular of the buccaneers, a "passinge longe sayle," a run of nearly one hundred miles across the heaving Atlantic rollers surging in through the Anegada Passage. But to one who loves the sea, the tang of salt spray high-flung by a plunging bow, and the heave of a tossing deck, it is a glorious sail. The *Vigilant* made fine weather of it, and sixteen hours after low-lying Anegada dropped below the horizon astern Anguilla rose like a cloud above the sea before us.

Anguilla, or the "Eel," was no doubt frequented by the buccaneers, but, as far as I know, there is nothing authentic to connect them with the island, and it holds but little interest. Its thirty-six square miles of brush and salt-grass have been abandoned to the negroes, who find it difficult to gain a livelihood. They do, to be sure, raise a few cattle and ponies, as well as donkeys; and, being forced to subsist on the meager rations nature has provided, these four-footed Anguillans are living examples of the survival of the fittest. They are noted throughout the neighboring islands for their hardiness, though they are diminutive beasts.

Passing Eel Island by, we headed for St. Martin, the one island of all the Caribbees which has the distinction of being under two flags at the same time. In days long past, when Briton, Don, Frenchman, and Hollander, as well as Dane and Swede, slit one another's throats over these bits of land, it was not uncommon for the islands to be in the possession of several nations in rapid succession. In fact, in those days it must have been difficult for the struggling inhabitants to know to what king or emperor they owed allegiance, for they were never quite sure, when they retired at night, what flag they would see flying above the fort and government house the next morning. It was a question of "O say, can you see" what banner is there? Often, within the space of as many days, they would be under British, French, and Dutch colors in turn. Often, too, one fort would be under one flag and another fort under another, or a portion of the island would be occupied by the troops of one nation and another part by the soldiers of a different power, while at times two nations agreed temporarily to hold an island in partnership, each keeping to its own side of the fence, so to speak; or by common consent an island was rejected by all and regarded as "neutral territory," the powers deciding that it was not worth the bloodshed necessary to hold it.

But gradually the islands became the acknowledged possessions of the various European nations, and only St. Martin remained through the centuries a land divided within itself, with the French flag flying from one port and the Dutch banner from another.

In the northern part the French rule, their half of the isle being a dependency of Guadeloupe, while the southern half acknowledges allegiance to the Netherlands. It would be hard to say whether France or Holland owns the better portion of the island, but unquestionably there are more people under the Dutch flag than under the French.

Marigot, the port and capital of French St. Martin, is a charmingly pretty town, and the greater number of the three-thousand-odd subjects of France dwell within its confines. Philippsburg, the Dutch capital and port, is less populous, but the Dutch subjects altogether number fully five thousand. Of course there is no hard-and-fast boundary between the two, no trocha or barbed-wire fence stretching across the island. No doubt the easy-going natives bother very little as to whether they dwell under one flag or another, and drift back and forth at will, or as their occupations demand, from West Indian France to Antillean Holland. There are few of the islanders who do not speak the Creole patois, and as the common language of the Dutch West Indies is English, and virtually all St. Martians speak what passes for that tongue, their dual linguistic troubles are almost nil.

Scenically, St. Martin is lovely. It is mountainous, its loftiest summit, Paradise Peak, rising nearly two thousand feet above the sea. The surface of the island is delightfully varied, with rolling conical hills, broad valleys, deep gorges, and, near the shores, immense salt-water lagoons. It is for the most part fertile, and its inhabitants—at least those in Dutch territory—industriously cultivate the land. Many of its hills and mountains are luxuriantly forested. The big lagoons serve the natives as salt farms or pans, and the production of salt, the crops grown, the raising of cattle, donkeys, and poultry, and the yield of the fisheries provide a steady if not munificent income, so that the St. Martians are comparatively prosperous.

Quite the reverse is the condition of the neighboring island of St. Bartholomew,—or, as it is always called, St. Barts,—within whose lovely harbor of Gustavia the *Vigilant* dropped anchor after her splendid run from Anegada.

St. Barts is diminutive, barely eight square miles in area, hilly, with one of its so-called "mountains" rising to one thousand feet. It is wholly destitute of springs or streams, far from fertile, and deplorably poverty-stricken—literally out at elbows. Its people (virtually all negroes and mulattoes) number about three thousand, and so wretchedly poor is their island, with so little in the way of opportunity or employment, that the bulk of them are scattered up and down the Antilles laboring for a livelihood, or, in their sloops, carrying cargoes from port to port or plying a fisherman's trade. Although St. Barts is a French dependency, nearly all its inhabitants speak English, and they are noted throughout the northern islands as industrious workers. Among them at times one sees fair-haired, blue-eyed individuals—weird-looking creatures at first sight, seemingly albino negroes with their pale eyes and flaxen wool, but merely the odd result of the commingling of Swedish and African blood, for St. Barts for many years belonged to Sweden. Not until 1878 did the Swedes relinquish this one possession of theirs in the Caribbees and turn the almost worthless bit of land over to France. Swedish blood still crops out, not only among the negroes but in the few "poor whites" who claim St. Barts as their native land, and Sweden's lost sovereignty is perpetuated in the name of the island's one port, Gustavia.

However, like many another island of the Caribbean, St. Barts has seen better days. Back in the good old times Gustavia's streets were almost literally paved with gold and its inhabitants fairly rolled in wealth. Here, as to few others of the Virgin Islands, flocked the buccaneers, for at St. Barts that most cruel and murderous of pirates, Montbars the "Exterminator," established his headquarters. So great was the fear he and his fellows inspired in all that no nation or official dared move finger to molest him and his gang. Wild was the life that ebbed and flowed in St. Barts in Montbars's day. Gustavia's harbor swarmed with swift, long-sparred pirate craft; in the sheltered coves the buccaneers repaired and refitted their ships; under the palms along the beach their rude shelters of sail-cloth were raised, and here after many a long cruise and desperate battle they came to divide their loot and squander it.

What a scene they must have presented, what a picture of lawlessness, as, gathered in the shadows of the palms, with chests of plate, coffers of jewels, and bales of satins, brocades, and velvets on the hard sand before them, they watched narrowly as their captains apportioned the treasures they had won by murder, rapine, and torture. And there too, upon the sand,—wild-eyed, disheveled, with blanched, tear-stained cheeks,—were their human loot, girls and women, wives and daughters of Spanish grandees, tenderly nurtured ladies torn shrieking from their murdered loved ones' arms, to be auctioned off like cattle here on St. Barts's shores,—souls to be bartered and gambled for, toys to amuse their black-hearted captors for a space ere being cast into the gutter or to the sharks. Surrounded by his brutish, blear-eyed crew, the pirate captain stood, a weather-beaten, mahogany-faced rascal, his long, ragged moustache and tangled mop of hair adding to his wild appearance, a cocked hat set rakishly upon his head, with bedraggled plume drooping upon his shoulder. His blood-stained ruffled shirt, open at the throat, revealed a hairy tattooed chest, and his long-skirted, gold-laced coat of crimson showed a round hole and a dark stain upon the breast, where some pirate's bullet had ended the life of the garment's former owner. His voluminous trousers of vivid blue, ending at the knees, exposed his stanchion-like legs clad in green silk stockings, while a heavy pair of Cordovan shoes with huge silver buckles covered his feet. His arms crossed upon his chest, a cocked and loaded pistol grasped in each hand, with hawk-like, piercing eyes and a sardonic smile he watched his men growling, wrangling, and cursing over the portion of loot meted out to them by the one-eyed, scar-faced boatswain.

Dumping a chest of coins upon a sheet of tarry canvas, this fellow would count them out in piles, one for each man, and to every coin he tossed on the piles for the crew he would throw five upon that which formed the captain's share. Pieces of eight crudely struck from silver bullion, dull-golden onzas, castellanos, doubloons, guineas, louis d'or, oddly shaped "cross money," in turn were divided. Then came ingots of gold and bars of silver; altar-pieces and chalices; dishes of beaten gold, jeweled girdles, rings, and bracelets; necklaces of pearls and emeralds—a collection worth a king's ransom. And these, after the glowering chieftain had taken his pick, were gambled for by the tossing of coins or with dice, for so varied and miscellaneous was the loot that to apportion the articles fairly was impossible. Last of all came the women; and then, as the great sun, in a sea of gold and blood, dipped below the horizon and the swift-falling tropic night wrapped the island in a mantle of black, torches flared, ribald songs rang out over the waters of the tranquil harbor, blasphemies and drunken curses mingled with women's screams, and debauchery held sway.

Such scenes, in the time of Montbars and his fellows, were of daily and nightly occurrence in St. Barts, and the island and its more peaceable and thrifty inhabitants waxed rich. But at last there came a reckoning. The nations, outraged by the effrontery of the pirates, joined forces to wipe them from the seas, and after many a gory battle the lairs of the buccaneers were cleaned up. Here and there a pirate ship still sailed the Caribbean and flew the black flag. On jungle-covered, out-of-the-way cays whose ownership had never been determined, the remmants of the Brethren still had secret retreats. From hiding-places among the reefs or landlocked coves those who survived dashed forth to murder and to pillage unsuspecting merchantmen, but the power of the buccaneers was broken. Like jackals they prowled about the Caribbean, and the Virgin Islands knew them no more.

Without the buccaneers, St. Barts continued to prosper. Within Gustavia's harbor swift privateers took the place of pirate ships. From this safe retreat the Americans sailed forth to settle scores with many a British merchantman,—and corvette, for that matter,—and while England strove to retain her revolting colonies in North America, and the United States was being born, vast stores of riches, brought by the privateers, accumulated in St. Barts.

But, though it was a neutral port and Sweden's banner flew above the fort, the English had no compunctions about violating another nation's rights, to benefit their own cause. Holding that might made right, Admiral Rodney swept down with his frigates upon Gustavia and sacked St. Barts of more than two million dollars' worth of merchandise. Then, for a time, the island lived on the fruits of its past, but ever losing ground, ever falling behind, ever becoming poorer, ever getting shabbier and shabbier, until to-day one could scarcely find as many copper cents in St. Barts as the British found dollars.

And the worst of it is that the island, like many of its moribund neighbors, seems to hold no promise of a future. There seems to be no industry that can retrieve its fortunes, no possibility of making it pay, for it is handicapped by nature. It cannot compete with the larger, more fertile and prosperous islands (who themselves are always in debt); its town is tumbling about its people's ears, and there is a steady exodus of its inhabitants to more flourishing lands.

While St. Barts is most interesting historically, and was for so long a haven of the buccaneers and the headquarters of one of the most notorious and bloodthirsty of pirate chieftains, yet there are upon the island few if any reminders of the good old days. Of course, there are tales of hidden pirate treasure,—the natives even going so far as to assert that Montbars himself secreted vast sums in the caverns along St. Barts's coast,—and a few years ago an earthen jug full of ancient coins was dug up on the outskirts of Gustavia. But, unfortunately for romance, the coins were not pieces of eight and doubloons, as all self-respecting pirate hoards should be, but Swedish and Dutch; and undoubtedly, instead of having been buried there by a thrifty buccaneer, they had been put away for the proverbial rainy day by some worthy and peaceable as well as foresighted citizen.

Even the old-fashioned, corroded cannon that one can find in nearly any of the islands seem totally lacking here, for so poverty-stricken and hard put to it have the people been that any such weighty pieces of metal have long since been taken from their resting-places and disposed of for junk, to eke out the resources of the natives.

But we should have a warm spot in our hearts for the little island, despite its lack of interest or attractions and its threadbare present. Had it not been for St. Barts and certain of its neighbors, where our privateers could lie, and from which they could prey on British shipping and harass British men-of-war, the result of our ancestors' brave efforts to throw off the British yoke might have been very different.

By the same token, we should think kindly of and doff our hats to St. Eustatius, whose magnificent volcanic cone rose majestically before the *Vigilant* five hours after she had spread her wings and sailed out of Gustavia's harbor. It was here at "Statia," as it is always called, that the Stars and Stripes—or, rather, its earlier prototype—was first saluted by the guns of a foreign power. And a pretty mess that courtesy made for stout old Governor De Graaf, for it brought the British under the redoubtable Rodney down upon this isle and resulted in the ruin of Statia.

It was in November, 1776, that the fort at Orangetown (Statia's only port) roared out its thunderous salute to the banner of the new republic as it flew from the masthead of the *Andrew Doria* of Baltimore, one of a fleet of privateers that found friends and safety in the Dutch, Swedish, and

Danish isles and did so much to help the cause of the American colonies. Like St. Barts, Statia, during our Revolution, proved a godsend to our privateers and merchantmen, for it was not only a neutral island but a free port as well. Hence, at a time when England's high-handed and short-sighted colonial policies had almost ruined commerce in the West Indies, virtually all trade between Europe and the American colonies became diverted to the tiny volcanic isle of Statia. Then, when the French threw in their lot with our forefathers, they too flocked to the Dutch port, until St. Eustatius became the richest and greatest center of commerce in the New World and rivaled the most famed marts of trade in the Old World as well. Ships flying the flags of all nations steered their course for Statia; the roadstead before Orangetown was a forest of masts and yards; immense warehouses and docks lined the waterfront, and the place became a vast storehouse and trading-post, a maritime and commercial exchange, such as the world had never seen before.

Often before little sun-bathed Orangetown fully two hundred ships would ride at anchor, and back and forth between them and the shore a steady stream of boats plied, heavily laden with goods from every corner of the earth. The streets were filled with crowds of stevedores, slaves, merchants, and sailors. Bales, boxes, and barrels overflowed the giant warehouses and were piled mountain-high along the thoroughfares and on the beach, and merchants and buyers, unable to find accommodations, set up their business in the open air, with packing-cases for chairs and tables and sail-canvas awnings for roofs.

And to Statia also flocked the privateering craft from Portland, Salem, Boston, New York, Baltimore, and countless other ports. Here they repaired and refitted, here they disposed of captured prizes and loot, and here they were welcomed with open arms by the thrifty Dutch. Perchance, had the Statians and their cosmopolitan visitors confined themselves to legitimate trade, the British might have said or done nothing, even though De Graaf saw fit to recognize the new-born republic officially by a salute to its flag. But the island had gone money-mad, and not only did Statia become temporarily the world's greatest center of commerce, but, in addition, it became a brazenly open dêpot for contraband of war, while, to add insult to injury, the Dutch made no bones of convoying American privateers with their men-o'-war, and did not hesitate to grant Dutch papers to American merchantmen. Thus matters stood until at last the

English decided that something must be done, and on February 3, 1781, Rodney swept unexpectedly down on Statia and, meeting with scarcely a show of resistance, took possession of the town and all it contained, to say nothing of over a hundred and fifty merchant ships lying in the harbor at the time.

It was a prize which would have made the greatest buccaneer of them all turn green with envy, for the loot consisted of over twenty-five million dollars' worth of goods, to say nothing of the ships. As it was manifestly impossible for the British fleet to carry off this treasure, and as Britain could ill afford to lose over five million pounds sterling so easily obtained, the invaders promptly inaugurated the greatest auction sale ever known, and there in Orangetown sold to the highest bidders that vast accumulation of merchandise which had poured from the ends of the earth into the little port.

Then, having seen the last of the goods taken away and the last ship sail, Rodney pocketed his millions in the name of the King of England and, feeling that it had been a good job well done, hoisted anchor and bore away for other adventures.

The blow was one from which Statia never recovered. To-day the ruins of the immense warehouses and docks are everywhere in evidence along the waterfront of Orangetown; from hoary old Fort

SABA Saba Island from the sea

SABA A Saban sedan chair

SABA "Going aboard"

SABA The town of Bottom from Saba Peak

Orange quaint cannon point their silent muzzles seaward through a tangle of weeds upon the parapets from which they roared out their welcome to the *Doria's* flag so many years ago; the tower of the church wherein Mynheer De Graaf attended services still stands above its ruined walls, and scattered over the island are the remains of princely mansions and vast estates. But the island and its port are almost as dead as the sturdy old Dutchmen sleeping beneath the great carved headstones in the cemetery on the hill.

Seen from the sea, Statia is very beautiful, with its two thousand-foot symmetrical cone rising in a magnificent sweep from the water, and with its northern slopes stretching into hills and plains that once were one vast luxurious garden. Statia's soil is exceedingly fertile and in the olden days an enormous income was derived from its plantations of cane and indigo, sugar and cotton, and from its orchards of fruit. But to-day there is little cultivation carried on, and the population of nearly one quarter of a million inhabitants has dwindled to a scant two thousand, most of whom are mulattoes or blacks.

The port of Orangetown is attractively picturesque, part of it straggling along just above the reach of the lazy waves and part clambering up a steep hill to where, three hundred feet above the sea, the Dutch flag still flies from its staff above the fort. For one who desires to escape from the noise and strife and worries of great cities and modern life Statia would be an ideal retreat, for its climate is excellent, it is extremely healthful, and anything and everything may be grown to perfection in its rich volcanic soil. Otherwise it is but another of those sleepy isles made famous in history and now content to bask in the tropic sun and dream of its past.

Far more interesting is Statia's neighbor to the west, a massive sheer-sided volcanic peak upjutting from the tumbling sea for nearly three thousand feet—the most remarkable island, the most topsyturvy, astonishing bit of land in all the seven seas, and known as Saba. Like Statia, Saba is Dutch, and, among its many other distinctions, it is the only island in the Antilles that has never changed hands and that has no bloody stories of battles or of ruthless slaughter of the aborigines to mar its history

Saba's feet are bathed in water thousands of fathoms in depth, its head is veiled in clouds thousands of feet in the air, its coast is forbidding, hemmed by thundering surf and beetling cliffs. It has no harbor, no anchorage, and no landing-place worthy of the name; and yet it supports a thrifty, happy, healthy population of nearly two thousand souls whose everyday lives, whose occupations, and whose habitat all go far to prove that it is indeed "hard to beat the Dutch."

Viewing the island from the sea, one would scarcely dream that a human being dwelt upon this mid-sea pinnacle, but a thousand feet above the water, snugly hidden in an extinct crater as though dropped from the clouds, is a delightfully neat, pretty, and typical Dutch village, which, with the habitual upsidedownness of the Sabans, is called "The Bottom" because it is at the top!

Completely out of the world is Bottom, and yet it is doubtful if any town on earth can boast that so large a percentage of its people have traveled far and wide. For, incongruous as it seems, nearly all the able-bodied Saban men are sailors by choice and profession, and, from early manhood until declining years force them to forsake the sea, they roam the ocean highways as officers of great sailing-ships and liners. But ever when done with sailoring they return to spend their old age in their strange island home, and from their lofty aery—which must remind them of the masthead of a ship

—pass their time watching the vessels that ply back and forth across the Caribbean, but never stop to make a call at Saba.

And to visit this remarkable ocean-girt scrap of Holland is not by any means an easy matter, either. To reach it one must travel from St. Kitts or one of the larger islands by sail-boat, and must choose propitious weather or the voyage will be for naught. Then, if the sea is fairly calm, the visitor lands, or "goes aboard," as the Sabans say, upon a steep bit of shingly beach on the southern shore of the island. Here, close to the water's edge, stands a wooden shack—the combined custom-house and harbor-master's office of this harborless isle, with the flag of the Netherlands fluttering above it.

Near at hand a flight of roughly hewn stone steps leads upward toward the clouds—the road or, as the inhabitants call it, "The Ladder," from the landing-place to the town. Eight hundred steps there are, a veritable Jacob's ladder; but the Sabans are accommodating and hospitable, and if the stranger views with trepidation the thousand-foot climb he can make the journey in comparative ease and comfort seated in a rocking-chair lashed between a couple of oars and borne upon the shoulders of herculean blacks.

The Sabans, however, think nothing of the climb, and carry up the ladder every ounce of merchandise which comes to their island. It is not unusual to see a colored Saban ascending the precipitous way with a half-barrel of flour or a tierce of pork upon his or her head, and when a cargo arrives these goat-like porters and portresses often make a dozen or more round trips in a single day.

But at the end of the climb all else is forgotten in the view that greets the traveler's eyes. Spread like a map in a great green bowl, surrounded on every side with towering peaks, are neatly walled, carefully tended gardens, and in the center the toy village of white, red-roofed houses separated by narrow lanes between cañon-like walls of stone. Here, in a temperate climate of perpetual June, the fair-haired, blue-eyed, rosy-cheeked people dwell, with a few yellow-brown and black Sabans as well, and here, a thousand feet above the surf, they raise potatoes, strawberries, and many Northern vegetables and fruits, as well as all those of the tropics.

Indeed, aside from the incomes of their sailor laddies, the Sabans depend largely upon the products of their gardens, and carry them regularly to the market at St. Kitts. But they have many another industry besides, and many a quaint and curious custom. Passing through the streets, one may often see an elderly pair, who might have stepped from some cottage in Holland, industriously brushing and polishing a coffin in their dooryard, for the Sabans believe in preparedness; and, knowing the futility and the uncertainties of life and the inevitability of death, they keep their coffins ready for emergencies and as much a part of their household furnishings as chairs or tables.

While the inhabitants of this strange little island are thoroughly Dutch in appearance, the recognized language of Saba is English, and, save among the older people, the tongue of the Netherlands is seldom used.

Owing to the absence of so many of the men at sea, women seem in the great majority at Bottom and like all the women of their race they are never idle for a moment, and they keep their homes and village so tidy and clean that one is convinced that here is the original "spotless town." In the intervals between scrubbing, dusting, washing, and cooking the Saban women find time to make beautiful drawn-work and lace, which find a ready sale and add many guilders and dollars to their pin-money.

But all that has gone before pales into insignificance when we learn of the leading industry of the

Sabans, the work with which the youths and older men occupy themselves, the business that makes the visitor pinch himself to make sure he is not dreaming; for who in the world would ever imagine that it is, of all things, boat-building! Yes; stanch, seaworthy boats, renowned throughout the West Indies, are built here in a crater a thousand feet above the sea, where every plank and timber used in their construction must be carried on people's heads up the ladder of eight hundred stone steps! And when at last one of these mountain-top boats is built, how, you may well ask, do the Sabans get it down to the water? By the simplest method in the world: they let it down the sides of the cliffs exactly as though their island were a ship and they were lowering their craft from the davits!

CHAPTER VIII

ST. KITTS AND THE GORGEOUS ISLE

DESPITE all their interest, neither Statia nor Saba held aught that linked them with the buccaneers,—indeed, I doubt if these adventurers ever visited either,—and so, dipping our colors to old Fort Orange in memory of the salute the ancient guns gave the *Andrew Doria,* we bore on to Basseterre, the port and capital of St. Kitts.

To one who has seen only the more northern islands, St. Kitts is a revelation,—a fascinating sight,—and even after one has viewed the more southerly isles with their overpowering grandeur of mile-high mountains and wondrous forests, St. Kitts still holds its own, for it possesses charms unlike those of any other of the Caribbees.

From the cloud-draped summit of Mount Misery—dark and sinister, four thousand feet above the sea—to the beaches rimmed with creaming foam, St. Kitts is a glorious mass of green,—green of a thousand shades and tints, from that of ripening cane to that of the deep, shadowy ravines of its mountain forests. Upward from the sandy beaches and rugged bluffs sweep the broad cane-fields, undulating over hill and dale and reminding one so strongly of the downs of Sussex that one no longer marvels that the homesick English settlers, weary of the long and tedious voyage, gazed with brimming eyes upon this smiling, sun-bright isle. Vividly, tenderly green are the fields of young canes, golden or russet the others, sienna-red the plowed acres between, but all are drenched with tropic sunshine, and all, from a distance, seem as well tended and as regularly laid out as a great garden.

And everywhere are the palms. As far as eye can see, the swaying coco-palms line the shores above the tumbling surf. Against the sky the plume-topped cabbage-palms show their sharp silhouettes above the lesser trees upon the mountain sides. For miles along the winding, perfect roads the towering royal palms form avenues of great columnar trunks and drooping, feathery fronds. They cluster above the lowly negro huts or shade the great plantation homes without discrimination and with equal beauty, and they nod like giant feather dusters above the roof-tops of the town.

Massive, majestic, and mountainous is the northern portion of St. Kitts, and it takes no very vivid imagination to see in towering Mount Misery the likeness of St. Christopher bearing the infant Jesus on his shoulder which caused Columbus to name the island after his own patron saint. But to the south the mountains with their dense, forest-clad slopes give way to hills covered with endless acres of cane, until at Basseterre the island is almost flat, and only isolated rounded Monkey Hill breaks the rolling, down-like land.

Basseterre is a fittingly pretty town for this lovely island, with its red roofs and its pastel-tinted houses shaded by palms above the wonderfully colored sea, on whose calm surface ride gaily painted sloops and schooners and bevies of row-boats of every color of the rainbow.

But it must be admitted that there is very little of interest here. There is a fairly attractive public garden; flowering shrubs and trees are everywhere; there are pretty embowered residences, and the people are friendly and hospitable. But there is nothing distinctive about the place: it might be any one of a score of *dolce-far-niente* tropical towns, and it is by no means either prosperous or over-clean. Time was when St. Kitts was a well-to-do island; its planters lived like princes or feudal lords, fleets of ships rode to anchor in its harbor, and thousands of toiling blacks planted and cultivated and garnered the golden canes which sent a steady flow of molasses and sugar from the isle and brought an equally steady flow of golden sovereigns back to the Kittefonians' pockets. But the omnipresent and lowly beet spelled St. Kitts's doom, as it spelled the doom of many another sugar-producing land, and though the island is by no means poverty-stricken, and during the late war became prosperous for a time, the golden days of the past will never return.

Efforts have been made to win back prosperity with sea-island cotton, citrous fruits, and other tropical products; but it is a hard matter indeed to wean a sugar-planter from canes; and even those who have taken up the cultivation of other things have not been over-successful.

As a winter resort, St. Kitts is delightful, for it boasts a good climate and a healthful one; its scenery is magnificent; it possesses splendid motor-roads that completly encircle the island; it offers excellent fishing and hunting, plenty of outdoor sports, and an active volcano, Mount Misery, with a wonderful climb through the virgin tropical forests to its crater.

The island has, like its fellows, had a checkered career, but it can boast of being the first of the British West Indies to be settled by the English, who established themselves here in 1623. However, they did not succeed in holding it in undisputed possession, and what with the Caribs, the pirates, and the French, those earlier colonists had a mighty hard time of it. More than once St. Kitts came wholly under the sway of France. At other times the two nations buried the hatchet temporarily, and while the English confined themselves to the northern half of the isle, with their headquarters at Sandy Point, the French were content with the other half, with Basseterre as their port; yet there was constant friction, and not until 1782 was St. Kitts definitely turned over to the British.

Except in the name of the capital, there are few if any traces of French occupancy, but at Brimstone Hill, close to Sandy Point, are the massive ruins of extensive fortifications built by the British. Here, on an isolated, precipitous mass of rock, for all the world like a young mountain gone astray, is a solid mass of loopholed and battlemented masonry completely covering every available portion of the eight-hundred-foot hill. It is an impressive and redoubtable fortification, well-nigh impregnable in the days of muzzle-loading cannon and black powder, and complete with sally-ports, moats, and drawbridges. But it is quite deserted and useless, the abode of countless monkeys—descendants of apes brought from Gibraltar as pets, by the garrison—which are eagerly hunted and esteemed by the Kittefonians as a great delicacy.

Looking upon this stupendous work of defense, one marvels that any enemy ever dared attack or even approach St. Kitts, but, to tell the truth, it never saw battle, for it was not built until 1793, ten years after France and England ceased quarreling over the island and its neighbors, and all too late to be of any value whatsoever to its builders.

As an imposing ruin it is well worth a visit, but its historical attractions are nil. Indeed, St. Kitts seems strangely lacking in anything connecting its present with its rather turbulent and not at all bloodless past. I do not think there is even the customary tale of buried treasure on the island; at least I have never heard one. The people do not claim to have found pirates' hoards in their cane-fields or caverns; and they do not even associate the name of any great pirate chieftain with their delightful home.

Nevertheless, St. Kitts was at one time a resort of pirates—or, rather, buccaneers—who were attacked by the Spaniards in 1629 and driven from the island. Many of these, of French blood, made their way to Tortuga, off the coast of Haiti, and there formed the nucleus of that famous headquarters of the Brethren of the Main. As far as records go there is nothing to show that the freebooters ever returned in large numbers or for an extended stay, and, according to a most interesting document which I was so fortunate as to acquire in St. Kitts, when they did appear they were met with so warm a welcome that it is not at all surprising they gave the lovely island a wide berth.

The faded and crumpled bit of worm-eaten parchment, which I value even more than the ancient coins so opportunely acquired at Anegada, is a fragment of the court records of St. Kitts in the good old days, and its scarcely legible writing relates the following:

An assize and generall Gaole delivrie held at St. Christophers Colonie from ye nineteenthe daye of Maye to ye 22n. daye off ye same Monthe 1701 Captaine Josias Pendringhame Magustrate &C. The Jurye of our Soveraigne Lord the Kinge Doe presente Antonio Mendoza of Hispaniola and a subjecte of ye Kinge of Spain for that ye said on or about ye 11 Daye of Apryl 1701 feloneousely delibyrately and malliciousley and encontrarye to ye laws off Almightie God and our Soveraigne Lord the Kinge did in his cuppes saucely and arrogantyly speak of the Governour and our Lord the Kinge and bye force and armes into ye tavernne of John Wilkes Esq. did entre and there did Horrible sware and cursse and did felonoslye use theattenninge words and did strike and cutte most murtherouslye severalle subjects of our Soveraigne Lord the Kinge. Of w'h Indictment he pleadeth not Guiltie butte onne presente Master Samuel Dunscombe mariner did sware that said Antonio Mendoza was of his knowenge a Bloodthirste piratte and Guiltie of diabolicalle practises & ye Grande Inquest findinge yt a trewe bill to be tryd by God and ye Countrye w'h beinge a Jurie of 12 men sworne finde him Guiltie & for the same he be adjuged to be carryd to ye Fort Prison to haave both his earres cutt close by his head and be burnet throughe ye tongee with an Hot iron and to be caste chained in ye Dungon to awaitte ye plesyure of God and Our Soveraigne Lord the Kinge.

We cannot but pity the luckless Spaniard who under the spell of Kittefonian rum, or possibly palm toddy, did "Horrible sware and cursse" and who may very likely have been quite innocent of any piratical or "diabolicalle" past, for the British had no love for the Dons and even when nominally at peace with Spain thought little of putting an end to any subject of the Spanish king who came their way. No doubt the very fact that the prisoner was a Spaniard was his undoing; and that worthy mariner Samuel Dunscombe probably perjured himself for the satisfaction of seeing a Don tortured. At any rate, it seems as though having both ears "cutt close" and having one's "tongee" perforated with a red-hot iron was pretty severe punishment for the alleged crimes. But it only goes to prove how times have changed, and how little we can judge, by present-day standards, of what in those days was cruelty or inhumanity.

Also in St. Kitts, though on another visit, I came into possession of an equally interesting souvenir of olden times—a remarkable little volume bearing the rather cumbersome title of: "The True Travels, Adventures and Observations of Captain John Smith, in Europe, Asia, Africa and America from Anno Domini 1593 to 1629; his accidents and sea fights in the straits; his service and stratagems of war in Hungaria, Transylvania, Wallachi, and Moldavia, against the Turks and Tartars; his description of the Tartars, their strange manners and customs of religions, diets, buildings, wars, feasts, ceremonies, and living; how he slew the Bashaw of Malbritz in Cambria, and escaped from the Turks and the Tartars; together with a continuation of his General History of Virginia, Summer Isles, New England and their proceedings since 1624 to this present 1629, published in Anno Domini 1630."

From all of which it will be gathered that our hero of Pocahontas fame was an adventurer of many parts in divers lands, and that his activities in Virginia were but minor incidents in his romantic career. In fact, for a space, Smith was something of a pirate himself, judged by our standards at least, and his accounts of sea battles and prizes taken are fascinatingly quaint. Of St. Kitts, too, he has much to say, and he gives us more of an in-

ST. KITTS Basseterre and Monkey Hill

ST. KITTS The Circus, Basseterre

A DESCRIPTION of The South Sea & Coasts of AMERICA Containing y^e whole Navigation and all those places at which Capt. SHARP and his Companions were in the years 1680 . 1681
The Tropick of Cancer
Tropick of Capricorn
Equinoctialis
MAR DEL ZUR
MARE BRAZILIÆ
MARE MAGALLANICUM
AMERICA Meridio:
PERU
CHICAS
CHILE
BRAZIL
SINUS MEXICANUS
Nova Hispaniæ Pars
FLORIDA
Bahama Islands
Hispaniola
Puerto Rico
Barbados
Jamaica
Sharp's Reditus
Sharp's Passage

sight into the troubles and tribulations of the first settlers on this "fayre islant" than any other writer. Aside from raids by the man-eating Caribs, being harasssed by pirates, and constant quarrels with the French, the early English settlers seem to have had a most unfortunate experience with hurricanes, which Smith naïvely explains are "overgrowne and most monstrous stormes." Indeed, the very year of its settlement by the English, 1623, a hurricane swept the island and wiped out the settlers' gardens, their tobacco-fields, their houses, and their fort. Hardly had they recovered from this when, in September, 1625, another hurricane hurled itself upon the island. This was even worse than its predecessor of two years before, and Smith states that, in addition to blowing down all the houses, the tobacco, and "two drums into the air we know not wither," it also "drove two ships on shore, that were both split." He adds: "All our provisions thus lost we were very miserable, living only on what we could get in the wild woods. . . . Thus we continued till near June that the Tortels came in, 1627." Six months later the colonists were once more made homeless through a hurricane, and until the end of the narrative hurricane followed hurricane.[1]

[1] This is an excerpt from a report by Captain Thomas Warner,

To-day, however, St. Kitts is by no means noted for its "overgrowne stormes," which may be of interest meteorologically as tending to show that hurricanes are not so frequent in the Antilles as formerly and may, in centuries to come, cease altogether.

Another interesting fact brought out by Smith is that St. Kitts was largely populated by malefactors and convicts bought at so much a head from British prisons, shipped to the West Indies like cattle, in the stinking holds of small ships, and auctioned off as slaves among the planters. When we stop to think of such things, of the unspeakable atrocities practised by the masters or owners of these unfortunates upon their own countrymen (whom they branded with red-hot irons and mutilated or tortured on the least provocation), to say nothing of compelling white men, women, and children to labor half naked from sunrise to sunset in the cane- and tobacco-fields, under a broiling sun and urged on by the cruel lash, the buccaneers seem tender-hearted gentlemen by comparison.

South of this emerald isle, plainly visible from Basseterre and separated from St. Kitts merely

the founder of the colony, who lies buried in Middle Island Church on the highway between Sandy Point and Basseterre, where his tombstone informs us that he "boughte an illustryous nayme with loss of noble blood."

by a narrow strait, lies Nevis. In a gigantic, absolutely symmetrical cone of green the massive volcano of Nevis rises against the sky, its brow crowned with a perpetual diadem of drifting fleecy clouds and at its feet the undulating green fields sloping to the sea.

Once the Mecca of the wealth and fashion of Europe and the Antilles, the world's most famous watering-place, a spot so thronged with notables, so gay with great balls, state receptions, and palatial gambling-resorts, so ablaze with silks, satins, and jewels, so flooded with gold and riches that it became known as "The Gorgeous Isle," Nevis to-day is almost as dead as its volcano's crater. And yet it is as charming, its climate is as salubrious, its thermal springs and mineral waters as life-giving, its fields and forests as alluring as in those days when its harbor was thronged with stately ships and its streets and hostelries rang to the song and laughter of satin-clad, bewigged gentlemen, and ladies with powered hair; and liveried negro link-bearers lit the way for sedan-chairs ablaze with gilded scrolls and cupids. But the vast estates, the palatial mansions, the great Bath-House, and the marvelously appointed casinos are but memories —crumbling ruins forlorn and overgrown. Nevis is but a ghost of the "Gorgeous Isle" of the eighteenth century, though a very beautiful ghost.

Aside from its one-time fame as a spa, Nevis is mainly noted as the birthplace of Alexander Hamilton and the place where Admiral Lord Nelson was married. The house wherein our statesman was born still stands on a hill near the town, though in a badly ruined state, and in the ancient but well-preserved "Fig Tree Church" there is still the thumbed and faded marriage register wherein one may read, under the entries for the year 1787: "March 11, Horatio Nelson Esq., Captain of H. M. S. *Boreas,* to Frances Herbert Nisbet, widow." What a matter-of-fact record of the mighty, one-armed old sea-fighter's love romance!

But to my mind the most interesting thing in Nevis is the submerged ancient capital of Jamestown, which in 1680 was destroyed by a severe earthquake. Then, as though Nature wished to hide the ruin she had wrought, the town with its tumble-down buildings, many of its inhabitants, and —so it is said—vast wealth, sank bodily below the sea. To-day, in calm weather, one may gaze downward through the crystal-clear water and trace the faint outlines of coral-incrusted walls of buildings that mark the resting-place of the drowned city.

History, unfortunately, has little information to give us concerning Jamestown and its destruction, or of the events of that awful day. One of the few survivors was a noted freebooter, a Captain Greaves,—otherwise known as "Red Legs,"—who, having seen the error of his ways, had abandoned his piratical career and had settled down in Nevis to a life of peace in the guise of a well-to-do planter. But the reformed pirate, being recognized and denounced by a former victim, was arrested and cast into an underground dungeon, only to be miraculously saved by the earthquake, which destroyed his prison and heaved him up quite unharmed. Finding himself floating upon the sea with the remains of the town fathoms deep beneath him, the ex-pirate clung to a piece of wreckage, and after numerous adventures safely reached another island, where he once more essayed a respectable existence, and lived and died a highly honored citizen.

This was but one incident in the romantic career of Greaves, or "Red Legs,"—which is a far more appropriate name for a freebooter,—who was a unique and fascinating character. Sold as a slave in Barbados, as were thousands of Scotch and Irish prisoners taken in the days of Cromwell, Greaves, in an effort to escape from a cruel master, sought refuge on a Dutch ship in the harbor. By some mischance, he swam in the darkness to the wrong vessel and found himself upon a pirate craft. Fate having thus taken a hand in shaping his destiny, the erstwhile slave boy took to the buccaneers' life as a duck takes to water. As all his unfortunate fellows were known in the islands as "red legs,"—as their descendants are to-day,—this new recruit of the pirates at once received the nickname, which stuck to him through all his years of buccaneering. While he was famous for his reckless daring, his almost uncanny luck in piratical undertakings, yet he was never dreaded as were many of his fellows. For Red Legs, despite his handicap, was a gallant and chivalrous gentleman at heart, and though he scuttled ships and sacked towns without end, yet he earned the reputation of never harming women or putting prisoners to death or torture. He was, in fact, that incredible paradox, a moral pirate, and in his declining years he devoted large sums—whether honestly earned from his plantation or loot from his piratical ventures is unknown—to charity and churches.

The island of Nevis can boast of association with one other pirate, who in a way was even more remarkable than Red Legs and accomplished the most noteworthy feat in all the annals of buccaneering. This was no less a personage than Bartholomew Sharp, who, after what was probably the greatest adventure experienced by any of those most adventurous men the buccaneers, sailed into Nevis, back in 1682, and, having decided to abandon the sea and rest on his laurels, departed thence to England.

CHAPTER IX

THE "DANGEROUS VOYAGE" AND THE EFFECT OF A NAGGING TONGUE

NO story of the West Indies in their relation to the buccaneers would be complete without some mention of Bartholomew Sharp and his marvelous cruise, which even Ringrose, his sailing-master and historian, dubbed "The Dangerous Voyage."

Of Sharp's earlier days of pirating we know little, but that he was an adept follower of the profession we may be sure, for his contemporaries spoke of him as "that sea artist and valiant commander" and, to use a slang expression, it took *some* pirate to win such praise from the corsairs of the Caribbean.

At all events, Sharp evidently found the pickings of the Spanish Main and its neighboring waters too poor for his liking, and, seeking richer fields for his art, gathered together a wild and daring company of some three hundred and fifty men and in April, 1680, sailed for the Isthmus of Panama. Among this choice assortment of companionable spirits were many noteworthy pirates, for Sharp had great deeds in view and aimed to outdo the redoubtable Sir Henry Morgan himself. Ringrose, the historian of the buccaneers, was there; Dampier the buccaneer naturalist [1]; Wafer the surgeon; Watling and Gayny; Jobson the chemist; Coxon and Sawkins and many another. Reaching the isthmus, they disembarked and, emulating Morgan, proceeded to cross the "Bridge of the World" afoot by way of Darien, the wildest and hardest route. This in itself was no mean task, but to the pirates it was only an incident, a somewhat disagreeable means to an end and nothing more. Having gained the shores of the Pacific, they promptly commandeered canoes and without hesitation boldly attacked the Spanish fleet lying in the lee of Perico Island, off the city of Panama.

Then followed a battle which must have satisfied even the most bloodthirsty. As usual, the pirates won the day, captured all the Dons' ships, and, having thus secured the necessary tools of their trade, they transferred armaments, ammunition, and such treasure as there was, from the smaller ships to a four-hundred-ton galleon known as *La Santissima Trinidad* or *The Most Blessed Trinity.* Finally, having scuttled the craft they could not

[1] See Introduction.

use, they started on a career of piracy which, as a record of successes, battles, murders, mutinies, and bloodshed, has probably never been equaled.

Indeed, so execrable a pirate did Sharp prove himself that even some of his most notorious fellows could no longer stomach him, and Dampier, Gayny, Jobson, and over forty others deserted the company and started back for the Caribbean via the Isthmus of Darien.

Thereupon Sharp was seized with a brilliant idea, an inspiration which had never come to his brother buccaneers, a wild scheme quite worthy of his rash spirit. It was nothing less than to ravage the entire western coast of South America, sail through the Strait of Magellan, and return by sea to his old stamping-ground in the West Indies.

This was "the dangerous voyage," and while it proved far more dangerous to the unfortunate peoples of the west coast than to the buccaneers, yet the mishaps and adventures of the latter were thrilling enough, and sufficiently numerous to fill a volume. No fiction ever written, no imaginings no matter how vivid could equal Ringrose's log of *The Most Blessed Trinity,* as, sailing down the coast, her crew landed and sacked towns, filled market-places with dead and wounded, ravished women, pillaged cathedrals, razed cities, and with sword and torch left a trail of blood and devastation from Panama to Patagonia.

Laden with loot,—with wines and spirits, silver bullion,[1] golden coins, jewels torn from the fingers of terrified women; plate and chalices from desecrated churches; embroidered vestments of murdered priests, treasure won through unspeakable tortures; satins and silks; even hides and tallow,—the battered galleon, scarred by shot and shell, her gilded stern castle hacked away to afford room for guns, her counter charred by fire, her decks bloodstained, cruised ever southward toward the Horn.

But the buccaneers did not escape unscathed. At many a town they were ignominiously defeated. Even Sharp had his troubles. As was often the case with such rascals,—incredible as it may seem,—the pirate crew, despite their ruthless and villainous lives, had certain ideas of religion. Finding their captain utterly regardless of the Sabbath, and so lacking in even a semblance of piety that he did not hesitate to sack a town or scuttle a ship on that day, they decided that the time had come to end such sacrilegious behavior, and, seizing Sharp, they placed him in irons and dumped him into the already

[1] One prize taken by the *Trinity*, the *San Rosario*, was laden with over seven hundred "pigs," or ingots of silver bullion, but the buccaneers, mistaking the precious metal for tin, threw overboard all but one bar which was retained by one of the men for a souvenir.

overcrowded hold. Then in his place they appointed a new skipper, one John Watling, an hypocritical old villain who would murder out of hand on Saturday and hold divine services the next morning, when his cutthroat crew would join in singing hymns or repeating prayers, the while wetting their throats with fiery rum. But the consciences of the men were quieted, and the new captain might have safely brought *The Most Blessed Trinity* safely to the Antilles, had not Fate, in the shape of a bullet through his liver, ended his sanctimonious and bloody career.

As there was no other capable of taking command, the mutineers were compelled to reinstate Sharp, who apparently had been meditating upon his own sins as he sat manacled in the dismal hold, and with only his own thoughts for company had decided to lead a better life henceforth. At any rate, one of the first things he did when the irons were knocked from his wrists and ankles and he found himself once more upon his ship's quarter-deck, was to intercede for the life of an aged Indian prisoner whom Watling, before his sudden demise, had ordered shot for supposedly giving false information about Arica.

Who would have imagined that the desperate and unconscionable pirate chieftain,—whose greatest enjoyment had been in the screams of captured women, the shrieks of tortured men, the groans of the dying and the roar of cannon—would ever come to this? But the scarred, leather-skinned, shaggy-browed old villain waxed eloquent and drew heartrending pictures of the poor Indian's empty home, of his wife and children seated in their lowly hut, waiting for the return of their lord and master; and his chronicler even asserts that the suddenly reformed Bartholomew's voice faltered and tears coursed down his cheeks as he spoke.

Unfortunately for the captive, the captain's plea was in vain, and his crew, still sullen and mutinous, being determined to put an end to the old Indian, Sharp called for a basin of water and ostentatiously washing his gnarled and blood-stained hands therein, wiped them on the bedraggled and grease-spotted velvet coat he wore, and then, with up-turned eyes, declared most impressively and solemnly that he was "clear of the blood of this poor man." He added, "I will warrant you a hot day for this piece of cruelty whenever we come to fight at Arica,"—a prophecy which was fulfilled in a manner far exceeding his expectations and believed by the freebooters, with their sailors' superstitions, to be the direct result of the Indian's death, as they later discovered he had told them nothing but the truth. At Arica scores of the invaders were killed or made prisoners, among them the ships' two surgeons, and a bare handful of her original crew remained to work the badly battered and strained ship, and reef and handle the patched and shot-riddled sails as she staggered and plunged through the tempestuous, ice-filled seas and freezing gales around the Cape and into the Atlantic through uncharted waters. For they failed to make the Strait of Magellan and won a way where no ship had sailed eastward before. Possibly during his short confinement and his compulsory resignation from leadership, Sharp really did find grace and decide to live an honest life thenceforth; or more likely, being a canny rascal, he had no desire to repeat his experience and determined to give his rebellious crew their full of righteousness. Whatever the reason, there was no further trouble, and *The Most Blessed Trinity,* having successfully weathered the storms and billows of the Antarctic, went wallowing on her way northward through the Atlantic.

Weather-beaten, storm-strained; her sails in tatters, her rigging gray, ragged, and slack, her spars patched and fished in scores of places; with yard-long weeds upon her leaking bottom, and bearing the scars of many a battle, the one-time Spanish flag-ship worked up the coast, through the doldrums, and into the trades. Her log reveals little but a constant succession of gales and hurricanes, of starvation rations and ceaseless work to keep the old ship afloat and able to sail, until, eighteen months after starting forth on her "most dangerous voyage" she entered the Caribbean and sighted Barbados—the first land seen since passing Patagonia.

But the sea-weary buccaneers were fated not to set foot upon the right little, tight little isle. Within Carlisle Bay lay H. M. S. *Richmond,* and Sharp, glimpsing the war-ship, promptly squared his battered yards and headed for Antigua.

A dozen or more of the men, among them Ringrose, landed here—eventually to make their way in safety to England—while *The Most Blessed Trinity,* with men working ceaselessly at her wheezing pumps, bore away for Nevis. Here, two years after Jamestown had sunk beneath the waves, the wraith-like galleon with her lawless crew came to rest, and the great "sea artist," having accomplished his harebrained undertaking, turned his battered old hulk over to his fellows and, well laden with riches, sailed for England arrayed in all the gorgeous finery of some murdered grandee.

Thus ended this most remarkable voyage, this greatest of buccaneer adventures; a cruise unequaled in the annals of the sea; the longest, bloodiest, and most successful pirate raid of history.

No doubt, like Red Legs, Sharp settled down in some quiet nook and spent the remainder of his life as a respected squire or gentleman farmer in Sussex or Surrey; for nothing seems to be known of him after he arrived in England, and, having been tried for and acquitted of piracy, he dropped out of sight. But Basil Ringrose, to whom we are indebted for the log of *The Most Blessed Trinity,* and who, as navigator, was mainly responsible for the safe consummation of her voyage, was far too restless a soul to be content with English lanes and hedgerows and a vine-clad thatched cottage. Once more taking to the buccaneer's life, he joined a pirate ship bound for the South Seas, and met death off the coast of Mexico after again rounding the Horn.

It was not at all unusual for a pirate to give up the sea and, under an assumed name, live quietly upon the fruits of his labors, with his past quite unsuspected by his neighbors, but it was rarely indeed that an honored and respected gentleman took suddenly to pirating.

Such, however, was the case with a certain Major Stede Bonnet, a rich and finely educated citizen of Barbados and a pillar of the church.

He was a gentleman most highly thought of, a leader of Barbados society, and apparently one of fortune's favorites. But it seems that there was a fly in the major's ointment in the person of a nagging, quarrelsome Mrs. Bonnet.

In fact, so unbearable did the major's life become that at last he decided to choose the less of two evils. Having purchased a sloop, fitted her with guns, assembled a crew, and named his acquisition *The Revenge,* Major Bonnet bade a thankful farewell to his wife and, on a dark night in 1716, sailed forth from Bridgetown Harbor, bound a-pirating.

Oddly enough, although the gallant if henpecked officer knew nothing whatsoever of seamanship, he seems to have been a somewhat successful and lucky pirate,—albeit a humane one, for it was he who rescued the marooned members of Blackbeard's crew from their desert isle,—and *The Revenge,* cruising off our Atlantic coast, took prizes right and left.

In a short time Bonnet's name was one to conjure with, and a mere mention of it brought terror to the hearts of shipping-men and sailors in every port from Salem to Savannah, while so bold did he become that he had the effrontery to make Gardiner's Island, in Long Island Sound, his headquarters at various times. For a space, too, he joined forces with the redoubtable Teach, better known as Blackbeard, but the partnership was rather unfortunate, for the scoundrelly Teach robbed the major of his ship and most of his possessions.

This treacherous behavior on the part of a supposed friend made Bonnet melancholy, if we are to believe his biographer, and may have led to his undoing, for shortly afterward—in 1718, to be exact—he was taken prisoner off the Carolinas. He managed to make good his escape in a canoe, but a reward of seventy pounds sterling was offered for him, and the following year he was captured at Sullivan's Island, was tried in Charleston, and, having been sentenced to death, was hanged at White Point. Possibly poor Major Bonnet was not sorry to find peace even at the end of the hangman's rope, for his adventures had brought him little more comfort or ease than his home life in Barbados; and it is even doubtful if his widow wept over his demise, or mended her ways. Of her we know nothing; she slips quite out of the story with the departure of her spouse on *The Revenge,* and even Johnson in his "History of the Pyrates" was too gallant to do more than hint at her character by stating that "This humour of going a pyrating was believed to proceed from a disorder of the mind said to have been occasioned by some discomforts in the marriage state."

However, we do know, from historical records, that poor Stede was subjected to so lengthy a diatribe by the judge who condemned him (it filled six closely written pages) that even his wife's scoldings must have seemed mild in comparison, and ere the judge's long-winded advice as to leading the higher life was ended the major must have become so utterly worn out as actually to long for death.

Aside from Red Legs and the unfortunate Major Bonnet, Barbados, or, for that matter, any of the southern islands, have little to link them with the buccaneers; and as I was following in the wake of these adventurers, and not endeavoring to make a cruise of all the Antilles, the *Vigilant* sailed away from charming St. Kitts with Santo Domingo as her goal.

There was a long sail ahead, nearly three hundred and fifty miles to cover before we reached our objective point at Samana Bay, but we planned to break the stretch by a stop at St. Croix, one hundred and twenty-five miles from St. Kitts. Over a sparkling, sunny sea, with the wind on our quarter, we sped away from the fair green hills and downs of St. Kitts, left the great cone of Statia and the isolated, beetling peak of Saba looming hazily and like phantom isles to the north, and with a broad wake of suds streaming far astern and a roaring, curling mass of foam beneath our bows, swept across Saba Bank.

It gives one a strange feeling to be sailing across the deep-blue Caribbean far from land and suddenly to look over a ship's rails and plainly see bottom with its masses of corals, its great starfish, its huge black sea-cucumbers, and its clustered sponges under the keel. Many times have I sailed over Saba Bank, and never can I overcome the impression that the ship is about to touch the ragged coral so clearly visible; and the effect is even more remarkable when one is crossing the bank on a big steamship. Saba Bank extends for nearly forty miles east and west, and almost the same distance north and south, with from six to twenty fathoms of glass-clear water over it; and while in heavy weather large vessels avoid it, because of the huge seas that pile up in the shoal water and the danger of touching a reef, in calm weather they pass unhesitatingly across it.

Beyond Saba Bank we were out of sight of land, and on that wide waste of waters stretching unbroken, even by a sail, to the horizon on every side, the little *Vigilant* seemed pitifully small. More than ever was I impressed with the courage, the confidence, and the faith in God which led the early voyagers and discoverers over this unknown, uncharted sea in craft far smaller and less seaworthy than the *Vigilant.* Rarely do we stop to consider what marvelous undertakings and great adventures those ancient voyages were. In miserable tubs—unwieldy, unfit for beating to windward with any degree of success, clumsily sparred, and uncouthly rigged—the daring navigators crossed the broad Atlantic and cruised hither and yon among the reefs and isles of the Caribbean. The wonder is that they did not all pile their timbers upon the ragged coral reefs and low-lying cays, or that they ever managed to find the same island twice. To steer a course across the Caribbean and raise one of the isles above one's bows is no small undertaking in a well-found vessel and with the aid of modern instruments, and how Columbus and his fellows ever accomplished it, with their crude appliances and with no charts to guide them, is a mystery which ever fills me with wonder.

And as I lolled upon the *Vigilant's* deck while our little ship with flowing sheets plunged on to the westward, I also wondered how big Sam could steer so unerringly for St. Croix—or if he could. But he seemed to be perfectly confident of himself, grasping the wheel in those great black hands of his, casting an occasional glance at the bellying sails, balancing himself on his huge sinewy legs to the heave of the deck, and peering straight ahead with no heed to the compass, as though his eyes could pierce the distance and see the hills of St. Croix beyond the horizon.

Each day I took the sun and worked out our position, purely as a precautionary measure; but I never revealed the results to Sam, for I was curious to see just how accurately he could sail by dead reckoning, or instinct, or whatever it was.

Once, as I stood near the taffrail and squinted through my sextant, Sam chuckled, and a broad grin spread over his black, good-natured face.

"Ah don' guess you think Ah kin mek Santa Cruz, Chief," he ventured.

"Oh, I 'm not worrying over that, Sam," I replied. "But it 's a good plan to know just where we are, in case of trouble—if a storm should come up and blow us off our course, or anything should happen to you."

"Tha 's right, Chief," he agreed. "But Ah reckon Ah 'd mek some islan' 'gardless o' all that. Ah don't need to know where we is for to get where we's goin'."

"Well, how on earth do you do it, Sam?" I asked.

"Lordy! Ah don' can' say," he declared. "Ah jus' knows where'bouts th' lan' is, an' Ah steers for he."

I had to let it go at that, for the Bahaman's sense of direction was as inexplicable to himself as to me; but, after all, while this ability to head directly for a definite speck of land in a waste of waters is staggering to a landsman, is it really any more remarkable than a woodsman's ability to head across country through forests or over trackless plains and unerringly come to his destination? Perhaps it is the same instinct that guides the carrier-pigeon, the migrating birds, the cat and the dog, and even the lowly toad, across long distances of unknown territory. And if we accept the latest scientific theory that all of these are unconsciously following vibratory waves or flows of electrons, then possibly big Sam was being led across the Caribbean by means of nature's radio, to which the ordinary mortal's intellect is not attuned.

As we tore along, reeling off a good eight knots, Joe strolled aft, armed with heavy lines and baited hooks, and, making them fast to the rail, paid them out rapidly astern. Hardly had the first whipping line run out for fifty feet in the creaming wake when there was a flash of silver and gold and Joe began hauling in. But his catch was more than he could handle alone, and I hurried to help him. A moment later we had a magnificent twenty-five-pound albacore flapping on deck, and for the next half-hour the fun was fast and furious. I verily believe we could easily have filled the *Vigilant's* hold with fish had we kept on, but when enough Spanish mackerel, albacore, dolphin, and bonito had been secured to provide a fish diet for all on board for the next twenty-four hours, Joe rolled up his lines and betook himself to the galley, carrying the particular specimen he intended for my meal and calling to the men to bring their own.

Sam grinned widely at Joseph's superior manner.

"Tha' Turk' Islan' boy act like he ain' th' same specie wi' other niggers," he chuckled. "On'y he Bahaman like mahsel' Ah guess he don' 'sociate long o' me. But, Lordy, Chief, he cert'n'y can cook! Ya-umm!"

"Yep," I replied; "Joe is inclined to be a bit of a snob, but, as you say, he 's a fine cook—and a mighty faithful boy, too. Are all the Turks Island boys his kind?"

"Not zactly, Chief," responded Sam. "But the' does mek to be a bit bumpt'ous. You see, Chief, the' says as how Gran' Turk was the islan' what

Columbus foun' first, n' the' argufies as how tha' meks they th' firs' qual'ty niggers in th' islan's, Chief."

I roared with laughter.

"That 's good, Sam!" I cried. "But it 's not so strange, after all. We 've got people in the States that put on just as many airs because their ancestors came over in the *Mayflower*."

"Lord! is tha' so, Chief?" exclaimed Sam. "Ah never did n' know white folks bothered 'bout such humbuggin'."

A moment later, Trouble shouted that land was in sight; and, sure enough, straight before the pitching tip of our jib-boom, a tiny opalescent cloud broke the horizon under the setting sun.

Sam's instinct had not failed him: he had, figuratively, hit the bull's-eye first shot, and a triumphant grin spread over his face as he stopped and peered ahead beneath the booms.

Rapidly the land rose before us, an indigo patch against the crimson sky, and ere nightfall we were close in to the island, rocking lazily along on an almost calm sea, our sails flapping, half filled, in the rapidly falling wind, and the boom of the surf and a chorus of night insects coming to us mingled with the scent of flowers, the pungent odor of burning canes, and the earthy smell of newly plowed fields. With scarcely steerage way, the *Vigilant* crept on through the night and past the twinkling lights of Christiansted; and, gazing up at the myriad brilliant stars, and lulled by the soft murmur of the rippling water and the gentle creaking of the rigging and spars, I fell asleep.

CHAPTER X

THE ISLE OF THE HOLY CROSS

ST. CROIX, or—to use its more euphonious Spanish name—Santa Cruz, seems an island fashioned from green plush. If ever there was a true Emerald Isle, it is this island of the Holy Cross; and while it lacks the majestic mountains of the larger islands, their dense forests and their impressive scenery, it possesses a wonderful beauty all its own. It is like a perfect gem, a jewel of radiant green, in a band of silver set in purest turquoise. Here Nature with a lavish hand has spread green of every imaginable hue; green such as no artist ever conceived or could reproduce. Then, to complete her chef-d'œuvre, she has added touches of brilliant scarlet in flaming poinciana trees, soft browns in unplanted fields, dull yellows in the groves of tibet-trees, and high lights in the shape of snow-white plantation houses and sugar-mills, the whole framed in dazzling coral sand, creamy surf, and water of wondrous hues, from deepest sapphire to palest acquamarine.

No towering mountain peaks distract the eye or

lead one's gaze upward to the clouds; no great cataracts hurtle over ragged precipices; no rugged cliffs rear themselves above the sea, and no mysterious, shadowy jungles clothe the hills. As in a true masterpiece, its composition is simple, its harmony of tones is perfection, and as though scorning comparison it hangs alone against a background of blue sky and bluer sea in the midst of the Caribbean.

From East Point to Fredericksted, near its western end, Santa Cruz is one unending succession of rounded green hills, smiling valleys, golden-green cane-fields, and white beaches. Sugar is, or was, king in this isle of the Holy Cross, and upward from the very edge of the sea to the summits of its highest hills the fields spread like a patchwork quilt over the land, outlined by smooth white roads or long lines of royal palms, and dotted with the towers of ancient windmills, the tall chimneys of the sugar-mills, white limestone estate houses, and groves and clumps of trees. Along the coast low limestone bluffs alternate with palm-fringed, white-beached coves, each lovelier than the preceding, until, as a culmination of all, Fredericksted is disclosed to view. Close to the sea, half hidden behind its screen of coco-palms, the little town nestles against its background of vivid green beyond a bay of marvelous, shimmering, multicolored water. Intensely tropical and foreign-looking is this town—known locally as "West End" to distinguish it from its only competitor, Christiansted or "Basse End"—with its softly tinted buff, pink, and pale-blue residences; its low, massive warehouses and stores with wide-arched doorways; its flower-filled balconies and patios, and its quaint red Danish fort.

Here in the transparent water the *Vigilant* came to rest in her own home port, where the Stars and Stripes flew in place of the scarlet flag of Denmark. Somehow, to me, Old Glory appeared out of place here, for always the Danish banner with its snowy cross had seemed most appropriate for this little isle of Santa Cruz. But aside from the different flag, a few khaki-clad "soldiers of the sea" in place of the blue-uniformed, "woodeny" Danish troops, and the fact that the official notices pasted on stuccoed walls were in English instead of Dansk, I could see few changes in the place.

Except in its beauty from the sea, Fredericksted has little to offer in the way of sights or attractions. Its streets of white lime are blindingly glaring, and reflect the heat and light of the intense tropical sunlight in a way that makes walking about at midday a torture. It has no noteworthy or impressive buildings, and under its new owners it appears no more prosperous than before. But as a resort wherein to pass a few weeks or months to avoid the rigors of a Northern winter St. Croix has many attractions. Its climate is noted for its salubrity; there are splendid motor roads about the shores and across the island from West End to Basse End; there is pigeon- and deer-hunting to be had; the tepid water on its perfect beaches makes sea-bathing an unending delight, and the hospitality and good-fellowship of its people are charming. Of tropical pests there are few. There are no poisonous reptiles, only one species of small, harmless snake being found on the island; there are no venomous insects; mosquitos are few, and though at certain seasons and in some places sand-flies are troublesome, house-flies are scarcely known. But do not assume from this that the island has no drawbacks, or is a perfect Eden. Its blacks—and about ninety per cent. of its population of fifteen thousand souls are of African blood—are discontented and surly and lack the happy-go-lucky good nature of the other West Indian natives. Since the United States came into possession they have caught the Land-of-Liberty idea, and have organized labor-unions, declared strikes, and made things generally unpleasant for the planters and whites.

Moreover, the otherwise delightful isle is subject to severe hurricanes and more or less disastrous earthquakes. In 1867, St. Croix was virtually devastated by a quake followed by a tidal wave which lifted the U. S. S. *Monongahela* from her moorings in the harbor, and, carrying her completely over the tops of the coco-palms along the shore, deposited her unharmed and right side up on dry land. From this unique position, this unexpected and unwelcome dry-docking, the cruiser was salvaged by digging a canal to the sea through which she was launched, whereupon she proceeded on her way none the worse for the experience.

In 1772, over five hundred houses were destroyed by a hurricane which whipped up such a sea that the water rose seventy feet above its normal level and destroyed a vast amount of shipping. Oddly enough, this hurricane was the direct means of bringing to our shores one of our greatest celebrities, Alexander Hamilton. At the time, Hamilton, who was then a lad of fifteen years, was an underpaid clerk in the counting-house of one Nikolas Cruger of Christiansted, and his letter to friends in the States, wherein he vividly described the devastation of the storm, attracted so much attention that it resulted in his being given a chance to come to this country and secure a college education. Had it not been for that hurricane on Santa Cruz, the great statesman no doubt would have lived and died an unknown accountant in the Antilles.

Again and again the island has been swept by these "overgrowne and monstrous stormes," as Captain Smith called them, and though they occur only during the summer, and therefore need not be taken into consideration by winter tourists or visitors, yet they have done a great deal to keep the island from gaining the prosperity it should enjoy, and have wrought incalculable damage to crops and property.

Historically, Santa Cruz has a most interesting past. It has been French, Spanish, Dutch, English, Danish, and American in turn, and enjoys the distinction of having at one time been under the banner of the Knights of Malta, who sought to establish a little kingdom of their own here in the Caribbean.

Originally discovered by Columbus in 1493, the island of the Holy Cross—a name, by the way, the significance of which is puzzling—remained unknown until 1587, when Sir Walter Raleigh landed on its shores on his way to Virginia. At that time, however, the island was the abode of fierce cannibal Indians, who made forays to the neighboring islands, especially Porto Rico, where they not only secured a supply of captives for their larder but also hewed the big trees into dugout canoes, a fact which would indicate that even at that period there were no extensive forests on Santa Cruz. Europeans did not see fit to attempt a settlement on the island until 1625, when Dutch, French, and English colonists occupied it jointly and apparently in peace. As no mention is made of trouble with the cannibals, we must assume that they had disappeared, though how they were so suddenly extirpated, or whether or not they betook themselves elsewhere, is a mystery. As usual, however, the settlers soon began to quarrel and the island was a scene of bloodshed and battles for possession for a quarter of a century, or until 1651, when it was sold by the French to the Knights of Malta. But after six years of occupancy, during which they were on the verge of starvation most of the time, the knights decided that establishing a West Indian kingdom was no sinecure, and, seizing a ship which had arrived from France, they compelled the mariners to take them with their goods and chattels to Brazil.

From that time until the Danes took possession in 1733–35, the island frequently changed hands, and for the next hundred years hurricanes and slave uprisings did almost as much to prevent any settled prosperity as had the battles and wars before. Even now, under Uncle Sam's régime, there is much room for improvement; for the isle is far from peaceful or prosperous. Perhaps, when we learn from bitter experience how to handle tropical colonies, Santa Cruz may come into its own; or, perchance through the cultivation of some commodity other than sugar, the island may attain prosperity; but at present matters are far from promising. As one of the greatest faults of Santa Cruz is its lack of good harbors, which were essential to pirates, and as there was nothing in particular to attract such visitors to the island, it is doubtful if the buccaneers ever did more than touch here occasionally. I did not come to the island because of its piratical associations, however, but merely for a visit with old friends, the owners of my little ship, as well as to break the long trip from St. Kitts to Santo Domingo. This having been accomplished, we once more hoisted sail and, leaving the isle of the Holy Cross behind, headed for Porto Rico, sixty miles away.

There was no need for Sam's uncanny instinct now; the veriest tyro could have steered a course straight for that largest of Uncle Sam's West Indian colonies, for scarcely had the green hills of Santa Cruz vanished in a filmy cloud behind us when the lofty mountains of Porto Rico rose against the sky before our bows. By mid-afternoon we were close under the land, with its tiers of sky-piercing peaks rearing their vast bulwarks beneath masses of heavy clouds, while above all towered the phantasmal form of El Yunque (The Anvil) lifting its head nearly three thousand feet above the ragged coast-line.

The island appeared vast as a continent, with its coasts stretching eastward and westward to the horizon for one hundred miles, but in comparison with the lush greenness of Santa Cruz, the down-like surface and clear-cut forested mountains of St. Kitts, or the luxuriance of the smaller Caribbees, Porto Rico is dismal, monotonous, far from attractive, viewed from the sea.

There is no doubt that the island has beauties of its own, but it lacks the transcendent loveliness of the smaller islands, isles not one twentieth its size but whereon are mountains clothed, from cloud-shrouded summits to breaking surf, with vast forests,—mountains almost twice the height of Porto Rico's loftiest peak,—and with a thousand times the scenic glories of Porto Rico compressed within an area of a few square miles, which the eye can take in as an entirety. Driving over Porto Rico's splendid roads by motor-car, the visitor is impressed more with the engineering feats that made these highways possible than with the scenery. The well-tilled tobacco-fields with acres of cheese-cloth stretched over them, giving the appearance of snow-covered hillsides, attract the eye more than the natural vegetation, which is scant and uninteresting. There is little of the intensely tropical vegetation, the luxuriance and riot of color one associates with the West Indies; and while the mountains are rugged, impressive, cut by stupendous cañon-like valleys, and in places wildly grand, the great forests of gigantic trees, the feeling of being in an untamed wilderness, and the charm of the primeval are lacking. One feels, no matter where he may be upon this island, that Man has conquered it, that there is nothing novel or unusual about it. While to some the ever-present indications of prosperity, of civilization, of Man's conquest of mountains, plains, and valleys, appeals more strongly than nature's greatest beauties, personally I prefer to be where the influence of human beings and the almighty dollar is less in evidence.

Nevertheless I have a warm spot in my heart for Porto Rico. Many delightful days—yes, even months—have I spent there; many are my friends upon the island, and thousands of miles have I toured over its splendid roads. San Juan is a delightfully interesting and picturesque city, with its ancient forts, its grim old Morro, its massive walls and quaint lantern-like sentry-boxes; and there are other towns and cities on the island which call to mind the days when America was in the making. But Porto Rico had little to do with the buccaneers, unless we include Sir Francis Drake and his lifelong friend Hawkins among them. For these two the island held a dream of conquest, and at San Juan they battered long and loudly at its doors and performed some mighty deeds of daring, seamanship, and battle under the frowning walls and grim guns of the never-conquered old Morro. But their efforts came to little, and in their hopeless attempt to take the place Drake received the wound that brought him to his death off Porto Bello, and Hawkins lost his life and was buried off the eastern shores of the island he had sought so long and hard to take. Never in all their long lives of valiant fighting and reckless courage had the two suffered such heartbreaking defeat and disappointment, for in the treasure-vaults at San Juan were stored over four million dollars' worth of plate, bullion, and coins—greater riches by far than Drake had ever taken in all his conquests, not excepting those of the famed Armada, which his seamanship and fighting ability had scattered and destroyed a few years before.

Neither Drake or Hawkins may be classed among the buccaneers, however,—although to the Spaniards they were nothing more nor less than pirates,—and so they really have no place in our story.

Three years after Drake's failure—in 1598, to be exact—a far more romantic figure decided to try his luck at capturing San Juan. This was no less a personage than George, Earl of Cumberland, a Cambridge graduate, a courtier, a gambler, and, to use a modern expression, an all-round "sport." He was extraordinarily brave, a good soldier, an expert seaman, and renowned for his immense physical strength. He was also a Knight of the Garter, and, for some reason which history fails to relate, Queen Elizabeth had seen fit to present him with one of her gloves, which, set with diamonds, he invariably wore like a plume in his hat. During Drake's encounter with the Armada this picturesque young peer had commanded a British ship, and, having once tasted the charms of sea-fighting, he then and there took to pirating, or privateering, whichever you will. At the age of forty he had won considerable fame and ever was distinguished by the claret-colored glove of his sovereign which he wore through thick and thin, evidently considering it a talisman. Perhaps it was his faith in this unique decoration which led to his attack upon Porto Rico, when on March 6, 1598, he sailed forth from Plymouth, England, with a fleet of twenty ships, the flag-ship bearing the odd name of *The Scourge of Malice.*

After a pleasant voyage, and the taking of a few prizes to break the monotony of the long sea trip, the earl arrived at Dominica, gave his men shore leave for a day or two, filled his casks with fresh water, and then bore away for San Juan. Profiting by Drake's dismal failure, My Lord of Cumberland made no attempt to attack the Morro or the shore batteries, but in true buccaneer fashion landed six hundred men at dead of night a mile or more to the east of San Juan, and then, dividing his forces into two detachments, rushed the city at dawn. The Dons, taken completely unaware, resisted stubbornly, but the guns of the Morro and the other forts were powerless to aid, and after two hours of savage hand-to-hand fighting Cumberland was in possession of the supposedly impregnable capital. The British lost no time in pillaging it as thoroughly as any of the later buccaneers could have done. Then, out of pure wantonness apparently, they fired all the wooden houses and buildings, destroyed the paintings, furnishings, and other articles they could not or did not care to carry off, seized or destroyed twelve ships which were in the harbor, and made a determined but unsuccessful attempt to raze the fortifications.

Meanwhile, all but a handful of the citizens had fled to the outlying country-side, leaving the hated British monarchs of all they surveyed, and we can easily picture the beruffled and begemmed pirate peer strutting about with the queen's glove still in his broad hat, vastly pleased with himself for his prowess—as, in truth, he well might be. Not only had he succeeded where the greatest of England's sea-fighters had signally failed, and secured vast treasure, but he saw in San Juan a glorious spot for a stronghold from which to make remunerative raids against the neighboring Spanish colonies and Spanish shipping.

But the dispossessed and robbed Porto Ricans had an ally that Cumberland had not taken into account, which, all unseen and unsuspected, was approaching, and which with all his courage and resources he could not overcome or even hold at bay. Before he realized it, the enemy was upon him: the deadly Yellow Jack had entered his camp by stealth, and like wildfire the plague spread among his hapless men. Within the fortnight Cumberland's force had been reduced one half; daily men died, raving and inhuman, their faces a ghastly yellow, eyes starting from their hollow sockets, their frames shaken and wasted by fever. Brave fighters though they were, the British were terrified by this enemy they could not fight; and, hastily packing his few surviving men upon his ships, the glove-plumed knight sailed away from the town he had won, never to return.

Perhaps it was the knowledge of Drake's failure, or the story—with hair-raising embellishments, like as not—of Cumberland's plague-stricken force that discouraged the buccaneers. They no doubt reasoned that a spot strong enough to repulse the famous Drake held little promise for their ruffianly if brave and hardy crews. At any rate, there is no record of their having made a serious effort to take San Juan; and while, from time to time, some particularly ambitious or daring pirate exchanged a few rounds of shot with the garrison of the Morro, and raided outlying towns, the buccaneers never accomplished anything of note and never looted enough treasure from the Porto Ricans to pay for the ammunition wasted and the blood spilled in their attempts. In fact, even the best of them, such as Morgan, Montbars, Lolonais, Sharp, and other notorious leaders, looked upon this island as too hard a nut for them to crack and confined their depredations to more promising fields.

But one attempt of the buccaneers to raid Porto Rico, though not San Juan, is well worth mentioning; for not only was it disastrous to the pirates, but it gives an excellent idea of their methods and persistence. As a matter of fact, it was in the first instance an accidental invasion, for Monsieur Ogeron, the buccaneer governor of Tortuga, having set forth at the head of a fleet, in a flag-ship named for himself and manned by five hundred pirates, had no intention of molesting the island, but was bound for the island of Curaçao, where he hoped to wrest town and treasure from the Dutch. Fate, however, interfered seriously with Monsieur's plans. Running into a storm, his new flag-ship was driven ignominiously upon the rocky Guandanillas close to the western shore of Porto Rico.

Fortunately,—or, rather, unfortunately, as it turned out,—his men all managed to reach dry land in safety, only to fall into the hands of their enemies the Spaniards on the following day. Thinking that as usual the buccaneers had landed on a piratical raid, the Dons fell upon the castaways tooth and nail, and killed a large proportion of the five hundred before they realized that they were dealing with unarmed, shipwrecked men. When at last they discovered that their hated enemies were quite incapable of defending themselves, they bound the buccaneers securely and marched them inland, meanwhile feeding them so sparingly on scraps from their own meals that the pirates were barely kept alive. Ogeron, crafty old rascal that he was, pretended to be a half-witted fellow, and his men stoutly maintained, when questioned, that their leader had been drowned—an excellent example of the buccaneers' faithfulness and loyalty to one another. Their captain, being looked upon as a fool and harmless, was left free and was treated far better than his comrades by the soldiers, who found much amusement in his capers and drolleries. Among the pirates was a French surgeon who was also left unbound in order that he might practise his profession among the Dons. So the medico and the governor put their heads together, and, having acquired a hatchet, slipped into the bush and managed to reach the shore. Their intention was to fell trees and construct a craft and then, putting to sea, gain Tortuga and rally their friends to attack Porto Rico and rescue the captive crew.

Such an undertaking, which would have appeared impossible to most men, did not daunt the resourceful pirates. Having managed to secure a quantity of small fish, which they killed near shore with their hatchet, and having kindled a fire by rubbing two sticks together, they dined heartily, and the following day proceeded to fell trees for their boat. Fortune, however, smiled upon them, and before the first tree was cut they spied a large canoe, in which were two men, making directly toward them. Hiding in the bushes until the canoe was pulled upon the beach, the two buccaneers discovered that the occupants were harmless fishermen, one a mulatto, the other a Spaniard. Leaving the white man in charge of the boat, the colored fisherman picked up calabashes and, all unsuspecting of the danger lurking in the underbrush, made his way toward a spring. This was the buccaneers' opportunity: they leaped upon the mulatto, and to quote Esquemelling, "discharged a great blow on his head with the hatchet and soon bereaved him of life." The Spaniard, alarmed at the noise, tried to escape, "but this he could not perform so soon without being overtaken by the two and there massacred by their hands." Now in possession of a seaworthy craft, the buccaneers set sail for Samana Bay in Santo Domingo, where there was a lair of their associates. Here Ogeron made a most eloquent speech to his fellow buccaneers, and persuaded them to join him in a raid on Porto Rico, partly for loot and partly to rescue his ill-fated men, who had so inadvertently fallen into their enemies' hands.

But Ogeron's luck seems to have deserted him once and for all, for the expedition was a failure. The buccaneers were surprised by the watchful Spaniards, a large number of the pirates were slain, and while Ogeron escaped with a few of his fellows, the raid was abandoned and they "hastened to set sail and go back to Tortuga with great confusion in their minds, much diminished in their number and nothing laden with spoils, the hopes whereof had possessed their hearts."

The unfortunate survivors of the shipwreck were taken to San Juan and, in a chain-gang, were forced to labor at building the great fortress of San Cristobal; while at night they were closely guarded in dungeons by their captors, who had a wholesome fear of the buccaneers and knew this handful of maltreated prisoners was quite capable of wreaking vengeance unless kept under lock and key. As Esquemelling puts it, "by night they shut them up close prisoners fearing lest they should enterprise upon the city. For of such attempts the Spaniards had had divers proofs on other occasions which afforded them sufficient cause to use them after that manner."

That manacled, overworked, half-fed captives could commit any great damage among the armed Spaniards in a city of thousands of inhabitants may seem incredible; but as their chronicler says, the Dons had had "divers proofs" on other occasions and they took no chances. Indeed, each time a ship left port they packed some of the prisoners off to Havana, to labor on the fortifications there; and they also transported some of them to Spain, taking good care to disperse them far and wide. But the buccaneers seem to have had a supernatural ability to find one another; and, notwithstanding all the precautions of the Spaniards, the deported ones, again to quote Esquemelling, "soon after met almost all together in France and resolved among themselves to return again to Tortuga with the first opportunity should proffer . . . so that in a short while the greatest part of these Pirates had nested themselves again at Tortuga where after some time they equipped a new fleet to revenge their former misfortunes on the Spaniards." Of such stuff were these adventurers made, and after a few such "divers proofs" we can scarcely blame the Dons if they promptly killed all pirates who fell into their hands. Unquestionably, the only good pirate was a dead pirate.

Departing from Porto Rico, with far more interesting places ahead, we coasted along the southern shores of this island of "Boriquen" from which Ponce de Leon set forth in search of his fountain, and, only stopping at Ponce overnight, sailed onward toward Santo Domingo.

Barely sixty miles of water separates Porto Rico from Santo Domingo,—or, as the Spaniards called it, Hispaniola,—and midway in this strait lies the island of Mona, from which the passage takes its name. Barren, gray, and forbidding, Mona is little more than a mass of austere rock rising above the sea, with Monita or Little Mona at her feet. The only signs of life are the lighthouse and the flocks of screaming sea-birds, but there is a stunted growth of scrub upon the island, and hunting-parties come here at times; while the guano deposits of Mona have been worked for years.

Beyond—vast, mysterious, overwhelming in its magnitude and majesty—is Santo Domingo, second largest of the Antilles, nearly two hundred miles in width, nearly five hundred in length; a territory close to thirty thousand square miles in area, or three times the size of Belgium, twice the size of

Denmark, almost as large as Portugal or Ireland, and, compared with more familiar places, about as large as the state of Maine; or larger than Vermont, Massachusetts, Connecticut, and Rhode Island combined.

Continental in the altitude of its mountains, with the summit of Loma Tina towering to a height of eleven thousand feet, in the vastness of its interior plains, its great valleys, its coastal lands, its rolling savannas, and its huge rivers, Santo Domingo is by far the most beautiful, the richest, and the most imposing of the West Indies. Here was the very cradle of civilization in the New World; here ebbed and flowed the life of New Spain. From Santo Domingo, Cortez, Balboa, and all those other famous conquistadors of old set forth upon their adventures. Here was founded the first European settlement in the New World; here Columbus came to grief and lost one of his ships on that first memorable voyage in 1492; here he was cast in chains into a dungeon; here his son ruled as viceroy, and here the discoverer's bones still rest in the great cathedral. It was upon Santo Domingo's shores, too, that the first skirmish between the Indians and the white men occurred. It was on this great island that the first gold was found in the New World; and for centuries millions of treasure poured from

SANTA CRUZ Plantation

PORTO RICO City wall and house of Ponce de Leon

PORTO RICO The Morro, San Juan

PORTO RICO San Cristobal, where Ogeron's men labored

its mountains and streams, its valleys and hills into the treasury of Spain, until Hispaniola became celebrated as the richest land in all the world.

No other part of America is so closely associated with the making of New Spain, so linked with those brave though cruel old Dons whose names will never die. And in no other spot are there so many or so well-preserved relics of the old days. The very house in which the son of Columbus dwelt still stands above the quay at Santo Domingo City. The massive wall which Drake found such an obstacle still hems the capital about. The first cross erected in the New World is yet preserved within the great cathedral. The stone cistern built by Columbus to supply water is still there. One may wander through the half-ruined arches of the first university in America, where Las Casas taught; and over the doorway of many a stately, ancient house one may still trace the elaborate coats of arms of Spanish hidalgos and grandees who won everlasting fame by hewing an empire with fire and sword from the untamed wilderness of the New World.

No part of the Western Hemisphere has a bloodier, more tragic history. The soil of Santo Domingo has literally been soaked with the blood of countless thousands of helpless Indians, tortured and put to death without mercy by the ruthless Spaniards; torn to pieces by bloodhounds; lashed to death in the mines; burned, quartered, flayed alive, massacred wholesale—all in the name of Christianity. And as though these atrocities were not enough, thousands of human beings were slain in battle, and negro uprisings swept the fair land with death in awful forms, and unspeakable cruelties and tortures. As one reads the record of this magnificent island, one feels that it must be a place accursed.

It was here in Hispaniola, too, that the buccaneers had their beginning; here that the Brethren of the Main first came into existence and pledged themselves to that piratical brotherhood; and toward one of their most notorious strongholds Sam shaped the *Vigilant's* course, and we entered the great Bay of Samana.

CHAPTER XI

THE GIBRALTAR OF THE BUCCANEERS

ONE must search far and wide to find a more beautiful stretch of water than the Bay of Samana. Blue as the azure dome above it, the vast, lake-like expanse cuts into the very heart of the wondrous island for over thirty miles. From the lofty, richly forested mountains that hem it in on the north, to the low, rolling green hills on the south, it stretches for ten miles, and dotting its placid surface are verdant wooded isles. Sheltered by the land from all hard winds, deep enough for the largest ships, protected from the seas and with an area sufficient to afford anchorage for all the navies of the world and to spare, Samana Bay has no equal as a natural harbor in all the Antilles, if, indeed, in the entire world.

Its strategic value is enormous; as a coaling-station and naval base it is without a peer in the West Indies, and once our Government, alive to these facts, came very near purchasing it from the Dominicans. But long before that time the sea-rovers appreciated the manifold advantages of the bay, and here they came to find a retreat wherein they could and did hold their own in safety, though surrounded on every hand by their arch-enemies the Spaniards. Here, almost midway between the shores, a charmingly beautiful islet, about three miles in length and a mile wide, juts, a mass of emerald and ivory, above the blue waters; and here the buccaneers made their headquarters, transforming this Cayo Levantado, as it is called, into a veritable miniature Gibraltar of their own. And toward this one-time stronghold of the pirates the *Vigilant* rippled, through the waters of the bay that once sheltered many a buccaneer ship, and upon whose shores the first battle between the Europeans and the Indians took place.

It was on the borders of a tiny bay that this memorable but insignificant skirmish occurred which sealed the doom of the red man—a quiet little cove at the edge of the jungle under the towering green hills, and still called by the name Columbus bestowed upon it, Golfo de las Flechas (Bay of the Arrows), in memory of the shower of darts that the Indians poured upon a landing party of Spaniards. The arrows, however, rattled harmlessly upon the invaders' coats of mail, while, with the answering volley from the armored men, a number of the naked savages were killed. To-day it is very peaceful, and as wild, as uninhabited as when Columbus first entered the great bay. Indeed, it is even more deserted, for the last of the aborigines of the island have been dead two centuries and more, the Spaniards having waged upon them a relentless war of extermination, as a penalty for daring to protect their homes from the white invaders.

Deserted, too, is the little islet The Upraised Cay, to give it a literal equivalent for its Spanish name, though to the corsairs it was ever known as Trade Wind Cay. And off its gleaming coral beach the *Vigilant* came to rest.

From the schooner's decks the isle appeared a single rounded hill sloping gently to east and west, with a stretch of abrupt gray limestone cliffs along the northern shore and covered with a wealth of luxuriant vegetation. Before our anchorage a dazzling crescent of white sand swept from a rocky point to a low cape, and just off the spot where the snowy beach ended at the headland a bit of detached rock rose from the sea, a curiously formed islet supporting a mass of tangled shrubbery and vines and worn by the waves to a remarkable semblance of a gigantic turtle. Upon the beach the lazy swell curled in translucent turquoise, and everywhere upon the sand, upon the sea, winging overhead and perching upon the trees, were countless clumsy pelicans and fork-tailed frigate-birds.

Here, undisturbed by man,—for the natives have a superstitious fear of the spot, although they occasionally come here to kill the wild cattle and goats,—the sea-birds breed by thousands and wheel in endless circles above the ruins of the buccaneers' old stronghold. And what a stronghold it must have been! As I wandered through the thickets and clambered over the old fortifications I no longer marveled that, from this vantage-point, the pirates defied the powers of the world and held it for years despite the efforts of Spain, Britain, France, and Holland to dislodge them.

Everywhere amid the tangled vines and thorny scrub are great cisterns, foundations of buildings, water-sheds, and vaults. Along the cliffs are battlements, embrasures, walls, and loopholes; and leading up the slopes from the landing-place are long flights of stairs, all hewn and carved from the solid rock. What herculean labor is here represented! What unremitting toil of tortured prisoners and slaves! What toll of blood and suffering and death! Here, side by side with the naked blacks, grandees and hidalgos cut and hewed the rock to form their captors' lair; toiling beneath the blazing sun from dawn to dark; sweating, half-starved, their backs raw and covered with great welts from their brutal driver's lash, their fingers torn and bleeding from the jagged stone, their faces wan and drawn, their eyes bloodshot and furtive, their bones aching from fever, and their only hope of deliverance the death which would be meted out to them as soon as exhausted muscles and sinews gave way or their work was done.

Centuries have passed since their racked bodies were cast like carrion into the sea or dumped in a common grave in the sand, but their work has endured. To-day, flowering vines trail from the loopholes in the massive battlements the captives chiseled, and great forest trees have sprung up from crevices among the rocks and slowly but surely have riven the walls that defied shot and shell. The houses wherein the buccaneers made merry are roofless and tenanted by land-crabs and lizards, and the hewn water-tanks from which they filled their casks ere starting on their forays are choked with fallen leaves, rotting vegetation, and the gnarled roots of the jungle.

Weird tales the natives of the mainland tell of sights witnessed at dead of night upon this little isle. With fear-widened eyes, they whisper of ghostly mail-clad sentinels pacing the old walls, of phantom ships riding upon the waves off the cay, of blood-curdling shouts, songs, and curses coming from no mortal throat but echoing across the bay from this ancient stronghold. Also, fervently crossing themselves the while, they tell of piercing screams, as of lost souls, heard by the humble fishermen plying their trade at night upon the bay, and of mysterious lights, like the flare of torches, that dance and move and flit among the trees of the cay.

Of course there is many a tale of treasure hidden on the island; of vast stores of pirate loot secreted in the subterranean caverns and hewn underground recesses; and one hair-raising story they relate of a treasure-chest in the sea close to the island's shores, which is plainly visible through the transparent water. Many times, if we are to believe the natives, some unusually brave and covetous man has grappled for this chest, only to find, when he tediously hauled it to the surface, that a hideous demon was seated upon it, who grimaced and leered, and, throwing his slimy, misshapen body upon the terrified man, carried him to the depths of the sea along with the chest of gold he guards so well.

And after all, who can say what treasures may not be concealed upon this Gibraltar of the buccaneers? Countless chests of loot have been carried from triumphant pirate ships to the strip of white sand upon the cay. Many a bale of wondrous silk and cloth of gold and velvet damask has been slashed open with blood-stained cutlasses and flung to the pirates' mistresses who swarmed about the incoming ships' cargoes. Here, in the shade of the gnarled sea-grape thickets, scores of the most notorious rascals have lounged and plotted and yarned while quaffing priceless wines from the holy golden chalices snatched from profaned altars. Under the very trees that still rear their green crowns above the ruins the groans of tortured men, the screams of ravished women, and the drunken shouts of rum-crazed rioters have rent the air.

As far as is known, no one has ever salvaged any treasure from Trade Wind Cay. The limestone rock is honeycombed with cavities and caverns wherein whole ships' cargoes might be stored and none the wiser. But if the pirates hid it here, they hid it well indeed, although so superstitiously afraid of the place are the natives that they would never dare to search.

But probably the buccaneers never secreted loot upon the isle. Indeed, from what we know of the lives and characters of these men, it is pretty safe to assume that they never hid their treasure, but no sooner put foot on dry land than they spent their gold in drinking and debauchery. Of course many of the leaders put away tidy sums for a rainy day, for, as we have seen, more than one of them retired from the wild life and settled down in the islands or in their native land well provided with the wherewithal to live as gentlemen to the end of their days. But it is far more likely that these canny pirate chiefs placed their loot in the keeping of some trusted merchant ashore than that they buried it on wave-washed bits of land, and all our searching among the ruins of Cayo Levantado resulted in the finding of but three corroded pieces of the quaint cross money of the old Spanish padres.

Joseph, who made the discovery, was as pleased as though he had unearthed a chest of pieces of eight, and Trouble and the others of the crew, including even Sam, delved and dug like navvies in the hopes of finding more. No doubt, by going carefully over all the ruins and sifting the earth and mold, one might find many relics of the buccaneers, but aside from a few gun flints, some broken clay pipes curiously ornamented with high-pooped ships upon their bowls, some bits of old crockery and a lead button, the labors of my men resulted in little.

This is scarcely to be wondered at. Unless

made of precious metal, bronze, lead, or brass, any small weapons, ornaments, or appurtenances of the pirates would long since have disappeared, for steel and iron corrode and go to pieces in a few years near salt water in a tropical climate, and even the three big cannon that I found below the embrasures of the pirates' fort were little more than flakes and scales of rust, and were so thoroughly rotten that they could be kicked to pieces.

Moreover, for many years after the buccaneers were at last driven from the island, the place was occupied by the Spanish, then by the French, then by the Haitians, and even by the British (for Samana Bay has belonged to all of these in turn), and no doubt the soldiers, and civilians as well, passed many an hour searching for any treasures or keepsakes they might find. Certain it is that they carried off the old guns, at any rate those of bronze, which the pirates left behind, as well as the stores of shot, for such is a matter of historical record. Some of the very cannon that roared defiance from the buccaneers' fort—bell-muzzled, highly decorated affairs, with handles on their barrels and elaborate scrollwork over their breeches, are still scattered over Santo Domingo, clumsily mounted on the toy forts or used as posts at street corners in the cities.

And what of the pirates who builded this impregnable fastness and fortified this isle in Samana Bay? Were they British, French, or Dutch? And who were the leaders who made their headquarters here? Mainly they were French, members of that great buccaneer colony at Tortuga; for in the days when Cayo Levantado became a buccaneer lair the majority of the British pirates had parted company with their former French associates and had made their headquarters at Port Royal, Jamaica. Unquestionably Samana Bay knew the ships and the ensigns of nearly all the most notorious pirate chieftains, both French and British, and the great Morgan himself, Bartholomew Sharp of *Most Blessed Trinity* fame, Sawkins and Wafer, Red Legs and Watling, Ringrose and Esquemelling, Bartholomew Portugues, Rock Brasiliano, and even that most execrable and bloodthirsty fiend of all, Francis Lolonais, made Samana Bay their rendezvous and spent many a day at Trade Wind Cay.

We know from Esquemelling's chronicles that in 1673 this isle was a stronghold of the French pirates, for, as we have seen, Monsieur Ogeron also landed here after escaping from his captivity in Porto Rico and recruited a large body of pirates to join him in a second attack on that island. A few years later, too, Le Sieur Maintenon and his corsairs set sail from Samana Bay for Trinidad, which they sacked, afterward accepting for it a ransom of ten thousand pieces of eight; and hence they went forth on their ill-starred attempt to pillage the city of Caracas.

Unfortunately, the history of the buccaneers is very incomplete, and such accounts as were left by Esquemelling, Dampier, Ringrose, and others are mainly concerned with the pirates' deeds and defeats, rather than with their home life, and dates are woefully lacking. Moreover, the writers were so familiar with the comparatively uninteresting life and doings in the corsairs' haunts that it never occurred to them that such matters might interest others, while, in addition, few had any fixed abode, but were quite equally at home in Tortuga, Jamaica, Samana Bay, or the Virgin Islands. They were a restless lot, veritable gipsies of the sea; and while certain islands were associated with certain pirate leaders, as Jamaica with Morgan, St. Barts with Montbars, and Tortuga with Ogeron, most of their refuges welcomed any or all of them, and the common run of those who thronged these places owed allegiance to no particular leader, but gladly threw in their lot with any one who proposed an undertaking that promised loot and adventure.

Hence we cannot say definitely what great pirate conceived the idea of fortifying Trade Wind Cay, but the chances are that several united to make it what it was, and it certainly was the den of many during the heyday of the freebooters.

In addition to this fortress of the buccaneers, Samana Bay has much in the way of beauty and attraction; and having roamed and delved and dug over the little isle to our hearts' content we hoisted anchor and cruised about the shores of this great lake-like arm of the sea.

A few miles beyond Cayo Levantado, and nestling at the foot of the green hills on the bay's northern shores, is the town of Samana, or, to give it its full name, Santa Barbara de Samana; which is charmingly pretty—from a distance. As a town there is little to it, once one steps ashore. It is neither over-clean nor attractive, and it can boast of nothing in the way of old or impressive buildings. It is, however, unique, inasmuch as the negroes who dwell therein and in the vicinity nearly all speak English, being, to use their own quaint phrase, "of American abstraction," descendants of blacks from the Southern States brought out as laborers when Samana was leased to an American company many years ago. While far more ambitious and industrious than the other natives, they do not by any means make the most of the rich and fertile land whereon they dwell. Never in any part of the tropics have I seen or tasted such enormous and delicious pineapples as are grown here; and wonderful navel oranges, that equal and even excel the much-praised California fruit, go begging at a few cents a hundred.

Farther up the bay—at the very head of it, in fact—and bounded at its western end by a vast mangrove swamp, is the ramshackle, dirty little town of Sanchez, a miserable hole, which, withal, is of vast importance, as it is the tide-water terminus of the railway to the great interior table-land or Vega Real and the cities of La Vega and Santiago.

On the southern side of the bay is wild, uninhabited, heavily forested land, rising in hills and ridges to the mighty bulwarks of the mountains, with their summits nearly two miles above the sea, and sloping eastward to the grassy savannas of the Seybo district. Here at the borders of the low land is Caña Honda Bay (a lovely landlocked body of water surrounded by vast mangrove swamps that are the haunt of countless water-fowl and manatees), whence a road, so called, leads inland toward the savannas and the southern coast of Santo Domingo. All about the entrance to Caña Honda Bay are odd conical limestone hills, resembling strikingly the conventional mountains on ancient maps, and in each and every one there is a cavern. Some of these caves are enormous, penetrating the hills for miles and wondrously hung with stalactites and paved with stalagmites; others are small. Some have entrances high and dry on land, others can be entered only by means of boats, and the mouths of many of them are completely submerged.

In ages past, these caverns were the dwelling-places, or at least the stopping-places, of Indians, and in many of them are vast quantities of sea-shells, among which one finds stone implements and prehistoric pottery. Here, too, the natives declare, is buried treasure, and while even the imaginative Dominicans do not contend that any has ever been found, yet, if the buccaneers ever did hide loot in Santo Domingo, here among these myriad caves was the ideal spot.

Beyond these hills and opposite Trade Wind Cay is a long, sandy point covered with a vast growth of coconut-palms, self-planted from the cargo of a wrecked vessel which went to pieces in the bay years ago; and along the beach quantities of amber may be found. To be sure, no perfect specimens and no large masses have been secured, but the natives gather it, when they are not too

TRADE WIND CAY The Gibraltar of the Buccaneers

PORTO RICO A "piragua," the craft in which the buccaneers first captured Spanish ships

lazy to take the trouble, and sell it to the padres, who use it for incense in the churches.

But we upon the *Vigilant* could spare no time to search for the bits of fossil gum, and so, having made the circuit of the bay, we stood once more to sea and swinging northward heeled to a thrashing wind upon our beam and sped on toward Puerto Plata.

CHAPTER XII

THE BIRTHPLACE OF THE BUCCANEERS

SAILING along the shores of Santo Domingo, one realizes the aptness of the graphic illustration of the island's appearance with which, tradition says, Columbus answered Queen Isabella's queries. The great discoverer, according to the story, seized a sheet of parchment, crumpled it in his hands, and, dropping it on the table before his queen, exclaimed, "That is like Hispaniola!"

And nothing could be more like a crumpled piece of parchment than the tumbled, serrated mass of ridges, hills, mountains, and peaks of this great island. Wild, forest-covered, sublime in their grandeur, the mountains of Santo Domingo rise in endless succession, and one marvels that the old Dons, a mere handful of men, could ever have penetrated its fastnesses and subdued and exterminated the Indians. But the Spaniards with all their faults were made of stern stuff,—real "he men,"—and fired with the zeal of conquest, the fanatical determination to spread their faith among the heathen, and an insatiable lust for gold, they accomplished marvels and performed deeds which seem well-nigh impossible. Let any one to-day, equipped with every device and convenience and in the lightest clothing, step ashore on the coast of Santo Domingo and penetrate to the interior through the unbroken jungle, and he will feel, when he reaches his journey's end,—if, indeed, he ever does,—that he has performed a mighty feat. Climbing precipitous mountain sides, swimming rivers, fording streams, crawling up dry watercourses, hewing his way an inch at a time through the tangled vegetation; beset by biting insects, drenched with rain, torn by thorns and razor-grass, and exhausted with the steaming heat, he finds such a trip enough to try the stoutest nerves and the strongest muscles. But imagine undertaking such an expedition when clad in armor! Think of attempting the journey weighted down with mail, carrying a clumsy matchlock or a massive cross-bow, a heavy sword, a pike or halberd, and harassed by hostile Indians at every step. But the old Dons did it, did it and won out, though literally living off the country, knowing not what might meet them at their journey's end, and completely cut off from civilization and their fellows.

Of course they achieved their object at the cost

of a tremendous loss of life. If one hundred men set forth and a dozen won safely through, it was doing well, and rarely did more than ten per cent. of their number return in safety from their expeditions into the untrod jungles of the New World. But to them the lives of men-at-arms, of the common soldier or adventurer, were nothing; and the more that fell by the way, the more loot there would be to divide among the survivors. We must bear this in mind when thinking of the early days of the West Indies and the Spanish Main, for it was this utter disregard of life that enabled both Dons and buccaneers to perform deeds which, were they not incontrovertible historical facts, we should consider absolutely impossible.

Here, on the northern shores of Hispaniola, the Spaniards landed and marched inland to the vast interior Vega Real or Royal Plain and the Cibao district with its golden sands; and there on the high interior plains they founded and built the cities of La Vega, Moca, and Santiago de los Caballeros, cities which still stand. In these cities are many lineal descendants of the conquistadors, and in their dwellings one may still find weapons and pieces of armor which have been handed down through the centuries. Indeed, in the ruins of La Vega la Antigua, which was destroyed by an earthquake in

1564, one may yet dig up ancient Spanish coins, old Toledo blades, and other relics; and throughout the island one sees the natives armed with home-made machetes fashioned from old swords they have salvaged from the ruins of this once rich and famous town.

To-day, however, one travels from the coast to the Cibao by railway, and takes the train at Puerto Plata, a delightfully situated port which the *Vigilant* passed the second day after leaving the Mona Passage and heading westward along the coast. Puerto Plata is beautiful from the sea, with its red-roofed buildings half hidden by palms at the base of the towering green cone of Plata Mountain; and in reality the town is by far the cleanest and most attractive in the republic. Its harbor is excellent, being almost landlocked, but the water shoals so gradually that despite a long pier jutting from the waterfront of the town into the bay the drays and trucks are compelled to drive out until the mules and horses are belly-deep in the water, in order to load or unload the boats.

It was off Puerto Plata that a vast treasure in bullion was recovered many years ago—one of the few authentic cases of the actual finding of ancient treasure in the West Indies. This happened in the latter part of the eighteenth century when Captain

William Phipps of Salem,—a worthy mariner with a love of romance and one-time governor of Massachusetts,—became imbued with the idea of recovering treasure-trove from a galleon which, in endeavoring to escape from the buccaneers, had been sunk off Puerto Plata. In those days, even as to-day, sunken treasure appealed to many otherwise hard-headed and practical men, and Captain Phipps found backers who provided the ships and wherewithal for his expedition. Apparently his information as to the location of the old wreck was somewhat hazy, and after a deal of search he had about given up in despair when one of his divers brought up a lump of coral growing upon an oddly squarish and heavy object. Knocking off the incrustation, the captain found an ingot of silver, and ere tempestuous weather came on several tons of bullion, together with gold and jewels,—in all amounting to over one and a half million dollars,—had been dragged from the depths of the sea and safely stowed under hatches.

Had the worthy Phipps been content with a comfortable fortune, he could have spent his declining years in a snug little home in Salem, where, surrounded by his grandchildren, he might have spun many a yarn of his treasure-hunt. But he was too avaricious, and, anxious to secure the last bit of treasure that might still lie among the corals of Silver Shoals, he spent his share of the salvaged bullion in outfitting another expedition. Unfortunately a storm came up, his ship was wrecked, and Phipps barely escaped with his life and came home as poor as when he had first started treasure-seeking.

A few miles beyond Puerto Plata, completely hidden in the interminable green jungle and with nothing to distinguish it from any other of the thousands of little coves that indent the coast, is the site of the first European settlement in the New World. Isabella, Columbus named it in honor of the queen who made his discoveries possible, and here in December, 1493, he built, on his second voyage to the New World, a tiny fort, erected a few houses, and left a handful of men. Near here the Dons found the first gold they had seen in a natural state in the lands they had discovered, the flakes of precious metal adhering with sand to the water-casks which the sailors filled at a near-by stream. This, with the Indians' information that they obtained all their gold from inland, convinced Columbus that untold wealth was to be had for the asking, so to speak; and, planting his little town of Isabella, he sailed away, expecting to return the following year to find the settlers surrounded with chests and bags full of the yellow metal. Instead, when he returned, he found most of them dead and buried, the settlement destroyed, and no gold. Maltreatment of the natives had brought swift vengeance upon the Spaniards; fever and the climate had aided the red men, and Isabella had passed out of existence. It was never rebuilt, and all that remains of this first town in America are a few crumbling, jungle-grown walls.

Beyond Isabella the green and luxuriant verdure gives way to barren hills and cactus-covered plains, until the frowning, red-cliffed headland of El Morro is passed, with the miserable, mosquito-infested mud-hole of a town known as Monte Cristo. Just beyond this God-forsaken spot we left the waters of the Dominican Republic behind, and, entering the territorial waters of Haiti, rushed westward toward the great bulk of Tortuga, the birthplace of the buccaneers.

Larger than any of the Lesser Antilles, Tortuga stretches its mass of wooded hills and mountains for nearly twenty-five miles, with a width of three miles. It is an impenetrable jungle for the most part, almost uninhabited, but it was once the greatest of all the resorts of the buccaneers and the home of the most notorious pirates of history.

Separated from the mainland of Santo Domingo

ST. BARTS Mending nets where the buccaneers divided loot

CARIB CANOES It was in such craft that the first buccaneers voyaged from St. Kitts to Hispaniola

TORTUGA The birthplace of the buccaneers

by only a narrow strait, Tortuga was an ideal spot for the sea-rovers, and for many a year they held it, having their own governors, their own laws, their own forts, and brazenly defying the world to dislodge them. Here their ships rode to anchor under the protecting guns of their fort; from here they fitted out fleets of heavily armed vessels manned by thousands of the most reckless, daring, ruthless men who ever lived; and from this stronghold—right in the Dons' dooryard, as we might say—the buccaneers ravaged Spanish cities and destroyed Spanish ships throughout the length and breadth of the Caribbean and beyond.

In the well-protected harbor where once the fleets of Lolonais, Morgan, Montbars, and many another corsair had swung to their moorings, the little *Vigilant* dropped her anchor. Although to-day the port is scarcely worthy the name of town, yet in the heyday of the buccaneers Cayona, as it was called, had a teeming population. It was divided into four sections, known as the Lowland or Basseterre, comprising the coastal land and the port proper; the Middle Plantation, which was a district mainly devoted to tobacco-culture; the Ringot, and Le Mont or The Mountain, which consisted of the oldest settlement on the slopes of the towering hills behind the port. Beyond these the island was uninhabited, as it is to-day. It is extremely mountainous and rocky, although heavily wooded, a fact which aroused the interest of Esquemelling and caused him to comment upon it. He says:

> Yet notwithstanding hugely thick of lofty trees that cease not to grow upon the hardest of these rocks without partaking of softer soil. Hence it comes that their roots for the greatest part, are seen all over, entangled among the rocks, not unlike the branching of ivy against our walls.

This is an excellent description, and one which will give a vivid idea of the difficulties to be encountered in penetrating the interior of the island, Moreover, the northern coast is forbidding, with precipitous cliffs along the shore and with no harbors or landing-places, so that the island was virtually inaccessible except on the southwestern end where the port was established. This natural formation of the island, which rendered it very easy to fortify, was no doubt one of the chief reasons why it was selected by the buccaneers as their headquarters. But there were other reasons, of perhaps even greater importance, to understand which we must look into the origin and history of the sea-rovers.

Tortuga had its beginning in a handful of refugees from St. Kitts, Frenchmen who had settled on that isle and had been driven off by the Spaniards in 1629. Fleeing from the Dons, they made their way in little dugout canoes to Hispaniola. To their wave-weary eyes this vast, heavily wooded, luxuriant land must have seemed a veritable paradise, and when, upon landing and penetrating a short distance into the interior, they found it teeming with wild cattle, wild hogs, and wild horses, they realized that fortune had indeed favored them. But the herds of wild cattle, horses, and swine were not the only denizens of Hispaniola, for the Spaniards had long been established there, and the refugees from St. Kitts knew that as soon as they were discovered by the Dons they would meet with a summary end. Near at hand, however, was the promising island of Tortuga, with barely a dozen Spaniards dwelling upon it, and, again taking to the miniature craft which had served them so well, the Frenchmen sailed across the strait, determined to do or die.

There was no occasion for bloodshed, however, for the handful of settlers upon Tortuga were peaceable and friendly folk, and instead of resisting the Kittefonians they welcomed them, and aided them in every way. Thus for six months the French and Spanish dwelt together on the best of terms in Tortuga. But this state of affairs did not endure for long. The French, finding Tortuga an agreeable spot, well stocked with game as well as wild hogs and cattle, crossed and recrossed the sea to French settlements and brought scores of their countrymen to the new land, until the Dons, feeling that the place would soon become wholly French, repented of their former friendliness and sent word of the newcomers' presence to the Spanish at Santo Domingo.

As a result, a strong force of Spanish troops was despatched to Tortuga, and the French, realizing the futility of resistance, promptly took to the woods and later secretly made their way in their canoes to the neighboring island of Hispaniola. Here they lived in the jungle and carried on a guerrilla warfare against the Dons, who were ever seeking to eliminate their unwelcome guests. Finding no French at Tortuga, the Spanish soon withdrew the bulk of the troops, to use them to better advantage on the larger island, whereupon the tactful French hied themselves once more to Tortuga, massacred the few Spaniards left there, and, taking possession, threw up hastily constructed fortifications. Then, aware that they could not hope to resist the mighty power of Spain for long, they despatched a boat to St. Kitts, begging the French governor of that island to send aid.

Being only too glad to add to the possessions of

France, the governor immediately responded by sending over a good-sized ship with a large complement of men, a plentiful store of arms, cannon and ammunition, and a quantity of supplies. The new arrivals at once began constructing a fort upon the summit of a rocky hill which overlooked the harbor, and which was so situated that it could be reached only by means of a defile barely wide enough to permit the passage of two persons abreast. Here a battery of two guns was erected, a house was built, and a natural cavern was transformed into a magazine, and, as a finishing touch, the natural passway was destroyed and the fort rendered accessible only by means of ladders.

Feeling that they were now quite secure, the French colonists set diligently to work, cultivating tobacco and other crops, fishing, hunting the wild cattle and swine, and, most lucrative of all, robbing the Spanish settlements on the coasts of the near-by Spanish islands.

At that time one of the principal articles of food and of export was the smoke-dried flesh of cattle and hogs, a product peculiar to Hispaniola and the neighboring islands and known by the Carib name of boucan or bucan. Tortuga, with limited agricultural resources but innumerable wild animals, was particularly well adapted to the bucanning industry, and a very large proportion of the settlers devoted virtually all their time to hunting and curing meat. As a result, the inhabitants soon became known as boucaniers, bucaneers or buccaneers, a name which was to become famed throughout the world. The original significance of "buccaneer" was wholly lost and, becoming synonymous with "pirate," it was destined to carry terror to the hearts of the Spaniards far and near. To Tortuga, the home of the buccaneers, flocked malcontents, adventurers, real pirates, seamen, and all sorts of wild rovers of the sea and land, until the island became headquarters for the most lawless of French and British wanderers and outlaws. But all were bound together by a common hatred of the Spaniards; all were willing to enter into any wild enterprise that promised loot; all were absolutely fearless, unprincipled, ruthless, and daring; and all took unto themselves the common name of buccaneers.

Do not imagine, however, that the Dons upon the neighboring island stood idly by and saw Tortuga fall into the buccaneers' hands without making any effort to prevent it. On the contrary, they did their best to recover the island, though without success. Upon a hill overlooking the French fort they established a battery of their own, and were about to make matters very uncomfortable for the buccaneers when the latter surprised them at midnight and took their fort by storm, slaughtering the defenders without mercy and throwing the survivors over the beetling cliffs. After this the buccaneers had it pretty much their own way for about thirty years, or until 1664, when the French West India Company was granted a royal charter to Tortuga, by the French crown.

But the West India Company soon found that to be granted a charter to the headquarters of the buccaneers was one thing and to secure their rights and privileges and bend the lawless rascals to their will was quite a different matter. Sending out their own factors and employees, the company established stores and plantations, but this effort was a failure; for no nation dared trade with Tortuga, so close to Spanish territory, and even the company's own ships were often seized and lost. Then the company sought to carry on trade with the buccaneers themselves, agreeing to supply them with goods and necessities on credit, the buccaneers to pay as they could from the fruits of their forays. But the company's factors soon discovered that the buccaneers were as inclined to questionable methods when dealing with their own country as when dealing with the Dons; and they received merely rude jests and laughter, or even blows at times, in place of money, when they sought to collect their accounts. Even when armed men were sent out to enforce a settlement, the buccaneers flatly refused to pay; and those of the guards who did not desert and throw in their lot with the freebooters cast aside their weapons and left the company at the first opportunity.

At last, convinced that these were far from desirable customers or neighbors, the French West India Company made the best of a bad bargain and, disposing of their few remaining possessions for what they would bring, withdrew from Tortuga and left it in undisputed control of the buccaneers.

This, then, was the beginning of that vast, all but unconquerable, incredibly valiant, and unspeakably cruel and unprincipled organization known as the "Brethren of the Main." Here in Tortuga the buccaneers came into existence; from a handful of despoiled Fenchmen from St. Kitts the band grew to thousands; from robbing Spanish corrals and chicken roosts along the shores of Hispaniola they progressed to the destruction of Spanish fleets, the sacking of towns, the capture of fortresses, and to unparalleled feats of bravery. From Tortuga they spread far and near, and the dugouts in which they were wont to make their first raids gave place to swift ships bristling with cannon and manned by hundreds of well-armed men; while from the harmless and peaceful occupation of drying meat, which gave them their name, they turned to bloodshed and piracy.

CHAPTER XIII

THE BRETHREN OF THE MAIN

ALTHOUGH from the time that handful of refugees took Tortuga from the Spaniards the island was nominally French, yet it was ever, to all intents and purposes, buccaneer. Even the governors, appointed by France, were in hearty sympathy with the freebooters and were no better than their fellows. Moreover, the inhabitants of the isle were not by any means all French. Attracted by the freedom of the place, the opportunities for the semi-wild life of buccanning, in its original sense, and the chances of "emprizing," as they put it, against the Dons, adventurous souls from far and near flocked to Tortuga.

Principally they were English or French, but there were not a few Dutch, a number of Portuguese, a sprinkling of Spanish, and an endless number of mixed breeds and men without any definite country. But, once in Tortuga, all differences of blood, religion, and profession, as well as of social status, were cast aside and forgotten, and they became once and for all buccaneers, [1] bound together as "Brethren of the Main." And, curious as it may seem, these men, although absolutely unprincipled and ruthless where others were concerned, were marvelously honest and square among themselves, and with the Indians with whom they came in contact. Of course this was a case of necessity rather than of choice, for they realized that only by faithfulness and integrity with one another could they succeed, and that the Indians were essential to them, as pilots, hunters, fishermen, and guides. It is also a fact, although lurid fiction and stories by those who know little or nothing of buccaneer history would have us believe otherwise, that as a rule these pirates were far more humane in their treatment of prisoners than the regular soldiery and naval forces of their day. But, like their dealings with the Indians, this consideration for their enemies and captives was to the buccaneers' advantage. They well

[1] Curiously enough, the term "buccaneer," from the French *boucanier,* was later adopted by the English freebooters and was applied exclusively to them, whereas the French corsairs took to themselves the English term "freebooters" and pronouncing it to the best of their ability called themselves *fribustiers* or *flibustiers,* which eventually became *flibustiers.*

According to some authorities, notably Van Esveldt in his work on the buccaneers published in 1756, the word "Filibuster" was originally derived from the Spanish "Flibotero," meaning one who uses a small boat. The British corsairs altered this to "Flybusters" or "Freebooters"; the French used the form "Flibustiers" and the Dutch "Vlieboters."

knew, "by divers experiences," that unless they gave quarter to their prisoners and released captives upon payment of ransom their own fellows would be put to torture and the sword when captured by the Spaniards. Moreover, through the gratitude of prisoners whom they spared, or even aided, the pirates gained much valuable information,—far more, in fact, than through torture,—and on more than one occasion the buccaneers who fell into the Dons' hands were treated courteously and were even helped on their way by those who had received similar treatment from the freebooters.

Of course there were exceptions to this. Such men as Montbars, Morgan, Lolonais, and a few others seemed to glory in torture and murder, and proved themselves fiends incarnate; and it was the deeds committed by such men that gave the reputation for bloodthirstiness to all. In addition, after the buccaneers had scattered and were no longer an organized body, but carried on their piratical ventures as individuals and were hunted by all nations, they deteriorated and became mere pirates, who robbed and killed friend and foe with equal impartiality. When the buccaneers first came into being, and for many years thereafter, France and England were at war with Spain, and so raids and attacks upon the Dons were considered legal warfare, and even long after peace was established between the powers the buccaneers preyed only upon their hereditary enemies the Spaniards. But as time passed and the authorities, in order to preserve peace, were compelled to apprehend and hang the most notorious of the buccaneers, the remainder looked upon every peaceful man as their enemy and considered legitimate prey every ship they could overpower. They burned, sacked, and destroyed whenever opportunity offered, regardless of flag or nationality.

At first the buccaneers were compelled to make their raids in small boats,—bateaux and pirogues, or dugout canoes,—for they had no ships of their own. But this handicap did not deter them in the least. The fact that a contemplated prize was a great galleon bristling with guns and swarming with armed men did not discourage them, but rather made them the more keen to take her. Manning their little craft, the buccaneers pulled or paddled or sailed toward their prey, steering in such a way as to avoid the heaviest fire of the enemy's guns (and it must be remembered that with the clumsy, short-range, far from accurate cannon of those days a moving small boat was a difficult mark to hit), and meantime keeping up a steady fusillade of small arms. Literally walking arsenals, trained marksmen, and accustomed to hunting wild cattle, the pirates usually succeeded in killing the helmsman of the enemy's ship, as well as many of the gunners. Running under the vessel's stern, they would make fast, wedge the rudder of their prize, and with knives in teeth swarm up chains and rigging and pour over the rail like a pack of fiends. Nothing could withstand the onslaught of this savage crew, who, yelling and cursing, poured over the bulwarks, cutlass in one hand, pistol in the other, and shooting, slashing, and thrusting like madmen, oblivious of wounds, regardless of death, hacked and slew and seemed to be everywhere at once.

It was thus that Sharp and his men took the Spanish fleet and came into possession of *The Most Blessed Trinity* in the harbor of Panama, and the annals of the buccaneers are filled with similar deeds. The ship in their hands, as a rule they either put the ordinary survivors of the battle ashore or set them adrift in a boat, retained the captain and his officers as prisoners for ransom, and took possession of any women who might be aboard.

Having by such means secured seaworthy sailing-vessels, the buccaneers were able to extend operations, and after eliminating the fancy gilt-work and lofty stern castles, the luxuriant fittings, and all unnecessary gear of their prizes, they would

FRANCIS LOLONOIS.

The Cruelty of Lolonois
LOLONOIS

man them with crews of several hundred each and set forth on their forays.

They seldom built ships of their own, but by selecting the handiest and swiftest of their prizes and rerigging and refitting them to suit their own special needs, they gradually accumulated a fleet of ships which were noted for speed and stanchness. Moreover, the larger vessels were seldom used. The pirates required craft which could dodge among reefs and slip through shoal waters where the big men-of-war could not follow, and it was only now and then that a buccaneer ship carried more than eight guns, the usual number being four or six. The pirates depended more upon seamanship and marksmanship than mere weight of metal or thundering broadsides, although on some of their later and larger enterprises they used ships carrying forty guns or more.

When we consider the heterogeneous character of their crews, and the varied antecedents and training of those who made up their number, it is not surprising that the corsairs succeeded against tremendous odds. In addition to the true Tortugan hunters and buccaneers there were logwood-cutters from the Central American coast and the bay islands, ex-soldiers and sailors, Indians, criminals from prisons and gaols, outlaws and bandits—all men who were trained in the use of arms, of immense physical strength and endurance, with an extraordinary power to undergo hunger, thirst, and other hardships, and with an utter disregard for death or bodily suffering.

The strangest part of it was that this riffraff of adventurers was amenable to discipline. When afloat or on one of their forays they obeyed their leaders implicitly and were true to them even in the face of torture or death. They never betrayed their comrades, would risk their lives to help another buccaneer, and would share their last centavo or their rags with a Brother of the Main at any time.

Another interesting fact is that these buccaneers were the inventors of life and accident insurance, or we might better say employees' compensation laws. Before starting on a cruise they made their preparations in a most efficient way and provided for all contingencies.

When a pirate leader decided that it was time to go a-pirating he would give out word of his intention and call for volunteers, each man who presented himself for the venture being supposed to bring his own arms, ammunition, and supplies. The next step was to provide food for the voyage, and the buccaneers, seeing no reason to use their own resources for the purchase of supplies which could be had for the taking, thereupon made a sortie against the nearest Spanish possession, held up and robbed a few corrals, and, buccanning the cattle and swine thus economically acquired, stocked the commissary department. The next step was to arrange shares of the prospective loot, and to draw up articles in writing very particularly setting forth the sum each man was to receive for his services, said sum to be taken from the "common stock" as it was called, or, in other words, the total value of prizes and loot secured; for their unalterable rule was "No prey, no pay."

First it was settled by vote what the captain was to receive for his services or the use of his ship (for very often the skipper was merely the owner of the vessel and was no navigator), then what the salaries of the other men, such as the carpenter, the steward, the gunners, the surgeon, were to be. Then it was agreed that the provisions and liquors should be paid for, recompense being given the individuals who had secured them. Finally came the matter of insurance, and a very complete schedule was drawn up, with exact provisions for payment for nearly every form of injury or wound. This varied somewhat according to the danger of the undertaking, but as a rule it was about six hundred pieces of eight for the loss of a right arm; five hundred pieces of eight for a left arm; the same for a right leg; four hundred for a left leg; one hundred pieces of eight for an eye, the same for a finger, and one thousand for total disability or death. In every case slaves might be taken in lieu of cash, the value of slaves, either white or black, male or female, being fixed at one hundred pieces of eight each. It was also provided that after the payment of all the aforesaid "salaries," refunds, and compensations the remainder of the loot should be equally divided among the survivors of the expedition, with the exception of the captain and other officers, the former always receiving five or six shares to each share of the men, and the others in proportion.

In addition to all this, each member of the company was compelled to take a solemn oath (not infrequently signed in blood) not to conceal, hide, or keep anything for himself, to turn all loot into the common fund, and to abide by the articles of agreement, obey his leaders, and not desert. The penalty for violation of this oath varied all the way from death to being marooned, forfeiting a share in the plunder, or being drummed out of the Brethren, according to the extent of the delinquent's offense.

Seldom, however, was it necessary to inflict any

ROCK. BRASILIANO

BARTOLOMEW PORTUGUES.

of these punishments, for it was extremely rare for a buccaneer to violate his oath or break his promises. It was largely this remarkable loyalty, this honor among themselves, their wonderful organization, their supreme confidence in their leaders, that enabled the buccaneers successfully to engage trained troops outnumbering them ten to one, to storm and take supposedly impregnable fortresses, and to sack towns in the heart of the enemy's country. To be sure, the prominent members of the brotherhood were born leaders, able executives, men of almost superhuman bravery and physical strength; in almost any legitimate undertaking they would have succeeded as well as in their chosen profession of piracy, and their personal courage and magnetism caused their followers to look upon them almost as demigods. The buccaneers would flock by thousands to the call of Mansvelt, Pierre le Grand, Michael le Basque, Alexandre, John Davis, Lolonais, De Graaf, or Morgan, and, regardless of how perilous the undertaking in hand, would follow them through untold horrors and sufferings, through hunger and thirst, through blood and fire; laughing at death, jeering at privations, and faithful to the last. To be sure, they were men to whom fighting and pillage were as the very breath of life, and in those days, when a man's life was valued at only one thousand pieces of eight (approximately one thousand dollars), the bait was large enough to warrant any one taking long chances. Not infrequently a successful foray would result in so vast an amount of loot that when the prizes were divided even the common sailors would receive as much as five thousand pieces of eight as their share for a few weeks' work. The purchasing power of such a sum was then equivalent to about a quarter of a million at the present time. We can readily imagine what risks men of the rough, buccaneer type would take to-day, what hardships they would undergo, and what atrocities they would be willing to commit with a reward of quarter of a million dollars dangling before their eyes, and with virtually no risk of punishment for their actions.

Moreover, the great buccaneer leaders rose almost without exception from the rank and file, by sheer force of character as well as through savagery and cruelty, and very often they were chosen by popular vote of the men. Roche or Rock Brasiliano, a German by birth, who was given his nickname because he had lived long in Brazil, was thus elected captain by men who with him deserted their ship after a disagreement with their commander. Within a few days, this fellow who hitherto had been an inconspicuous sailor succeeded in taking a great Spanish galleon and a vast amount of loot. This at once gave him prestige as a leader, and followers flocked to his standard. But Brasiliano was a degenerate and brutal rascal, who, in the words of Esquemelling (who served under him) "had no good behavior or government over himself in his domestic or private affairs and would oftentimes show himself brutal or foolish, running up and down the streets in drink, beating and wounding whom he met." A most unpleasant personage to have about, even in a buccaneer town! His cruelty was such as even to bring protests from his fellow pirates, his favorite pastime being to roast prisoners alive on revolving spits over slow fires. But he was undeniably brave, and on one occasion, when shipwrecked on the coast of Yucatan and marching overland with less than thirty survivors from his ill-fated ship, Brasiliano and his men attacked and routed over one hundred Spanish cavalrymen. Taking possession of the Dons' horses, they continued on their way, and made themselves masters of the Spanish fleet riding to anchor off the coast of Campeche. Brasiliano was a resourceful scoundrel, and when later he was cast into a dungeon after being captured during an espionage tour of the city of Campeche, which he planned to take, he won his freedom by sending the Spanish governor a letter purporting to come from the commandant of a buccaneer flotilla and threatening dire vengeance if the prisoner were not instantly released.

John Davis, a native Jamaican, also was elected captain and later admiral of the buccaneers because of his signal bravery as a common mariner. His most noteworthy venture was the sacking of San Juan, Nicaragua, and the taking of over fifty thousand dollars' worth of loot. Later he attacked and sacked St. Augustine, Florida, without the loss of a man. Moreover, Davis, according to his historians, was a gentlemanly rascal and very "kind and considerate even when in his cups," a decided contrast to Brasiliano in this respect.

Probably the most atrociously cruel of the buccaneers who made Tortuga their home was Francis L'Ollonais (usually spelled Lolonais), who, born in France, was sold as a slave in the West Indies, and, escaping, reached the French settlement at Tortuga. Like Brasiliano and others, Lolonais was for some time an ordinary seaman, but his daring and ability attracted the attention of Governor de la Place, who provided the promising young pirate with a ship and grub-staked him in the gay game of buccaneering. For a time Lolonais was extremely lucky and took ship after ship and sacked town after town successfully, meanwhile piling up a comfortable fortune for himself and his sponsor, Monsieur de la Place. But the inhumanities he practised were so unspeakable that even his own men became disgusted with him. Moreover, his fortunes turned, and after he had lost his ship on the coast of Yucatan his men were routed and he himself was seriously wounded. Eventually, however, by marching overland, he reached Campeche, entered the city in disguise, secured the services of a few slaves, and in a small boat returned to Tortuga. Here he equipped an expedition and sailed for Maracaibo, which he took and held for over two months, finally departing, after having committed every form of atrocity and abomination, with booty valued at more than half a million dollars.

Thus having recouped his fortunes and again established himself in the favor of his fellows and the governor, this "most execrable scoundrel," as Esquemelling calls him, set sail to ravish the coasts of Cuba and Central America. For a time he succeeded beyond all expectations, taking countless ships and towns, his blood-lust and cruelty ever increasing with his victories. He had, in fact, become a veritable monster in human form, no doubt actually insane, until his men openly expostulated. The culmination came when, in Honduras, marching on Puerto Caballos, Lolonais took a number of Spanish prisoners, whom he questioned regarding the routes to the city. Being dissatisfied with the replies, he flew into a passion and, seizing one of the prisoners, he slashed open the fellow's breast with his cutlass, tore out his still living heart, and began to bite and gnaw at it with his teeth, like a ravenous beast. Shortly after this cannibalistic exhibition of his fury he was again shipwrecked, losing all the booty he had won and many of his men. Nothing daunted, Lolonais prepared to build a long-boat in which to continue his depredations. At the mouth of the San Juan River in Nicaragua he was attacked by Spaniards and Indians, and most of his surviving men were killed. Defeated for the first time, he decided to go southward and attack Cartagena, depending, as was the custom of the buccaneers, upon securing canoes and provisions from the Kuna Indians of Darien. But so utterly despicable had he been that even the savage Kunas had turned against him. To quote Esquemelling once more:

> Hither L'Ollonais came (being rather brought by his evil conscience that cried for punishment of his crimes) thinking to act in this country his former cruelties. But the Indians within a few days after his arrival took him prisoner and tore him to pieces alive, throwing his body limb by limb into the

fire and his ashes into the air, to the intent no trace or memory might remain of such an infamous inhuman creature. Thus ended the life and history and miserable death of that infernal wretch L'Ollonais who, full of horrid, execrable and enormous deeds, and also debtor to so much innocent blood, died by cruel and butcherly hands, such as his own were in the course of his life.

Surely, when a fellow pirate and one of his own companions penned such an indictment, we may safely consider Lolonais the most outrageous rascal who ever scourged the Spanish Main.

It was owing partly to the inhuman methods of the French buccaneers, such as Lolonais, partly to jealousies and the fact that the French were favored, partly to natural distrust and dislike for one another, and partly to more or less loyalty to their own governments, that the British pirates and the French freebooters of Tortuga began to quarrel. At first it was merely a matter of brawls among the men, but gradually the breach widened; armed parties of French and British clashed, riots took place, and at last open antagonism broke out and the French, outnumbering the English, in 1641 drove their erstwhile allies from the island. Scattering about the Caribbean, the English freebooters established themselves here and there among the Virgin Islands, on the Bay Islands, in Samana Bay, and elsewhere, until in 1654, when Penn and

Venables sought to take Jamaica from Spain, they rallied under the British ensign and joined the navy of their king.

It was largely owing to the part the English buccaneers took in this concerted attack on Jamaica, in which they won the admiration of the British admirals and officers for their courage and resourcefulness, that Jamaica became a colony of the English crown. The acquisition of this island by the British provided the English buccaneers with a base for their operations and a safe refuge, and for many years Jamaica—or, rather Port Royal, its chief port—became the most notorious resort of the pirates.

CHAPTER XIV

THE GRANDDADDY OF THE DOLLAR

HAVING seen all that was to be seen at Tortuga, even clambering up the rocky heights to the ruins of that first ancient buccaneers' fort overlooking the harbor, we boarded the *Vigilant* and bore westward for Jamaica.

As Tortuga sank low upon the horizon astern and faded into a soft gray cloud, the lofty mountains about Cape Maysi, Cuba, showed dimly above the sea over our starboard bow, with the mighty bulk of the towering Sierra Maestra of the Pearl of the Antilles faintly outlined, somber, forbidding, in countless peaks against the sky. Then ahead loomed the lonely isle of Navassa, with Haiti's mountain ranges to the east, and through the Windward Passage the *Vigilant* swept on.

Navassa, a barren mass of rock fringed with surf beating upon its jagged ledges and wave-carved cliffs, rising in odd terraces from the angry sea to the dull-green summit whereon stands a solitary lighthouse, may hold pirates' treasure as the Haitians assert, but if it does, that is the only worth-while thing upon the isle. At all events, if the buccaneers hid treasure here they must have chosen their time in good weather, carried their chests ashore in small boats, and hoisted them upon the forbidding rock by tackle, for there is no natural landing-place, and owing to the swift tides and currents there is no sheltered lee under the shore. Everywhere the rocks rise directly from the waves, and the construction of the lighthouse, radio station, and other buildings proved a colossal task owing to the extreme difficulty of getting material ashore. But Navassa can lay claim to one unique distinction, inasmuch as it is the only island which ever sent an S. O. S. call speeding through the ether.

This happened when the first occupants of the station found themselves on the verge of starvation and almost dying of thirst, the steamer with supplies having failed to arrive. But the "Sparks" in charge was a resourceful chap, and he sent broadcast his plea for help exactly as though Navassa were a derelict ship, and thus brought succor to himself and comrades.

We sped past Navassa, giving it a wide berth, and the only signs of life we saw were the countless thousands of boobies, frigate-birds, and pelicans that make this isolated spot their home. Behind us stretched vast Gonaives Bay, with the island of Gonaives looking like a continent itself, though a mere dot on the map compared with Santo Domingo.

No doubt in the good old days Gonaives was a stamping-ground for the buccaneers, although there is little mention of it in either history or the chronicles of the freebooters. Across the way in Cuba, too, the Spaniards more than once felt the hand of these sea-rovers, and many a Cuban town was sacked and pillaged, notably Puerto Principe (now known as Camaguey), originally built on the northern coast of the island. Indeed, it was the frequency of pirates' attacks on the town that induced the inhabitants to move inland. But this failed to save them, and Morgan took the inland "port" and burned and slew and robbed.

It was this exploit of Morgan's which first stamped him as a pirate of prowess. It was his first noteworthy enterprise, and paved the way for all his other famous deeds, or misdeeds. His original intention was to attack Havana, but he was evidently unable to resist Puerto Principe with all its riches—which proved a most unprofitable venture.

The Isle of Pines, now almost exclusively an American settlement, also was once a favorite resort of the buccaneers. Though it was Spanish territory and a dependency of Cuba, yet the few Spaniards who dwelt upon it were friends of the pirates, —an exceptional circumstance,—and gladly welcomed them. But it was merely used as a stopping-place whereon to secure fruits, vegetables, and sea-turtles, being far too near Spanish strongholds to be permanent. The most interesting thing about it which the buccaneers' chroniclers recorded was the fact that it was infested by huge crocodiles or alligators which, to quote Esquemelling, were "of a corpulency very horrible to the sight" and did not hesitate to attack men. Indeed, he states with all seriousness that the giant reptiles actually attempted to climb up the ship's gangway and invade the vessel.

But we could stop neither at Cuba, Gonaives, the Isle of Pines, nor Haiti, and ere nightfall only the heaving sea stretched to the horizon on every hand, and into the golden west the *Vigilant* bore onward, bound for Jamaica. It was with no little regret that I looked forward to seeing Jamaica, despite its interest and associations with the buccaneers, for it was at this island that I was to part company with the *Vigilant* and my crew and continue on the last lap of the journey by prosaic steamship.

What a wondrous procession of ships and hardy

adventurers had passed this way through centuries past, I thought, as the schooner glided through the gleaming phosphorescent water. Westward from his new-found isles and Cuba, which he thought a continent, had sailed Columbus in his caravels. Across this same sea had come the pennant-bedecked ships of Balboa, Pedrarias, and those countless other adventurers who carved a new world for Spain out of the jungles and mountains of Central and South America. Through these same waves had wallowed the battle-scarred *Golden Hind* and her fellow ships, with Drake and Hawkins fresh from the conquest of impregnable Porto Bello. Back and forth across this vast blue waste had sailed stately galleons laden with riches, with gilded towering poops gleaming in the sun, scarlet and yellow banners outflung to the breeze, mail-clad grandees and black-robed friars pacing the decks. And swift in their wake had come the dingy, menacing ships of the buccaneers. What scenes of battle and bloodshed had taken place on this tranquil sea beneath the brilliant tropic stars! What shrieks of agony and deadly fear had rung out upon the night; what awful tragedies had the serene moon looked down upon; and what countless rotting hulks and bleaching bones might still lie upon the ocean's floor countless fathoms under the

Vigilant's keel! Treasure, too, might be there—plate and bullion, precious stones and pearls, which had gone down with the sinking galleons ere the pirates had time to complete their pillage. There, deep in the ooze or on the hard shell sand, they would lie forever: dull, corroded ingots of silver, bars of gold, priceless gems, doubloons and onzas and pieces of eight that men had slaved and murdered and tortured and fought for, then had lost to the world forever.

And speaking of treasure, of pieces of eight, of doubloons, and of onzas,—terms which occur so persistently in every tale or song or history of buccaneer days,—a word or two regarding these coins may not come amiss.

Particularly interesting are the pieces of eight, the coins which are as much a part and parcel of any story of pirates or treasure as the black flag with its skull and cross-bones or the ear-ringed, fierce-whiskered buccaneer, for the piece of eight was the granddaddy of our own American dollar. Not only was it the basis for our standard "cartwheel," but our dollar sign, $, is merely an evolution of the ancient symbol for the piece of eight. This famous coin (which is still very common and is known as the "Spanish dollar") was a silver piece approximately the size of our dollar and with a value of four pesetas or eight reales, from which latter fact it received its name. Roughly, a real was worth twelve and a half cents, or one one hundredth of a doubloon, so that the approximate value of the piece of eight was one dollar; and a doubloon was worth twelve dollars and a half. The onza, or double doubloon of two hundred reales or one hundred pesetas, was equivalent to about twenty-five dollars although to-day the onza, weighing twenty-five grams, is worth intrinsically about seventeen dollars.

In addition to these coins of Spanish mintage there was a fractional currency of a very odd and interesting type known to-day as "cross money." This consisted of slugs of various sizes cut from the pieces of eight and so hammered as to obliterate the lettering and inscriptions with the exception of the cross-like portion of the Spanish coat of arms. This served as a sort of hall-mark or guarantee that the coin was of sterling fineness, and at times, when the slug did not happen to have the desired portion of the shield upon its surface, a cross was stamped upon it by the priests, as proof that the bit of metal was from a piece of eight.

To this day these quaint and curious coins are still in use among the natives in some portions of the interior of Panama, and while no two are alike in size or shape, yet they all have definite weights. The ancient pieces, dating from the days of the conquistadors and buccaneers, pass from hand to hand as reales and pesetas.

In the early days of the American colonies, virtually all the trade of the world was conducted on the basis of the Spanish piece of eight, and most accounts in America were kept in them. The ordinary symbol used in designating the coins was an eight with a line drawn through it, and on many old invoices and manifests we may find such entries as "10 sacks of coffee $60. Later, when the new-born republic decided to coin its own silver, and melted down the old pieces of eight for bullion, the new coins were based on the Spanish piece of eight; and it was only natural that clerks and accountants should still use the old symbol, and by merely running another line through the figure eight the well-known dollar mark was evolved.

Moreover, the piece of eight, with the doubloons and onzas, paved the way for our metric monetary system, for the doubloon was one hundred reales and the piece of eight one hundred centavos, and the mere change in name from "piece of eight" to "dollar" caused no confusion or difficulties in accounting, as long as the metric system was adopted.

Nevertheless, accountants must have had hard times of it in those days, and the buccaneers, when dividing their loot, must have found it no little task to compute the relative value of the cosmopolitan lot of coins they accumulated. We can picture them there under the palms on some tropic beach, waiting expectantly and impatiently, cursing and passing rough jokes, while one of the crew, who perchance spent his early days upon an office stool, seated upon a cask of rum, with a dirty scrap of paper and a scratchy quill is setting down lists of louis d'or, ducats, pounds sterling, pistoles, guilders, and Heaven knows what, and with a puzzled wrinkle on his scarred brow and chewing at his ragged mustache is striving to convert the heterogeneous loot into understandable terms.

Or perhaps, no clerkly corsair being available, the buccaneers took a shorter cut to the division of their spoils, and, weighing the gold and silver regardless of its origin or its minted value, divided the loot by pound or hundredweight like any other commodity. Such minor matters, apparently, were not of sufficient interest to the pirates' chroniclers to be recorded; and moreover, in those days, almost any coin, provided it was of gold or silver, would pass freely in any seaport of the Antilles. No doubt the buccaneers were outrageously cheated by the tradesmen and the keepers of bars and gambling-dens, more especially when it came to converting their bullion and jewels into ready cash or its equivalent. Esquemelling remarks on this, and states that gems and jewelry of priceless value were bartered for a song, the buccaneers being utterly ignorant of their worth. But these adventurers cared not a jot whether they were cheated or not as long as they had enough to keep themselves uproariously drunk and to gamble to their hearts' content. To them money meant merely carousal, and it was not unusual for the rascals to spend several thousand pieces of eight in a few days.

Especially was this true in Port Royal, Jamaica, the richest and wickedest spot in the world, as it was called; the clearing-house of the buccaneers; their most noted headquarters, which undoubtedly harbored more execrable villains and more brave and reckless men than ever have been gathered together in one town before or since. And it was toward Port Royal the *Vigilant* was sailing through the night.

Still no faintest haze of land showed above the rim of the sea when another glorious day dawned. It is a long sail from Tortuga to Jamaica, and here Sam's instinct or sixth sense was of no avail and observations were necessary. He had never sailed the course before, and while no doubt he could have found a spot on Jamaica's bulk (for he could scarcely have missed it if he had come within thirty miles of its shores), to save time and make sure I "shot" the sun and worked out our position, all of which seemed a sort of witchcraft to the members of my crew.

"How are you going to get back to St. Croix?" I asked Sam when, having found our position, I had corrected the Bahaman's course slightly. "Are n't you afraid you 'll get lost and go on sailing the Caribbean forever, like the Flying Dutchman?"

"Ah don' 'fraid, Chief," chuckled Sam. "Ah don' knows 'bout th' Dutch gentleman, but ef he did n' manage for to mek po't Ah 'm thinkin' he mos' cert'n'y was a stoopid nigger', like Joe say. Why, Lordy, Chief! yo' jus' got for to sail east an' yo 's boun' for to mek some islan'! Yo' can' 'void doin' of it, Chief, no, sir. Yo' can' sail outen th' Caribbean 'less yo' parse 'twix' some o' th' islan's, an' yo' boun' for to see he. An' Ah can fotch St. Croix all right, Chief. Ah 'll sail nor'-east till Ah sees Cuba or Sant' Domingo or Port' Rico an' gets mah bearin's an' heads for Fredericksted. Don' worry 'bout me, Chief."

"Well, it 's your funeral, Sam," I laughed.

"But I suppose the longest way round is the shortest way home in your case."

Sam looked puzzled, and a perplexed frown wrinkled his forehead.

"Yaas, sir," he ventured at last. "Ah guess tha 's so, Chief; but, beggin' yo' pardon, Ah don' un'erstan' 'bout the fun'ral. Ah thinks yo' mus' be mistook, Chief; it 's mah weddin' Ah 's goin' to, an' not a fun'ral, Chief."

"Oho! so that 's it!" I exclaimed. "Why, you rascal, I thought you were too old to get married! Who 's the lucky young lady, Sam?"

The Bahaman shifted uneasily, and half turned his face; I could almost imagine that he blushed under his black skin.

"Tha' s why Ah 'm goin' to mek to get married," he vouchsafed finally. " 'Cause Ah 'm gettin' 'long in years, Chief. Long 's Ah 'm young an' fit the' ain' call for to take on th' troubles o' a companion, Chief. Lordy, the 's trouble 'nough by mahself! An' Ah don' have a home, rightly speakin', Chief. But when Ah mek to get ol' Ah jus' mus' cert'n'y fin' some companion for to look arfter me."

I roared. The idea of Sam needing any one to look after him was ludicrous; and, moreover, he was far from old—barely forty, I imagined.

"But who 's the girl?" I queried. "Some one you

met this trip, I suppose. What is she—black, brown, or yellow, Sam?"

"Lordy, Chief!" exclaimed Sam, in genuine surprise. "Ah can' say. Ah ain' foun' her as yet, Chief! Ah 'm goin' for to—"

But whatever Sam was "goin' for to" do was left untold, for at this stage of the conversation the man who had been sent aloft called out that land was in sight, and all attention was turned to the faint and misty outlines that rose, dream-like and unreal, like pearly shadows against the sky.

Rapidly the mountains took on form and shape, though still many miles away, and presently we spied ahead a slender column of sooty smoke, the first sign of a ship we had seen since leaving Navassa astern. Soon the masts and funnels of the steamer rose above the horizon, below them a shimmering white hull developed, and half an hour later we swept past one of the "great white fleet" of the United Fruit Company, outward bound from Kingston. Upon her decks were scores of passengers and her rails were lined with curious tourists as the *Vigilant,* burying her bows under the sparkling froth-capped waves and reeling onward before the trade-wind like a drunken man, passed the big liner to which the tumbling seas were merely ripples.

Perhaps they took us for some island packet;

perchance they thought us fishermen; or, maybe, when we ran up the Stars and Stripes in salute, they realized that we were simply cruising. Probably not a soul among the hundreds that crowded the steamer's deck dreamed that they were gazing at an historic craft; that the little schooner—a mere speck beside the towering fruit boat—had sailed the seas a century and more before the first sailing-vessel of the fruit company carried bananas from Jamaica to New York. For that matter, a lifetime before Fulton's first steamboat trundled slowly up the Hudson.

No doubt those curious, kodaking voyagers, whose interest in the old haunts of the buccaneers center mainly on cocktails, jazz, and the cuisine of the hotels, pitied us poor beings who must needs travel by schooner rather than by steam, and thanked their stars that palatial steamships were at their disposal. For my part, I pitied them because they knew not the real joys of cruising the Caribbean, and missed all the romance and fascination that the islands held. And as the sleek white hull dropped lower and lower in the distance and the Blue Mountains of Jamaica rose ever clearer before our bows, I could not help wondering what old Morgan or Sharp would have thought had they raised a steamship on one of their forays.

The Towne of Puerto del Principe taken & sackt

SPANISH COINS USED IN BUCCANEER DAYS

1–2 Pieces of eight
3–4 "Cross money"
5–6 Doubloons
7–8 Onza or double doubloon

CHAPTER XV

WHERE A PIRATE RULED

AGAINST the soft azure of the tropic sky Jamaica lifts its lofty peaks, crowned with a diadem of clouds, above a sapphire sea. Faint and phantasmal as a vision it hangs above the waves, beautiful as a painting by a master's hand, as slowly the hills and valleys take on form and substance. Opulently rich, with wooded mountain sides, wide fields of golden cane, and endless banana walks, it is as fair a scene as one could hope to see. As the *Vigilant* bore steadily toward Kingston, and we watched valley after valley, wave-washed beaches, surf-beaten crags, and endless rows of palms unfold before us, the island seemed a veritable earthly paradise.

But Jamaica's history is far from that of an Eden, for its past has been one of bloodshed, debauchery, and death. From both God and man it has suffered much, and, as the *Vigilant* passed the long, low sand spit known as the Palisados and dropped anchor off the quarantine station at Port Royal, we were floating above what was once notorious as the wickedest city in the world; for beneath the placid waters here at the harbor mouth are the ruins of old Port Royal, the metropolis of the buccaneers.

Above the beach with the lazily lapping waves, modern Port Royal straggles upon the low, sandy point, a sleepy, sun-drenched spot of no importance save as a barracks and quarantine station. It is hard to realize, as one strolls through the roughly paved lanes or across the broiling-hot parade-ground, that this was once the chief port in the West Indies, the richest city in the New World, and one whose name was synonymous with every deviltry and vice known to man.

And yet there is much of interest to be seen in Port Royal to-day. There is the ancient, crumbling Fort Charles, looking seaward, with its moats and drawbridges, its quaint corners and damp underground rooms. And from the grass-grown embrasures the same ornate guns look grimly forth as in the days when Admiral Nelson was stationed here. Upon a tablet let into the coral-pink bricks is inscribed:

In this place
Dwelt
HORATIO NELSON
You who tread his footprints
Remember his glory

Also, leading from a heavily beamed guard-room in one corner of the ancient fortress is a little flight of stairs that opens on a paved platform known as "Nelson's Quarter-deck." Here, upon these time-worn flagstones, the famous admiral paced to and fro, no doubt regretting it was not in reality the deck of a great ship, and with longing eyes looked seaward for the French fleet which was expected to attack Port Royal. But the fleet never arrived. Had it attacked Jamaica, the history of the isle would, mayhap, have been very different, for the garrison at Fort Charles was pitifully weak, while the French flotilla was of immense strength. Perchance, too, had the attack been made, Nelson might never have won fame, for he was a mere lad of twenty-one when in 1779 he was placed in charge of the fort at Port Royal.

A year later he was once more in Jamaica, near to death with dysentery contracted on the San Juan expedition, and in the home of a noted black nurse, Cuba Cornwallis, he slowly regained his health and strength.

Strange sights and famous men has this old fort of sun-faded brick seen. It has seen Port Royal in all its vicious wickedness and flamboyant sin; it has seen the heaving earth and angry sea sweep the city and all its villainy into the depths. It has seen shot-riddled buccaneer ships returning, triumphant and deep-laden with loot, from piratical forays. It has witnessed many a wild revel of drink-flushed, foul-mouthed corsairs, and has listened to many a plan and plot of the freebooters as they argued and swore over some projected raid on the Spanish Main. Within its walls Morgan as well as Nelson and many a lesser light have dwelt and drunk the health of the king, and through storm and battle and cataclysms its walls and battlements have passed unscathed. The earthquake of 1692 wrought devastation and took thousands of lives, but left the old fort solid and strong. And even in 1907, when in a space of a few seconds modern Kingston crumbled to dust and newer forts fell like houses of cards, the flower-decked old fortress at the tip of the Palisados remained unharmed save for a single crack in one of its hoary walls.

Of the ancient buccaneer Port Royal, Fort Charles alone remains, and great indeed have been the changes the antique pile has seen take place about itself. From the ruin of the pirates' stronghold has risen the sleepy little town,—a village of narrow streets and darkey houses, of stately residences with balconies and balustrades richly carved by shipbuilders now long dead, of trim, well-kept gardens and struggling lawns, and with a naval yard wherein repose the giant figureheads of many famed old British ships and frigates—while across the harbor has grown the island's metropolis of Kingston. Few visitors now stop at Port Royal, few strange feet tread the old flagged esplanades and weed-grown ramp; and yet the little hamlet is well worthy of a visit, for it has a strange Old-World atmosphere and a fascination entirely lacking in Kingston. Its huge barrack square and parade-ground might well be those of some English port, were it not for the nodding palms and scorching sun. There is the old court-house, stately, austere, with shingled roof and flanked by arcades. There is the naval hospital, woefully damaged by the earthquake of 1907, and so out of place in the tropics with its typically English gardens and uncompromising architecture that it reminds one of the conventional houses equipped with chimneys which the old engravers and artists always introduced into their pictures of tropical scenes. And there are the swarded cricket-pitch, the bowling-green, and the tennis-courts on which the British officers and their women folk pass the cool of the afternoons. But the pirates' church, built from the proceeds of robbery and murder, is gone like its builders beneath the sea; the once-busy docks are silent and all but deserted; the warehouses, once filled with casks and bales and barrels, are empty save for rusting chains, bits of cordage, and other odds and ends; the great sail-lofts are bare, and the whole place has the air of a town aloof, communing with itself over its sins and errors of the past, and, like some once-famous courtesan, living in a state of faded gentility away from prying eyes and wagging tongues.

How different was the Port Royal of olden days—a flourishing, noisy, hustling town of several thousand houses, of thousands of inhabitants, of great warehouses filled almost to bursting, of busy shipyards and a "hard" whereon always a dozen vessels might be seen careened; a port before which scores of armed ships rode ever at anchor; a place whose people were as familiar with the Jolly Roger as with the British ensign; and withal the notorious rendezvous of the English buccaneers. Indeed, Jamaica's prosperity was built upon the business of the corsairs, and the port was scarcely more than a clearing-house for them.

Here came the Brethren of the Main from far and near, bringing their treasures: chests of plate and bullion, doubloons, onzas, and castellanos; pieces of eight and louis d'or; altar-pieces ablaze with precious stones; bales of velvets and satins, of silks and brocades; casks of brandy and wines, tobacco and coffee; the cargo of many a scuttled ship and galleon; the booty from many a ravished and sacked town; the holy vessels of countless desecrated churches; vestments heavy with gold and silver thread dragged from the bleeding bodies of butchered priests; jeweled trinkets torn from tortured, shrieking women; the output of many a famous mine; aye, and many a weeping, hapless captive girl, many a groaning slave, until within Port Royal so vast an accumulation of riches was gathered together that it was celebrated far and near as the greatest center of wealth the world had ever known.

And with its fame was coupled an even greater reputation for wickedness. Proud of the one as of the other was Port Royal; its evils were never hidden, never denied; brazenly to the world it proclaimed itself the nearest thing to hell on earth that man could devise.

Here came the swaggering, red-handed cutthroats to spend the gold they had won by robbery and murder, and ever the streets of Port Royal echoed to the drunken shouts and curses of the buccaneers. Sin in every form ruled; murder was of hourly occurrence, and far and wide the depravity of Port Royal was a byword.

A huge, bewhiskered rascal, clad in filched garments of many hues, would land fresh from a successful foray and, striding into a tavern, would fling down a handful of coin and order the cringing innkeeper to broach a pipe of wine in the street. Then, standing beside it with drawn pistols and with a drunken leer on his ill-favored face, the pirate captain would command all who passed to drink. Gladly enough would most accept this pressing invitation, and those who dared refuse would be shot down and their carcasses kicked into the gutter. Or again, merely to show the wealth at his command, he would buy out the tavern's stock of liquor and order it poured into the highway, meanwhile dipping it up in a pannikin and playfully throwing it over the garments of passing men and women. Such were mere pleasantries as recorded by Esquemelling; harmless jokes, to the pirates' minds; the forerunners of less-appreciated amusements such as running amuck and slashing or shooting all who were met, or, again, hanging prisoners in chains or roasting them over slow fires on wooden spits, or perchance flogging a slave to death for an afternoon's sport. Luckily the debauches did not last long. In a single night the revelers would often spend two or three thousand pieces of eight, not "leaving themselves peradventure a good shirt to wear on their backs in the morning," their chronicler tells us, and being compelled to lead a quiet life thereafter until the next corsairs' ship set sail.

But among themselves and to one another the buccaneers were liberal and loyal, and a contemporaneous account states that "If any one of them has lost all his goods, which often happens in their manner of life, they freely give him and make him partaker in what they have."

By some queer whimsy in their complex make-up, some inexplicable, paradoxical twist in their psychology, the pirates felt that their sink of iniquity in Jamaica was incomplete without a church. So forthwith, in this hell-hole, they builded themselves a house of worship, erecting it with the gold won by rapine and murder, fitting it with the candlesticks and altar-pieces, the holy vessels and chalices, the tapestries and paintings looted from other houses of God. And, as they never believed in doing anything by halves, the pirate chiefs decreed that now they had a church all buccaneers must attend services therein.

Indeed, it is said that the notorious Morgan more than once shot down some scoffing buccaneer who had the temerity to interrupt the sermon, and that, on his own ship, whenever a clergyman fell into his clutches, he compelled the prisoner to hold service. History fails to relate what disposal the famous chieftain made of the unfortunate priest or minister thereafter, but he probably compelled him to walk the plank or ended his career in some equally abrupt and pleasant manner, for that was "Harry Morgan's way," as he was fond of boasting.

But the church at Port Royal was the veriest mockery, and not one jot did it influence the behavior or the lives of the town's execrable denizens. Notoriously a pirates' resort, winked at by the British (indeed, encouraged by the government as long as the buccaneers preyed upon the Spaniards and left British ships in peace), the city grew and prospered until one pleasant day in June—the seventh, to be exact—in 1692, when, as though an outraged God could no longer suffer this blot upon the universe, Port Royal was wiped from the face of the earth in an instant. Without warning, with no time granted the carousing, roistering fiends to repent, an earthquake shook the island to its foundations, and Port Royal, with over three thousand of its houses, nearly all its inhabitants, and all its vast accumulated treasures, dropped bodily into the sea.

One can picture the awful scenes of that fatal day: the terror-stricken people rushing, shrieking, from the crumbling houses and through the heaving, rocking streets as the first tremors rent the town; the drunken pirates stumbling red-eyed and cursing from brothel and drinking-place, as timbers splintered and masonry fell, and ruthlessly cutting down all who hampered their flight. And all in vain. Tripping over the bodies of their fellows, choking the narrow streets, felled by tumbling walls, milling, pushing, crowding; befuddled with rum; the solid ground dropping from beneath their feet; blaspheming, screaming, the mob fought madly to save their worthless lives, until, swallowed by the inrushing water, overwhelmed by the relentless sea, men, women, and children, merchant and pirate, harlot and slave, innocent and guilty, were buried deep beneath the waves, while on the placid surface of the harbor floating bits of wreckage, a few struggling figures, and countless corpses were all that marked the scene of the awful punishment meted out.

And above the limit of the devastation, serene, uninjured, aloof, Fort Charles still gazed seaward. Of all Port Royal the old fortress alone remained —this and a few gruesome, buzzard-picked skeletons turning, twisting in the wind, swinging by their creaking chains from the gibbets beyond reach of the waves.

At one fell swoop Port Royal, the buccaneers' stronghold, had been wiped from the face of the earth, never to be rebuilt. To-day, when the water is calm, one may still trace the coral-incrusted outlines of the ruined town, while the negro boatmen relate uncanny tales of ghostly pirate ships sailing in the teeth of the wind, riding the crest of storms, ever striving to make the lost port, and of the phantom bells of the pirates' church tolling the requiem of the dead buccaneers beneath the tempestuous waves.

A few survivors there were, who had found refuge in boats or ships or who had escaped from the stampede to higher ground, and these, spared as by a miracle, saw the error of their ways and, repenting of their sins, moved across the bay and founded the city of Kingston. They had been taught a wholesome lesson. Piracy was given up in favor of honest pursuits, and as, in the years that followed, the buccaneers were driven from the Caribbean, Kingston grew and prospered, order reigned, and peaceable planters, honest merchants, and vast estates brought wealth and riches to the isle in place of pirates' loot and corsairs' treasures.

But Nemesis seems ever to hover above the fair island whose early prosperity was built on bloodshed and villainy. From time to time destructive hurricanes have swept it, leveling buildings, destroying crops, and killing people, as in 1880, when thirty lives were lost in Kingston and most of the wharves as well as countless houses were destroyed. Fire swept the town in 1882, leveling over six hundred buildings, and then came the earthquake and fire of 1907, which snuffed out the lives of over one thousand persons, crumpled Kingston to dust, and wrought awful havoc upon the isle.

And as though these acts of God were not enough, between times there have been wars and bloodshed and to spare. Uprising slaves burned, slaughtered, and destroyed. The Cimmaroons or runaway blacks waged a relentless guerrilla warfare, and bandits and brigands made life and property insecure for years. From the very beginning of its history, Jamaica has been a stage for deeds of violence. Indeed, its turbulent days were inaugurated when first Columbus beached his unseaworthy ships on the northern coast in June, 1503. Here he remained for a year, until rescued by an expedition from Santo Domingo,—twelve months of mutiny, suffering, and hardship,—and here he saved his men and himself from death by impressing the Indians with his famous prophecy of the moon's eclipse.

The site of his encampment, known as Christopher's Cove, is between St. Ann's Bay and Anotta Bay, and is one of the most historic places on the island, although, aside from its natural beauties, with its lovely beaches, its transparent water, and its setting of luxuriant foliage, there is nothing to be seen. Needless to say, Columbus, who discovered Jamaica in 1494, claimed it for the King of Spain, and Spanish it remained until 1655, when the British, under sturdy Admiral Penn and General Venables, vanquished the Dons and established the capital at Spanish Town in 1664.

It was during this period of warfare between the great nations that thousands of negro slaves escaped and, fleeing to the fastnesses of mountain and forest, became transformed into a half-savage race known as Cimmaroons, or, more commonly, Maroons. Fortifying themselves in the almost impenetrable mountain jungles, the Maroons harassed the planters, murdered and robbed travelers, burnt estates and outlying hamlets, and wreaked deviltry and destruction for years. Expedition after expedition was sent against them unsuccessfully, until, in the end, the British were forced to meet the wild negroes halfway, and, despairing of conquering them, made a treaty whereby the Maroons were granted their freedom and twenty-five hundred acres of land.

Then, for a space, the Jamaican whites breathed freely, but not for long. In 1760 the slaves rose, burning, butchering, and pillaging with their usual savagery, and five years later the Maroons once more burst out, leaving a wide trail of blood, of smoking fields, and of blackened ruins behind them, until a second treaty was made and half a thousand of the blacks were exiled to Sierra Leone. But even after this the islanders were seldom left in peace. In 1838 slavery was abolished, and yet in 1865 the negroes rose and slaughtered the whites and burned their homes at Montego Bay, brigandage was rampant in the hills, and altogether the wonder is that Jamaica has survived at all.

Just as Jamaica's old-time prosperity was founded upon the Brethren of the Main, so the island's present prosperity depends almost wholly upon the modern prototype of the pirates—a gigantic trust. In place of high-pooped, low-bowed ships with grinning guns along their sides Jamaica's harbors now shelter the spotless white hulls of the fruit-boats. While the telling arguments of shot and shell and the pistol and cutlass have given way to the all-powerful dollar and the peaceful if no less persuasive methods of modern business to compel others to come to terms, yet the Fruit Company is scarcely less domineering in its line than were Morgan and his associates in theirs.

Not that the Fruit Company has not done much for Jamaica and the other lands where it has holdings. The worst enemy of the great organization, the most rabid anti-trust fanatic, cannot deny that the company has improved land, made for livable conditions, instituted sanitary reforms, circulated money, given employment to thousands, established hospitals, built railways, erected palatial hotels, maintained a steamship service, and done countless other admirable things. But one and all have been done with an eye to personal gain and not for the good of the world or of the countries where it controls politics, finances, policies, and the very existence of the inhabitants. Like every trust, it is utterly selfish, and in Jamaica it has a strangle hold, controlling business and people, body and soul. With the octopus-like grip of this colossus on the lands about the Caribbean, there can be no successful competition, no open market, no independent profitable enterprise where fruit, and especially bananas, are concerned.

Let any one who doubts this attempt to establish an industry where the trust holds sway, and see how long it will be ere he feels the effects of the political influence, the control of labor, the monopoly of shipping which the owners of the White Fleet hold in their hands.

Sr. HEN: MORGAN

JAMAICA A road in the hills

As an example, let me mention the experience of a friend of mine who, finding that little Samana in Santo Domingo produced the largest and finest pineapples in the world and that luscious navel oranges were a drug on the market there at fifty cents a barrel, thought to establish a tiny fruit business of his own. Samples were sent to the leading commission fruit merchants in the States and to the big fancy-fruit and grocery houses, and one and all declared the fruit exceptional, and marketable at high prices, and stated that, coming as it did in midwinter, it would be in great demand. But one and all regretfully stated that they could not handle it, could not touch it, for if they did they would be boycotted and blacklisted by the Fruit Company!

Jamaica may have prospered through the banana industry, fostered and built up by the Fruit Company, but already there is dire complaint among the planters, in regard to the treatment they are getting. The prosperity built upon such a basis will be no more lasting, of no more benefit than the affluence the island once obtained from the buccaneers, and sooner or later the Jamaicans will wake up to find they have sold their birthright for a mess of pottage.

CHAPTER XVI

JAMAICA AND ITS PIRATE GOVERNOR

KINGSTON, the successor of Port Royal, is so well known and has so often been described that little need be said of it. It is not particularly attractive; it has no outstanding architectural beauties and no great historical interest, and is an unbearably hot and glaring town. Since the great earthquake and fire of 1907 it has been even less attractive than before, for many of its ruined buildings have never been rebuilt, tumble-down walls, blackened timbers, and weed-filled spaces are seen on every hand, reminding one of unsightly ulcers on an otherwise healthy body.

But as the chief port and largest city, as well as the capital of the island, Kingston is of importance, and is a busy, bustling little place with huge docks, a wealth of shipping, innumerable shops, and at least one first-class hotel, the Myrtle Bank, which is, of course, run by the Fruit Company.

Compared with other Caribbean ports, Kingston is modern, and owing to repeated catastrophes in the way of fires, hurricanes, and earthquakes there is little of the original town left and there is nothing foreign, quaint, or Old-Worldly about it. But within easy access are many very attractive and interesting points. There are the Hope and Castleton Gardens, the Blue Mountains, and countless charming spots in the hills. Jamaica can boast innumerable excellent automobile roads, and well-equipped railway trains are ready to carry visitors across the island to the huge Hotel Titchfield at Port Antonio (also the Fruit Company's), to Anotta Bay, Montego Bay, et cetera, while delightful short trips may be taken by motor-car to Gordon Town, Newcastle, Old Harbour, and Spanish Town, all of which may also be reached by trolley-cars if desired.

At the foot of the Blue Mountains—which always seem to have a sort of lure, like the mysterious mountains of childhood's fairy tales—is the Constant Springs Hotel, amid charming surroundings. Gordon Town, beside the Hope River and nearly one thousand feet above the sea, is a favorite place of residence, while Newcastle, nearly four thousand feet in the air and in the midst of magnificent mountain scenery, looks superciliously from its heights upon Kingston on its green plain bounded by the sea and the lofty hills, with the thin golden strip of sand connecting the mainland with Port

Royal like (as one enthusiast has put it) the eye at the tip of a peacock's feather.

In point of scenery Jamaica has nothing to be ashamed of, for while the island cannot boast active volcanoes, mountain-crater lakes, geysers, or some of the other features of the smaller Antilles, it possesses several magnificent cataracts. The most noted is Roaring River Falls, a beautiful cascade one hundred and fifty feet in height and two hundred feet wide, a roaring, tumbling cataract in a wonderful setting of luxuriant tropical jungle.

Much nearer Kingston is the Cane River Fall, in whose deep gorge the air is deliciously cool even on the hottest days. At the upper end of the cañon the falls plunge over a lofty ledge into a deep bowl of rock rimmed with giant ferns, and here one may pass behind the veil of water to a cave famed in Jamaica's history.

Within this cavern, so tradition says, once dwelt a desperate and notorious brigand known as Three-fingered Jack. For a long time the triple-fingered outlaw had things pretty much his own way. He was a sort of tropical Jesse James, in fact, and piled up a comfortable little fortune in his lair back of the falls. But at last he "met his meta," as the blacks say, and was killed in a desperate hand-to-hand conflict with a Maroon. In order to prove his victory the Maroon amputated the outlaw's hand with the three digits and brought the gruesome trophy to the authorities, who, as a reward for having destroyed the bandit, settled one hundred dollars a year for life on the Maroon. No doubt the half-savage black was sorry that every cascade did not hide the den of an outlaw, for fighting was the favorite pastime of the Maroons, and to put an end to a man in a good scrap must have seemed a very easy way of earning a handsome annuity.

Another natural wonder which the Jamaicans boast of is the Stone or Natural Bridge across the Rio de Oro, where the cañon walls, through which the stream flows, meet in an arch sixty feet above the water and are capped by an enormous slab of rock.

Perhaps the nearest and most worth-while point of interest is the old capital of the island, Spanish Town. Owing to Jamaica's having been so long a colony of Spain there are many Spanish names remaining there, and the memory of the old Dons' ownership is kept fresh by Rio Cobre, Rio Nuevo, Rio de Oro, Sabana la Mar, and so on. But—probably because the euphonious Spanish names were too difficult for Anglo-Saxon tongues —certain places have had their original names so twisted or altered that they are scarcely recognizable. Thus Bog Walk is merely a corruption of Boca de Agua, and has no connection with either a bog or walking; and the once stately Santiago de la Vega has been dubbed Spanish Town for so long that no one remembers its real name.

Aside from its name, Spanish Town has nothing Castilian about it. One may seek in vain for crumbling battlements and quaint lantern-like sentry-boxes, massive buildings with arched portals leading to flower-filled patios, embrasured windows with iron grilles or jutting balconies. It is, instead, more like a country village in England, or an old colonial town in New England, with white-painted, green-shuttered houses, grass-lined street and lanes, neat gardens, and a sleepy, quiet air as though it thoroughly enjoyed the delightful occupation of dozing in the sun beside the Rio Cobre with not a worry in the world.

But, after the fashion of every self-respecting Spanish city, it boasts a plaza (which is rather more like a village green) with an open market flanked by the old buildings of the days when it was the capital. On one side is the old House of Assembly. Across the drowsy street is the King's House, of red brick with white trimmings, like the typical court-house of a New England village. Near by is the Rodney Monument, and beyond, on the outskirts of the town, is the sole remaining relic of Spanish occupancy,—the oldest church in Jamaica and paradoxically called the English Cathedral. Mellow with age, the bricks have faded to a soft coral pink. Above—no doubt erected by the British, for the Dons were not given to such things—rises a lofty white steeple. Within, the old church is literally floored with tombs, in which rest the bones of many of the most notable personages of Jamaica's past. Some of the tombs are beautifully wrought works of art by Bacon; others are ornate with escutcheons and coats of arms, and not a few are exceedingly quaint and amusing. For example, we may read upon the slab that marks the grave of an officer who came to take the island from the Dons, along with Penn and Venables, that the occupant of the tomb "died amid great applause," while another, we are informed, "came to an untimely end by just cause." After reading that epitaph one feels very much as one does after being asked, "How old is Ann?" or "Why does a mouse?" and one is inordinately curious to know what that "just cause" might have been.

And speaking of that young officer who "died amid great applause," a word or two about that remarkable pair with whom he threw his lot, Penn and Venables, may be of interest. Oddly enough, the two warriors who took Jamaica from Spain and turned it over to Britain are always referred to as though they had been partners in some business enterprise,—"Penn and Venables,"—and never as Admiral Penn and General Venables. Why such an ill-assorted pair were selected by Cromwell to undertake the conquest of the West Indies will ever remain a mystery. Venables was an ardent fisherman, who much preferred writing essays on the sportsmanlike taking of trout and salmon to fighting, and in spare moments he wrote a book known as "The Experienced Angler." No doubt he was an experienced angler, but he was neither an experienced nor a brave warrior. In the first brush with the Spaniards at Santo Domingo he was disgracefully repulsed by a handful of negro and Spanish irregulars, although he had seven thousand men under him. And when the strangely assorted pair of commanders reached Jamaica the angler-general declined to land his troops until all fighting was over; and according to the historian, "he continued to walk the deck, wrapped in his cloak with his hat over his eyes looking as if he had been studying physic more than the general of an army."

In sharp contrast to this curious warrior was Penn, a jolly, rotund, blond man who looked far more like a good-natured village parson than a tough old sea-dog, but who nevertheless showed his mettle and proved himself a worthy upholder of Britain's traditions of the sea. Attacking the old Passage Fort at Jamaica with a small party of his sailors in a tiny galley, the cherubic-faced Penn led the assault in person and, storming the defenses, at one stroke took Jamaica. As a reward for his success he was promptly arrested and thrown into prison in the Tower on his arrival in England, the charge being that he had returned without leave; and as a companion in his troubles the morose and faint-hearted Venables was incarcerated along with him. Penn was soon released, however, leaving his erstwhile partner to his meditations on angling and other matters and no doubt pacing back and forth in his narrow cell much as he had done on his ship off Jamaica.

Another hero of Jamaica, whose body lies in the old Parish Church at Kingston, is Admiral John Benbow. Above his grave is a black stone slab bearing a coat of arms and the following inscription:

Here lyeth Interred the
Body of John Benbow
Esq Admiral of the White
A true Pattern of English
Courage who Lost his life
In Defence of His Queene
And Country November. ye 4th
1702 In the 52nd year of
His Age by a wound of his Legg
Receuid in an Engagement
with Monsr Du Casse Being
Much Lamented.

Not only did the "wound in his legg" mark the end of one of the most glorious and heroic battles against overwhelming odds in the annals of the British Navy, but it was also the sequel to one of the most disgraceful episodes in British maritime history. Perhaps that last line on old Benbow's gravestone has a double meaning, for if ever there was an engagement which should have been "much lamented" it was that with "Monsr Du Casse."

The British fleet of seven ships, carrying over three hundred and fifty guns, sailed from Port Royal and met the French fleet of five large and four small vessels off Santa Marta on August 21, 1702. From the first it was a running fight, and had the British ships stood together it would soon have been over, but the British captains held aloof, and refused to come within range of the enemy despite the admiral's urgent orders. As a result, old Benbow in the *Breda* carried on a single-handed battle with the enemy for four days, hanging on the heels of the French and pouring broadside after broadside at them, until his spars were carried away, his bulwarks shattered, his sails in ribbons, his ship riddled with shot, and the bulk of his men wounded or killed. Each night the doughty old admiral would work feverishly to repair damages and keep the *Breda* from sinking, and as soon as day dawned would begin pounding away again at the French. On the morning of the 23d, a chain shot smashed Benbow's right leg, but as soon as he recovered consciousness he ordered his bed carried to the quarter-deck, and there, mortally wounded, he continued to direct the hopeless battle.

But the odds were overwhelming; no single ship of seventy guns could hope to vanquish the entire French fleet, and when at last the indomitable admiral saw that his ship had barely enough rigging left to carry her to port he regretfully gave orders to withdraw. Shattered and torn, a veritable wreck, the *Breda* turned and headed for Jamaica with her tattered British ensign flying defiantly from her splintered masthead; the wounded admiral shaking his fists at his craven fellow officers, whose ships slunk below the horizon, homeward bound, and, despite his loss of blood and the fact that he was almost blind from shock, volubly cursing the French, while over his head was still flying the orders for a general attack to which the other ships had failed to respond.

Upon his arrival in Kingston, Benbow's leg was amputated, but gangrene had set in, and after a long and lingering illness, and suffering agonies, the gallant admiral passed away on November 4th, over two months after being wounded.

No doubt the failure to obey orders, on the part of the British commanders, was partly due to personal animosity, for Benbow was a surly and unlikeable man, noted for his rough and bullying attitude and cordially hated by his subordinates. But notwithstanding his peculiarities he was indisputably brave, and it is a satisfaction to know that the British captains—Kirkby, Constable, and Wade—were court-martialed, and that Kirkby and Wade were convicted and shot and Constable was cashiered and imprisoned and died in confinement. Of the others, Vincent was suspended, Hudson died before the trial was held, and only Walton of the *Ruby,* who had taken part in the early stage of the battle, was exonerated.

But Penn and Venables, Benbow and Rodney and all the others are of little interest and pale into insignificance as far as Jamaica's history is concerned beside that most remarkable and strange character, Sir Henry Morgan, the pirate chieftain who was knighted and who as lieutenant-governor ruled Jamaica with an iron hand.

Much has been written of Morgan, in history and in fiction, and his exploits have become so well known, his unprincipled ruthlessness such a byword, and his cruelties so notorious that we always think of him as having scourged the Caribbean and the Spanish Main for years. But as a matter of fact this most famous buccaneer's entire career spanned but a scant five years, and all his most notable deeds were performed within a space of two years. As in the case of all the noted pirate leaders, his career of bloodshed and robbery was meteoric. It is hard to realize that he rose from nothing to be the greatest buccaneer chieftain of his day, performed feats which had never before and have never since been equaled for sheer bravery and daredevil recklessness, was knighted, became the ruler of Jamaica, and dropped out of sight all within five years.

Morgan was a Welshman, the son of a well-to-do farmer. Finding farm life irksome, he decided to set forth in search of adventure and succeeded beyond his wildest dreams. Reaching Bristol, he shipped on a vessel bound for Barbados, where, almost as soon as he arrived, he was sold as a servant or virtually a slave. Little is known of his life in Barbados, or whether he escaped or worked out his serfdom, for we next hear of him in Jamaica, where, still seeking excitement, he joined a buccaneer's ship. He was an apt pupil, and, what was unusual among the pirates, a thrifty soul, and after his third or fourth trip as a buccaneer he had accumulated enough cash to buy a share in a ship with a few chosen comrades.

His fellows unanimously elected him as captain and, with a crew selected carefully from the hordes of pirates who infested Port Royal, Morgan sailed for Campeche. From the very first he was marvelously successful, and upon his return from Campeche he threw in his lot with Mansvelt, a hoary old rascal who was then preparing an expedition to the Main.

Mansvelt, recognizing the spirit and promising possibilities of the new accession to the buccaneers' ranks, selected Morgan as his vice-admiral, and with fifteen ships and over five hundred men the pirate fleet set sail on a glorious program of pillage and murder. Their first blow was struck at Old Providence Island (then known as St. Catherines), which Mansvelt planned to transform into a pirate kingdom of his own. With little loss the pirates took the island, established a garrison of their own men, and sailed for Costa Rica and the coast of Panama, where they pillaged and destroyed to their hearts' content, until finally driven off by the Spanish troops sent by the Governor of Panama.

Returning to Jamaica, Mansvelt laid before the governor of Jamaica his plans for establishing a buccaneer stronghold at Old Providence, and asked for men and ships as well as supplies. Oddly enough, his Excellency failed to fall in with the old pirate's plans, and Mansvelt, realizing he had bitten off a bigger slice than he could swallow by himself, sailed for Tortuga. Here, as Esquemelling says, "death suddenly surprised him and put a period to his wicked life," and Morgan found himself sole chieftain of the pirate fleet.

In the meantime the governor of Jamaica had thought matters over, and, Mansvelt being gone, he despatched a ship-load of men and women to Old Providence. The governor's underhand actions were, however, brought to naught, owing to the fact that the island had again been taken by the Spaniards, and the British ship and its people fell into their hands.

Morgan had not abandoned his predecessor's

dreams of a buccaneer stronghold so near the Spanish Main, and had written to merchants in Virginia and New England, asking for cash and supplies to enable him to fortify and colonize the island. But before a response was received his plans were frustrated by the Dons' again regaining possession of St. Catherine.

Morgan then turned his attention to other places. He sailed for Cuba, where with twelve ships and seven hundred men he prepared to sack the interior city of Puerto Principe. The Spaniards, having been warned, by an escaped prisoner of the pirates, of Morgan's approach, had secreted the greater part of their valuables and had prepared for defense. As usual, however, despite the brave resistance of the Spanish, the town fell easily to the buccaneers, and Morgan at once began to put into practice the cruelties and inhuman behavior for which he became notorious. Shutting the people into the churches, and leaving them without food or water—"much to their discomfort and inconvenience," as the historian naïvely informs us—Morgan and his men made merry, punctuating their feasting and drinking by torturing the Dons and striving by unspeakable cruelties to compel them to reveal their hiding-places for their money. At last, finding all their inhumanities in vain, the buccaneers withdrew after obtaining a big herd of cattle which they accepted in lieu of a ransom for the town. Compelling the prisoners to drive these cattle overland to the port, and then forcing the unfortunates to kill and dress the beeves, Morgan at last departed from Cuba's shores.

It was while the cattle were being slaughtered that an incident occurred which showed strikingly the curious combination of honor and rascality which went to form Morgan's make-up. One of the French pirates was cutting up a carcass when an English buccaneer robbed him of the marrow-bones. In the dispute that arose the Englishman challenged the other to a duel, but treacherously wounded the French pirate in the back before he had time to draw his weapon. This murder seemed about to start a revolt of the French members of the expedition against the British, but Morgan at once ordered the treacherous Englishman to be manacled, and carried him to Jamaica in chains and had him hanged at Port Royal for his offense.

Much to the pirates' disgust, the total receipts from the sack of Puerto Principe amounted to barely fifty thousand pieces of eight,—not enough to pay their debts in Jamaica,—and the French members of the company, still indignant at the murder of one of their number and disappointed at the insignificance of the loot, withdrew, and hied themselves to Tortuga.

The success of this first great victory of Morgan as an independent pirate chieftain brought hundreds of men clamoring to join him, and within a short time he again sailed away with nine ships and nearly five hundred men bent on what was the most daring exploit of pirate history up to that time. This was nothing less than an attack on the supposedly impregnable fortress at Porto Bello. It met with phenomenal success, and the pirates found themselves the richer by over a quarter of a million dollars in ready cash, aside from vast quantities of merchandise.

By this victory, Morgan was raised to the pinnacle of fame as a pirate chieftain. Flushed with success, he set forth with a large fleet and a veritable army of pirates to undertake the sack of Maracaibo. Again fortune favored, and Morgan, exhibiting marvelous strategic ability, not only took the town but managed to destroy the Spanish fleet which had sought to block his escape, returning to Jamaica with nearly half a million dollars' worth of loot.

Up to this time Morgan had been really within the pale of the law; for, Spain and England being at war, he and his men, as well as the other buccaneers, were regarded as legitimate privateers. But soon after his sack of Maracaibo peace between the nations was declared, and Morgan, foreseeing that Jamaica might become unpleasant for him and his fellows, withdrew to Tortuga, where he planned his most famous exploit, the attack on Panama.

Upon his return from this astoundingly daring and successful expedition Morgan was promptly arrested when he reached Jamaica, and in company with the governor (who had favored the pirates) was sent to England for trial. By his wonderful personality, specious arguments, and probably a wise distribution of a part of his loot where it would do the most good, the redoubtable Harry managed to escape the penalties of the law provided for pirates and was looked upon as a hero rather than a malefactor. Indeed, instead of being hanged in chains, Morgan was knighted, and sent back to Jamaica as lieutenant-governor. No doubt the king believed that it took a pirate to catch a pirate, and realized that Sir Henry was unprincipled enough to turn traitor to his former associates as long as the government paid him well.

In this his Majesty was not mistaken, for Morgan ruled the island with an iron hand. On his return from Panama he had cheated his men, and had made way with the greater portion of the booty, leaving his fellows to shift for themselves. When, later, these deserted rascals made their way to Jamaica they denounced his treachery in no measured terms. As a result, Morgan was as unpopular among the buccaneers as he had formerly been popular. But it did little good for the disgruntled pirates to rail and threaten reprisals when the object of their venom was the ruler of Jamaica. Morgan had it in his power to make short shrift of the pirates, and despite the fact that they had served under him and had stood by his side in many a desperate battle, Sir Henry hanged them out of hand, often without trial of any sort, until Jamaica became so hot for the lieutenant-governor's one-time associates that the majority betook themselves to Tortuga and rejoined their former French partners.

Morgan, however, was as crooked as a governor as he had been when a pirate; and the fact that he was a Sir altered his character not one jot. He had never believed in letting his one hand know what the other was doing, and while he publicly hanged pirates in chains he secretly furnished cash and outfits for his brother and a few chosen friends to go a-pirating. Rumors of this leaked out; Morgan's severities became so onerous that even the law-abiding inhabitants of the island rebelled, and as a result, he was recalled. Virtually nothing is known of his life after his recall; there is a deal of confusion as to where he lived or how he died, and not a monument, a tablet, or an inscription in Jamaica keeps green the memory or the deeds of Sir Henry Morgan, pirate, governor, and villain.

CHAPTER XVII

THE BRIDGE OF THE WORLD

ALTHOUGH Morgan rose to fame in Jamaica, yet in the island he is unhonored and unsung; and it was across leagues of heaving sea and along the shores of the Spanish Main that his marvelous, execrable enterprises were carried out. In order to follow in his wake I was compelled to bid farewell to my men and the stanch little *Vigilant* and continue my way by steamer.

It was with deep regret that I parted with faithful Sam, hideous-faced Trouble, dignified Joseph, and all the other care-free, happy-go-lucky black and brown members of my crew, for we had got along famously together and they seemed more like old friends than employees. But I knew that sooner or later I should see them all again: in the West Indies one is ever meeting old friends and acquaintances, and as Jules, the half-Carib Dominican, expressed it when he said good-bye, "Morne pas ka encountre; moune ka encountre tojou. [Only mountains never meet; people always meet again.]"

Out of the harbor the *Vigilant* sailed, past sleepy Port Royal at the tip of the Palisados and, heading eastward, bore off toward the distant Virgins. Outward after her forged the big steamer and, swinging her sharp prow westward, surged onward toward Central America, over the same course that Sir Henry sailed as with his crew of ruffians he swept down upon Porto Bello. Standing at the steamer's taffrail, I watched the little schooner heeling to the breeze. Wider and wider spread the stretch of heaving blue between us, until, like the flash of a sea-gull's wings, her white sails twinkled upon the horizon and were gone.

I was on deck at daybreak the following morning, gazing through my glasses at the gray and lofty peak of Old Providence,—the St. Catherine that Mansvelt had thought to make a pirate kingdom and which Morgan later had sacked and pillaged on his way to Panama.

In those days Old Providence was an important stronghold, a miniature Gibraltar guarding the approaches to the coast and ever heavily fortified and garrisoned. But to-day it is a forlorn and all but deserted spot, the home of fisherfolk and a few farmers who cultivate their precarious crops upon the rugged hillsides, and of so little worth that Panama left it in the undisputed possession of Colombia when she gained her independence. Passing the sea-girt volcanic isle to-day, one marvels that the pirates ever should have wasted ammunition and lives upon it; but to them it was a strategic point, and could they have but held it, the fate of Central America might have been very different. Instead of a series of small republics, the land from Mexico to Colombia might now be a colony of Britain.

Beyond Old Providence the wide, unbroken sea stretched away to the horizon, until at last dim mountains, the tip of the Andes, rose before our bows, and clearer and ever clearer grew the land, the coast of the Spanish Main. Rising in green hills from the water, it swept inward, an undulating sea of verdure, to the cloud-draped blue peaks: a vast, untamed wilderness with no vestige of settlement or civilization, until, as the hills became lower and the mountain ranges more distant, we passed the half-hidden entrance to Porto Bello and far ahead saw the smoke-pall and the low land that marked Colon and the entrance to the Panama Canal.

Past the lofty wireless towers, the huge hangars, and the white buildings of Coco Solo, past the great Hotel Washington, past the vast breakwater we steamed, and, gliding through the narrow entrance between the two long ridges of rock and concrete that protect—or, rather, are supposed to protect—the harbor, entered the waters of the Zone, where our steamer was warped into the huge concrete-and-steel piers at Cristobal.

How old Morgan and his fellow buccaneers would stare and rub their eyes could they but glimpse this terminus of the great ditch that links the two oceans, with its puffing locomotives, its row of huge docks, its scores of mighty steamships, and its innumerable honking motor-cars! It was a morass in their day, and for nearly two centuries thereafter; for Colon was built upon a swamp and enjoys the distinction of being one of the few towns, if not the only town, constructed in order to establish a starting-place for a railway, instead of the railway being built to accommodate a town. Originally the place was called Aspinwall, in honor of the projector of the trans-isthmian railroad, and there resulted a ludicrous state of affairs, a petty squabble between two nations that probably has no equal.

Although the Americans who built the town called it Aspinwall, the Colombians had their own ideas on the subject, and to perpetuate the name of the great discoverer they christened it Colon.

The United States Government then took a hand and, refusing to recognize any such town as Colon, declined to deliver mail addressed thereto. But that was a game which two could play, and the Colombians promptly refused to accept or deliver mail addressed to Aspinwall. As in most cases, possession was nine points of the law, and as the binomial port was unquestionably on Colombian territory, the United States at last backed down and grudgingly agreed that "Colon" it should remain.

Colon is a far from interesting city, but it is clean and sanitary and no longer the sordid, disease-ridden, filthy hole that it was in pre-canal days. Moreover, despite the lurid tales of fiction-writers, Colon is as orderly and law-abiding as any port, and while it possesses an inordinate number of cheap cabarets and cheaper bar-rooms, and is frequented by hundreds of Uncle Sam's sailors nightly, not to mention a multitude of seamen, canal-zone employees, and natives, yet serious crimes are rare and vice hides itself in out-of-the-way streets in a restricted district. But Colon's reputation as the "wickedest city in America" has not long been a thing of the past. Five years ago both Colon and Panama were such hotbeds of iniquity that the commanding general of the

United States forces on the isthmus was compelled to issue a general order prohibiting sailors and soldiers from entering Panamanian territory.

As a result of this order, Panama was compelled to clean up its two chief towns, for without the patronage of the Americans they would have been in sore straits, and while the Government was slow about it (for the average Panamanian is far from squeamish in regard to either physical or moral filth), the herculean task was at last accomplished and our men of the army and navy were once more permitted to roam through the streets and frequent the resorts of the Panamanian towns.

Little need be said of Colon, or of Cristobal, the spick-and-span little American town on the zone side of the railway which forms the boundary between American and Panamanian territory, or —what is of more importance to the majority of visitors—the boundary between a very dry and a very wet land.

Neither possesses any historical associations, and neither had been dreamed of in the days of the buccaneers. But near at hand, a scant twenty-five miles down the coast and easily accessible by motor-boat, is the ancient stronghold of Porto Bello, the grim old citadel that defied Drake, the treasure-house that fell to Morgan and his men, the Atlantic terminus of the celebrated Gold Road.

Within the vaults of Porto Bello have been stored countless millions of treasure. To this port, winding their way through the jungles, along the roughly paved road from Panama, came the long mule-trains, laden with the riches of the despoiled Incas; with the output of the marvelous mines of Darien and Veraguas; with the gems and jewels of Aztec kings and princes; with bullion and plate; with the treasures of the Indies. With jangling bells the gaily caparisoned mules trotted over the rough cobbles, splashed through the rivers, and plunged up the steep slopes; with cracking whips and hoarse shouts the sandaled drivers ran beside them, in picturesque Spanish cursing their beasts and urging them forward; chained together in groups, the bronze-skinned Indian and ebon-hued African slaves stumbled along, groaning, footsore, bleeding from the lash; while leading the way and bringing up the rear were the mail-clad soldiery, the plumed officers, the proud hidalgos and such well-to-do travelers as saw fit to travel from ocean to ocean across this Bridge of the World.

Long centuries have passed since the last treasure-train wound its slow way across the isthmus by the Gold Road. Huge trees have sprung from between its cobbles and have spread their vast network of branches above the spots where fever-stricken slaves dropped dying under the hoofs of the gold-laden mules. The forest has obliterated the once broad way; the jungle has hidden with its impenetrable curtain long stretches of the celebrated highroad; steeply arched bridges have crumbled into the tumbling rivers, and wayside stopping-places, where the long mule-teams halted for rest and refreshment, are mere mounds of giant ferns and huge-leafed plants. But still, so the natives say, ghostly figures may sometimes be seen traversing the highway. Through the silence of the midnight jungle come the tinkle of mule-bells and the clatter of hoofs on stone; weird lights flicker and dance between the trees, and the screams of mortals in agony and the groans of the dying make one's blood run cold. No natives willingly go near the old road after nightfall, for to them it is accursed, a way paved with dead men's bones, a trail of blood and death; and piously they cross themselves and speak in hushed and fearful voices at mention of it.

No one can say how many millions in gold and silver and jewels have been carried over this forest road from Panama to Porto Bello. For years it was the only route from the Pacific to the Atlantic, or vice versa, and over it flowed all the treasures that the ruthless Dons wrested from the New World; over it passed thousands of hardy Spaniards who sought to win fortune and fame from the new-found lands, and who left their bones in morass, jungle, and sea, from California to Patagonia.

Rich indeed were the pickings to be had in those days, and the loot of Inca and Aztec, of Toltec and Maya, the output of countless mines, and fortunes in pearls from the outlying isles were carried over the Gold Road and stored in the vaults of Porto Bello to await the plate-fleet with its convoys which was to bear the stupendous treasure across the sea to Spain.

A tempting spot to rob was Porto Bello, a vast coffer fairly bursting with riches, and many an avaricious buccaneer sighed regretfully as he cast covetous eyes toward the town and thought of the incalculable wealth that reposed in safety behind the grim walls and bristling guns of San Jerome Castle, on the heights above the quiet harbor.

But San Jerome had been builded with all the art and skill of the best Spanish engineers; it had been devised to guard the treasures of New Spain, and to guard them well. No ship could enter the port without passing under its guns; no man could approach by land without exposing himself to the ever-watchful sentries and a withering fire of musketry and cannon. It was not only a castle and a group of forts but a citadel as well—a vast pile of massive walls, of moats and battlements, of outjutting sentry-boxes—and ever garrisoned with a thousand men or more.

It was thought impregnable, beyond the possibility of capture; the Dons believed the riches within were as safe as though in the treasury of Madrid itself. But the very year that the fortifications were completed William Parker with two hundred rough-and-tumble pirates took the place by storm, burned a part of the town, and got safely away with a tremendous amount of booty.

Alarmed and chagrined to think that the hated British had cracked the vault they had thought so safe, the Spanish had the castle strengthened and enlarged; more heavy guns were mounted and the garrison increased, and the Dons again breathed freely. For sixty years and six the treasure lay safe; the mighty walls resisted all assaults; the cannon roared defiance, and above the battlements Spain's banner of blood and gold defied the world.

And then, like a bolt from a clear sky, came Morgan. With a fleet of nine ships and a scant five hundred men he landed on a wild, uninhabited stretch of coast and marched on the town at dead of night. Guided by an Englishman who had been a captive in Porto Bello, his forces approached the castle and a few men were sent forward, to steal silently upon the outermost sentry. Leaping on the unsuspecting Spaniard, they bore him to earth ere he could utter a sound, and, binding and gagging him, took him to Morgan. At threat of death by torture the poor fellow gave what information he could of the citadel and its garrison, and promised as well to follow out the orders of the pirates. Creeping like shadows under the walls of an outlying fort, the buccaneers posted themselves with weapons ready and ordered their prisoner to call out to his fellow soldiers, advising them to surrender, as an overwhelming force was about to attack.

In reply, the garrison at once began firing into the darkness, and with wild shouts and yells the pirates rushed this outer fort and, aided by the darkness and the terror which they always inspired, soon took the place. Having once threatened to destroy all within if they refused to surrender, Morgan was as good as his word. Herding the defenseless soldiers and officers in a single room, he set fire to the magazine, blowing the prisoners and the fort to atoms. The shouts, shots, and explosion had aroused the city and the other forts,

PANAMA

Ruins of the fort at Porto Bello

PANAMA The jungle, Darien, through which Sharp and his men tramped

and, believing that a tremendous force of the enemy must be upon them, the inhabitants became panic-stricken, rushing hither and thither, throwing their valuables into wells and cisterns, striving to escape to the near-by forest, and utterly demoralized. As a result, there was little resistance, and, slashing and shooting their way through the wild-eyed throngs, the pirates dashed to the cloisters in the town and, battering in the doors, made prisoners of the priests and nuns.

Meanwhile the governor, unable to rally the townspeople, retreated to the main fort, San Jerome,[1] and from this point maintained an incessant fusillade upon the pirates. Unable to approach closely, the buccaneers sought what shelter they could find, and, being accomplished marksmen, picked off the Spanish gunners each time they attempted to recharge their cannon. For hours,—from daybreak until noon,—the conflict raged, and for a time it seemed doubtful which side would be the victors. Several times the pirates took their lives in their hands and, dashing under the walls, attempted to start fires at the castle's doors, but each time they left dead and dying behind as the Dons threw bombs and blazing pitch upon them

[1] Of the several forts of the citadel or castle of San Jerome, the largest was also called San Jerome.

from the parapets. Finding they were making no headway, even Morgan himself began to despair, and with ready devilishness he proceeded to carry out a scheme of such downright villainy that it could have been born only in the mind of a monster. Hastily constructing a number of broad ladders, he notified the governor that unless the place were surrendered, he would force the nuns and monks to place the ladders and scale the walls. He knew full well that the Dons would hesitate to shoot down the holy men and women.

But the governor of Porto Bello was a man of no ordinary courage and determination, and replied that never would he surrender as long as he remained alive. Thereupon the nuns and monks were dragged forward and, prodded and flogged, were forced to lift the ladders, place them against the walls, and form a screen for the pirates swarming in their rear.

Praying and crossing themselves, beseeching the governor to surrender, the monks in blood-stained cassocks, the white-faced nuns with garments stripped from their quivering bodies, swollen and bruised from cruel blows, lifted the heavy ladders only to fall dead and wounded by scores from the shots of their own countrymen. But others were forced forward, until at last the ladders were in place and, with pistols and cutlasses drawn, the buccaneers swarmed up the walls. Heedless of the fire from above, shouting, swearing, and ever pressing on, they gained the parapet and like fiends incarnate leaped among the Spaniards, cutting and hacking, shooting and stabbing, and so terrorizing the soldiers by their onrush that many threw down their arms and fled.

Presently only the governor remained, fighting alone, his back to a wall, his sword flashing, his dark eyes gleaming defiance, his gray beard streaked with blood. Amazed at his courage, appreciating his bravery, the buccaneers offered him quarter, and even his own wife and daughters pleaded with him to surrender. But the old hidalgo would have none of this, and defiantly he shouted that he would die as a valiant soldier rather than be hanged as a coward. Over and over again the pirates, at Morgan's orders, strove to rush the old man and make him prisoner, but each time his flashing sword formed a circle of death beyond which none could pass until he fell, shot down by the pirate chieftain.

Porto Bello was now in the buccaneers' hands. Herding the people, wounded and well alike, into cells where, as Esquemelling says, "to the intent their own complaints might be the cure of their hurts for no other was afforded them," they were left under guard while the victors fell to eating and drinking. Soon the majority were outrageously drunk, and had the Dons rallied and attacked they might have retaken the place, for, again to quote Esquemelling, who was an eye-witness, "if there had been found fifty courageous men they might easily have taken the city and killed all the pirates."

For several days thereafter Porto Bello was such a scene of debauchery, of inhumanity, of agony and suffering as the sun has seldom looked upon. The buccaneers went about looting and ravishing, and, realizing that much of the treasure had been hidden, they tortured the prisoners to compel them to divulge the hiding-places. Every devilish device of the Inquisition, and worse, was brought into play. Men and women were broken on the wheel and torn on the rack; they were spitted and roasted over fires, quartered and hacked to bits, flayed alive, blinded, dipped in boiling pitch, subjected to unspeakable agonies before their loved ones' eyes, until, satiated with bloodshed, convinced that every centavo had been found, the pirates desisted. For fifteen awful days they remained in the stricken town, dying like rats of fever and excesses, daily casting scores of festering corpses into the sea, but so drunk with victory that no heed was given to their own losses or to the threats of an overwhelming force approaching from Panama.

Then, realizing that he must leave, Morgan demanded that the stricken inhabitants pay a ransom for the deliverance of the city, and, ambushing the approaching Spanish troops, he drove them back along the Gold Road. Knowing that his threats to burn the town and to massacre the few remaining inhabitants would be carried out if the ransom were not paid, the people scraped from hiding-places the sum of one hundred thousand pieces of eight, and turned them over to the ruthless conqueror. Rarely did Harry Morgan break his word to an enemy (which was about his only redeeming trait), and so, the ransom being paid, he prepared to evacuate the town with all the treasure he had won, which amounted to more than a quarter of a million dollars in cash and as much more in merchandise—truly, a rich haul!

But before he departed there entered into this awful tragedy a bit of that humor that ever was cropping up with Morgan. Marveling how any one could have taken Porto Bello with its supposedly impregnable forts, its mighty guns, and its horde of soldiery,—to say nothing of its citizens, who were reputed to be brave fighters,—the Viceroy of Panama despatched a messenger to the pirate, begging him to "send him some small pattern of those arms wherewith he had taken with such violence so great a city." Courteously (now that hostilities were over and the ransom paid) Sir Henry received the messenger, entertained him,—with stolen wine and looted provender, of course,—and sent him back to the viceroy bearing a pistol and a handful of bullets along with a message to the effect that he "desired the viceroy to accept that slender pattern of the arms wherewith he had taken Porto Bello and keep them for a twelvemonth; after which time he promised to come to Panama and fetch them away."

We can readily imagine with what thanksgiving the harried, tortured, robbed inhabitants of Porto Bello saw the last of the pirates leave, and watched the sails of their ships as they sank from sight below the horizon. But never again would they trust to the old forts to safeguard their treasure. As a result of Morgan's raid the Gold Road was abandoned between Porto Bello and Las Cruces on the Chagres. The mighty fortress of San Lorenzo at the river's mouth was strengthened, and the treasure bound for Spain was brought via land and the Chagres River to the ships lying in safety under the guns of San Lorenzo.

CHAGRES CASTLE (FORT SAN LORENZO)

But Porto Bello remained; its forts stand, and to-day one may wander about old Fort San Jerome. The ruins are in a good state of preservation, the chapel, the house of the valiant old governor, the cloisters from which the nuns and monks were dragged to form a human shield for the pirates, the massive treasury, and the huge barracks still stand; and one may yet trace the outlines and foundations of the old town.

Nearly as strong to-day as in the time of Morgan is old San Jerome, with its massive walls, its lantern-shaped sentry-boxes, the deeply carved coats of arms above its portals, its embrasures, and its battlements; but the modern Porto Bello is merely a native village of squalid huts and unkempt streets. Its glories have long since departed; the Gold Road is no more. Once the most fabulously rich of New-World cities, the third greatest stronghold of Spain on the Spanish Main, and the storehouse for millions, Porto Bello is to-day almost forgotten and unknown.

The splendid harbor that once sheltered pennant-gay galleons and proud frigates now gleams beneath the sun with only the humble fishing-boats and dugout canoes to ripple its blue surface. Over the spot where Drake lies fathoms deep beneath the sea, the speeding keels of steamships pass unheedingly. Where the white-faced friars reared the ladders under a storm of bullets, tangled lianas and broad-leafed vines drape the gray walls. Gay flowering shrubs hide the scars of battle and the rusting cannon on the slope up which the pirates stormed, and lizards sun themselves upon the spot where the proud and valiant governor sold his life so dearly.

Peaceful and calm is Porto Bello above its lovely bay. The age-gray fort is set in entrancing scenery, and it is hard indeed to realize that it was once the scene of bloodshed and carnage, that the green hills have echoed to the roar of cannon and the shrieks of the dying, that here, upon these very stones, Don and Briton, soldier and pirate struggled in mortal combat.

PANAMA San Lorenzo fortress as it is today

PANAMA The new city of Panama

PANAMA A street in modern Panama City

CHAPTER XVIII

THE CASTLE OF GOLD

SO marvelously rich was Panama, so vast were the quantities of gold wrested from the Indians and from the mines, that the Spaniards called the isthmus *Castillo del Oro* or Golden Castle. For years the precious metal flowed in a steady stream from the mines of Veraguas and of Darien, and rapidly accounts of these riches spread until Panama became known as the greatest gold-producing country in the world at that time. Hence the name "Costa Rica" then applied to all the country from Honduras to Darien. The quarter of a million dollars that Morgan looted from Porto Bello was but a drop in the bucket compared with the annual output of Panamanian mines.

No one can say how much gold was taken from the mines of Darien and Veraguas by the Dons, for most of the records, if any existed, disappeared with the burning of Old Panama; and others have been lost or destroyed in the revolutions and disturbances since then. But here and there, in the musty files of sleepy, half-forgotten old towns that once were great and prosperous cities of the gold districts, one may find stray bits of information which throw some light on the gold output of Panama's mines in early days.

Thus, in Veraguas we learn, from papers still preserved in Santiago, that it was customary for the Crown to receive a royalty of five per cent. or a *quinto* of all gold exported from the province. We also find from the age-yellowed treasury bills that in one year the Crown received over twenty thousand castellanos as its share of Veraguas gold. In other words, considerably over two tons of the yellow metal, or about two million dollars' worth of gold, were annually exported from this one district! And this was only a fraction of the total amount mined. That which went into private pockets, that which was expended for supplies, transportation, et cetera, that which went to the Church did not enter into these figures at all. Going further into the records, we learn that in 1570 over two thousand slaves were employed in the Veraguas gold-mines, and contemporary writers state that a placer that did not yield at least a castellano of gold to a "common kneading-trough" was not considered worth working.

And Veraguas was not the only gold-producing district, by any means. The mines of Chiriqui produced stupendous quantities; the mines of Darien were world-famed; there were mines in the present province of Cocle, in Los Santos, and in many other districts; and the total value produced staggers the imagination. It is stated in official documents that one small private mine produced enough gold in one year to build the college in Panama, a church, and several lordly mansions, and provided a comfortable fortune for the owner in addition! Moreover, incalculable sums were taken from the Indians and from the prehistoric graves.

No wonder, then, that Panama was the richest and most prosperous of Spain's possessions in the New World; for in addition to its own wealth it was the receiving and shipping point for all the treasures from ports of Mexico, Central and South America on the Pacific, and the East Indies.

Besides all this, its wealth in cattle was enormous; vast quantities of valuable woods, dyes, and medicinal plants were obtained from the forests; the yield of pearls from the Pearl Islands and the waters of Panama Bay was worth a king's ransom yearly, and the fertile lands produced great crops of sugar, tobacco, coffee, and cacao.

This being the case, we naturally wonder why Panama has fallen to its present state; why not a single mine is being worked to-day; why the "Castle of Gold" has become an insignificant republic perpetually bordering on bankruptcy; why it has fallen from its former proud estate as the richest country in the New World to a poverty-stricken land that would find it impossible to make both ends meet if it were not for the revenue it derives from the canal and trade with Zone employees, the army and navy, and the annual influx of tourists.

First and most important of all in the cessation of Panama's gold output was the fact that the Spaniards worked their mines by slave labor, usually making use of the native Indians. These often rebelled, and when opportunity offered massacred their cruel masters, destroyed the workings, and concealed or obliterated the approaches, so that the mines were lost. The negro and Moorish slaves brought in, ran away, became allies of the buccaneers and the Indians, led a wild bush life, and were a constant menace to the outlying settlements. Still later, with the emancipation of the slaves, many mines could not be worked at a profit and were abandoned, while in numerous cases the incredibly rich placers, which were mere pockets, were worked out and exhausted.

Revolutions, rebellions, and wars did their part

as well. The cattle ranges were deserted, outlying estates were destroyed, unprotected settlements were abandoned, and the jungle took possession of fields and lands.

But all this took many years. Even as late as 1850 virtually all the commerce of the isthmus was paid for in raw Panamanian gold, and such tumble-down, half-deserted interior towns as Santiago de Veraguas, Las Minas, San Francisco, and a score of others were busy, populous centers of wealth, fashion, and commerce.

And all the former prosperity of the country might have been won back and Panama might still be a rich and thriving country, had it not been for its people.

The old Dons, despite their ruthlessness, and their insatiable lust for gold, were daring, indomitable men. No hardship was too great for them to endure if there were riches to be won or new lands to conquer. No undertaking was too difficult, no dangers could deter them; even death mattered little, and, fighting the savages as they went, they overran the land, established towns, discovered mines, cultivated the soil, built cities, and endured every privation in building up the wealth and prosperity of the Castillo del Oro.

But not so their descendants, the decadent

people that have inherited the land which once was the brightest and richest jewel of all the colonies of the Spanish Crown. With very few exceptions the Panamanians are of a mongrel breed—a mixture of the Spaniard, the negro, and the Indian, with all of the worst and few of the best qualities of the three. Add to this a goodly sprinkling of Chinese blood, a dash of that of the old Moorish slaves, a seasoning of all the races of Europe which have passed across the isthmus during four hundred years, and we have the Panamanian of to-day. A few old families there are, to be sure, in whose veins the blood of the Castilian conquistadors runs fairly unmixed, and in certain outlying villages in the interior the people pride themselves on their pure Spanish descent. But the average Panamanian is the product of a melting-pot wherein the blood of a dozen races has been blended. Moreover, the blood has been of a far from desirable kind. It is the blood of adventurers, of soldiers of fortune, of remittance men, of those who have sought refuge where no extradition treaties were in force; the blood of gamblers and seamen, of down-trodden slaves and cowed and beaten Indians—the heritage of that vast horde that passed over the Bridge of the World from the days of Balboa to the building of the canal.

In the various portions of the republic the Panamanian varies somewhat, but only in the matter of blood, not in character. In the northern and western provinces he is mainly of Spanish and Indian extraction; in the Darien district and the east he is largely African, and in the cities he is a combination of everything—a hodgepodge of races, of colors, and of ancestry such as can be found on few spots on earth. But, whatever his blood, the character, temperament, and point of view of the Panamanian are virtually the same everywhere. He is conceited, arrogant, lazy, and weak in physique. For centuries the people have been content to live from the traffic across the isthmus, to cull a livelihood from those who passed from ocean to ocean, and to neglect their country's resources. In the interior they have degenerated into listless, abjectly poor, hook-worm-infested, undernourished, unspeakably miserable creatures whose lives are as aimless as the scrawny, tick-ridden cattle, and whose intellects are scarcely greater than those of the beasts about them. In the cities the common people are hardly superior, as far as physical or moral conditions are concerned, and they are absolutely lacking in initiative, foresight, or ambition, save in playing politics or in securing a soft government job.

Of course there are exceptions. There are many decent, intelligent, progressive, up-to-date and industrious men who have the interests and the good of their country at heart; men who are honest and advanced in their ideas and who would be a credit to any land. But these are a woeful minority. And, moreover, even the best of the Panamanians are neither builders, creators, manufacturers, masters of industry—or even good business men. What few industries there are in Panama are run by Americans; all the leading stores are in the hands of foreigners and Hebrews. Chinese and East Indians control the bulk of the smaller shops, and even the coal-black negroes from the British and French West Indies outdo the native Panamanians as far as business ability and progressiveness are concerned.

Is it any wonder, then, that Panama is undeveloped, largely unsettled, backward, and poverty-stricken? Were it not for the canal and the Americans, the country would have been ruined long ago. The towns were pest-holes until our engineers stepped in and sanitized them. The country was always in debt until an American fiscal agent took charge of Panamanian finances and checked the wholesale robbery among the officials. Panama's income is almost entirely derived from Americans

PANAMA Darien Indians wearing wooden crowns exactly as described by Dampier and Ringrose in their accounts of the buccaneers' trip across the isthmus

PANAMA The Tuira River down which Sharp and his men traveled

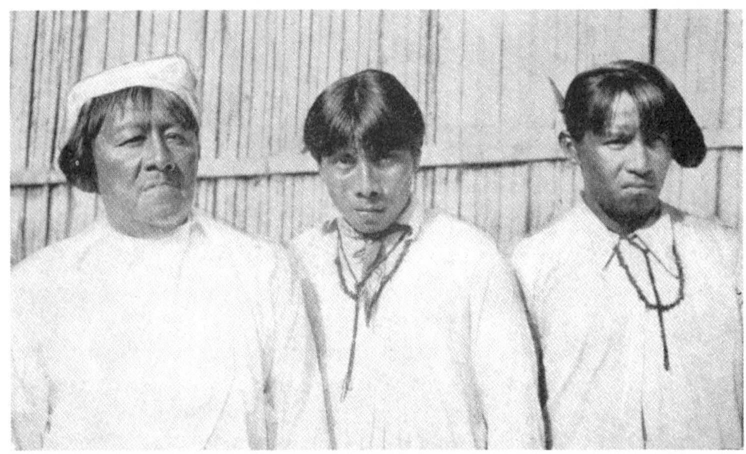

PANAMA Darien (Kuna) Indians, the Indians who guided Sharp and his men

and the canal, and without our aid and support the people could not even have won their independence or have maintained it afterward.

But there is not the least gratitude for what we have done. There is no more self-sufficient, egotistical, conceited man on earth than the average Panamanian; and while he is wise enough to know on which side his bread is buttered, he detests the Americans from the bottom of his heart, and particularly resents the fact that under American supervision the treasury cannot be looted at will by every political hanger-on, grafter, and protégé of the officials.

The stranger does not at first realize the true condition of affairs in the country, and is prone to take the Panamanians at their own valuation; for they are smooth talkers and prate loudly of their enlightenment, their progress, and their appreciation of the Americans. But, like all Latin Americans, they are born diplomats, and laud America publicly and curse her privately. Indeed, were it not for the ever-present power of Uncle Sam, the lives and property of Americans would be worth nothing in the republic; and, even as it is, crimes against Americans are whitewashed whenever possible.

Do not think from the above that the Panamanian is totally lacking in good qualities or redeeming features. He is intensely patriotic, he is fond of music and art, he is outwardly a polished gentleman, and while, as a rule, he has a streak of yellow in his make-up, yet individuals have shown time and time again that they possess a high degree of courage and self-sacrifice. On the whole, however, after one knows the Panamanians and has lived among them, one is rather sorry that Morgan did not make a clean job of it and wipe out all the inhabitants of Old Panama when he had the chance, or that old Mansvelt did not hold St. Catherine and from that vantage-point subdue the isthmus and add it to Britain's domains.

Panama is as rich, as fertile, and as fair a country as in the days of its greatest prosperity—an almost virgin land of limitless forests, stupendous mountains, vast rolling plains, great rivers, luxuriant valleys, high table-lands, and untrodden wildernesses.

One may cross the isthmus by railway trains hauled by oil-burning locomotives or may steam through the canal on huge liners. One may whirl about Colon or Panama in motor-cars or may ride on trolleys. One may live luxuriously in the palatial Tivoli or Washington Hotel, and may find every convenience and comfort of New York in the shops; and from morn to night one hears the bustle and the hum of modern progress and activity. And yet, within a few hours of all this, within a hundred and fifty miles of the teeming towns and the up-to-date Zone, is a vast unknown territory, a land that the foot of no white man has ever trod, a district wherein dwell Indians as primitive as those who gazed in wonder at the ships of Columbus.

And, oddly enough, it was in this district, in Darien, that the first Spanish settlement was made on the isthmus. It was across this wild and untamed land that Balboa made his slow and difficult way to look upon the Pacific, and it was through the Darien jungles that Sharp and Dampier and their fellow buccaneers forced their way from the Atlantic to the Pacific on that marvelous "dangerous voyage."

Darien has changed little since then. The jungles are as impenetrable as when the first Dons and the later buccaneers slashed through the tangle of creepers and vines. Within the forests dwell the same Indians as those Balboa fought and the same tribes that aided the pirates to attack the hated Spaniards. One may still find the Chokois garbed only in breech-cloths and wearing the strange wooden crowns described by Ringrose and

Dampier. One may still see the Kunas wearing the palm-wood combs and the golden nose-rings that attracted the buccaneers' attention and curiosity. And, just as in the days of Ringrose and his fellows, there are friendly or "tame" red men and wild Indians, or *bravos,* in Darien. As ever, the brown-skinned Chokois are friendly and peaceable, although as primitive as at the time of Balboa's expedition, while the yellow-skinned Kunas are as implacable, as aloof, and as unapproachable as when they tore the cruel Lolonais limb from limb.

But in addition to these wild tribesmen, who never permit a white man or a strange red man within their territory, there are also "tame," or, as the Panamanians say, "mansos" Kunas, descendants of those who helped and guided the buccaneers across the isthmus and were ever the allies of the pirates—or, for that matter, any enemies of the hated Dons.

Wonderful tales are told in Panama and Colon of the wild Kunas, or, as the people call them, "San Blas" Indians, of the forbidden district. It is said that they either kill whoever enters their land, or else slice off the soles of one's feet and then turn one loose in the jungle; and the Panamanians, as well as the Chokois, are in deadly fear of them.

As a matter of fact, while the Kunas *do* prevent strangers from entering the territory they control, which extends from the upper Chukunaque to the headwaters of the Bayano River, yet I doubt very much if they ever kill or even maltreat a white man. Personally I have gone into their forbidden district for a short distance, and have dwelt among the wild Kunas for a fortnight, and I was treated well and made many friends among them. But the *bravos* have seen the results of contact with civilized or supposedly civilized man, and they have no intention of permitting the native rubber-gatherers or gold-seekers to secure a foothold in their country. And when one has seen what association with other races does to the red men, one cannot blame the Kunas if they adopt stern measures to keep their tribc purc and undefiled.

Inhabitants of this same Darien are the true San Blas Indians, who have ever been confused with the Kunas, but are quite distinct—a peaceable, friendly tribe dwelling on the Atlantic coast and the neighboring islets. In the old days they were sworn friends of the pirates, and rendered every British freebooter inestimable aid, from the time of Drake to that of Patterson. As sailors they are unexcelled, and many buccaneer ships dropped anchor off the San Blas isles and picked up the stocky brown Indians to act as pilots on their forays up and down the coasts.

The buccaneers treated the Indians fairly wherever they met them, although no doubt their attitude toward the red men was due to selfish motives rather than to any sense of humanity or decency. They well knew how the Indians were treated by the Spaniards; they knew that by treating them kindly and fairly they could win their confidence and friendship and thus enlist them as allies against the Dons; and, most of all, they were compelled to depend upon them very largely for food.

But, whatever the reason, they never molested or disturbed the aborigines. Even when, as often happened, the Indians of some hitherto untouched locality attacked them, the buccaneers never retaliated. Instead, they endeavored to mollify the savages, made overtures of friendship, gave them presents, or, if they found it impossible to make peace with them, left the spot and the natives to themselves. In all their records there is not a single instance of the pirates' maltreating or killing Indians except on occasions when the Dons had Indian friends who took part in battles against the buccaneers or in case of those who were the Spaniards' servants.

As a result, the corsairs always were welcomed to the Indian villages; they always found refuge there in time of need; and the Indians gladly supplied them with game, grain, and vegetables, and even with canoes and guides. Indeed, without the guides and the craft supplied by the Kunas and Chokois, Sharp's "dangerous voyage" could never have been accomplished, for it would have been out of the question for the buccaneers to cross the isthmus, to gain the Pacific, and to attack the Spanish fleet.

But even with the Indians' help the feat was marvelous. When one attempts to follow their route to-day and sees the country through which they traveled, one realizes the odds against them. So dense is the jungle that in many places it is impossible to proceed a yard without cutting a way through the tangle of lianas, thorny bush, spiny palms, poisonous plants, and tangled, razor-edged saw-grass. There are deep, swift rivers, precipitous mountain sides, impassable ravines; and yet through this wilderness these daring men forced a way led by their Indian friends—and got through safely.

It is bad enough to cross Darien afoot in the dry season, with every convenience, but the pirates, three hundred strong, undertook the journey in the rainy season, April, and for provisions had only "four cakes of bread" apiece, while their equipment consisted of a fusee, a pistol, and a hanger each. In order that there might be no mistake and their fellows be taken for enemies, the company was divided into seven parties, each carrying a flag of a distinguishing color. With six Indians as guides the three hundred and twenty-seven men set forth. Through the jungle and up the mountains they toiled, fording or swimming the streams, often crossing the same river a dozen times, beset by noxious insects, filled with superstitious fears of monstrous fabulous beasts, constantly drenched with rain but never halting, never hesitating. Here and there they came to Indian villages which, according to descriptions by Ringrose and Dampier, were exactly like those one finds in Darien to-day, and everywhere the friendly Indians supplied them with plantains, cassava, corn, and game. At last, without the loss of a man, and with fifty Indians who had joined the expedition, they reached the Santa Maria (now Tuira) River and embarked in sixty-eight canoes supplied by the Indians.

But Ringrose says:

> If we had been tired whilst traveling by land before, certainly we were in a worse condition in our canoes. For at a distance of every stone's cast we were constrained to get out of our boats and haul them over sand or rocks or over trees that lay across and filled up the river, yea, several times over the very points of land itself.

All of which very vividly and precisely describes the conditions one meets when traveling in Darien to-day, as I know from personal experience.

And when at last they gained the broader reaches of the river and swept down upon the little frontier town of El Real de Santa Maria, and with fifty men took the fort despite its garrison of two hundred and sixty men (with a loss among the pirates of only one killed and two wounded), they found to their chagrin that they were just too late. Only three days previously the accumulated treasure from the Caña mine—over three hundred pounds of gold ingots—had been taken by ship to Panama, and El Real was as bare as old Mother Hubbard's cupboard.

But the pirates had no mind to return empty-handed. The treasure had gone to Panama, and other riches were there, too, no doubt. So, tumbling into the frail dugouts, they started for the great city, nothing daunted, and, as already described in a previous chapter, boarded and captured the Spanish fleet, took possession of the flag-ship, and, transforming her into a pirate vessel, ravished the coast of South America, and eventually rounded the Horn, and reached the Caribbean in safety.

El Real is still in existence, and just below the present village one may yet see the crumbling ruins of the town Sharp and his men took at the conclusion of that terrible journey, through the jungle, from the Atlantic.

In the old days El Real de Santa Maria was an important outpost, the heavily guarded, stockaded repository of vast quantities of gold taken from La Caña and scores of other mines in the district; while to it from what is now Colombia were brought gold-dust and emeralds. But Sharp's raid spelled the doom of Darien. The Dons, realizing that where pirates had once crossed others could find a way, felt that treasure was unsafe there; mine after mine was abandoned, in fear of piratical forays and owing to constant uprisings among the Indians; garrisons were withdrawn and towns deserted, and the once incredibly rich district was left to half-wild negroes and primitive red men. What settlements are there to-day are miserable, squalid holes; the inhabitants are lazy and shiftless, and while Darien's forests are still dense with dyewoods, valuable timber, and medicinal plants, while its rivers still flow over golden sands, and while its mountains still hold fortunes in mineral wealth, it is for the most part an untamed, impenetrable wilderness.

CHAPTER XIX

PANAMA NEW AND OLD

THE Panama which Sharp and his men approached in their bobbing little canoes after that memorable trip across Darien, was the same city which still looks forth across the Pacific from the shadow of Ancon Hill. But it has altered greatly since the time when the pirates, knives in teeth, swarmed over the taffrails of the Spanish ships and in hand-to-hand battle won the day. And yet in many ways the description given of the town by Ringrose would serve as well for the present town. He says:

> It stands in a deep bay and in form is round, excepting only that part where it runs along the sea side. Formerly it stood four miles to the east where it was taken by Sir Henry Morgan but then being burnt they removed it to the place where it now stands. This new city of which I speak is much bigger than the old one and is built for the most part of brick, the rest being of stone and tiled. The churches (not yet finished) are eight in number, whereof the chief is called Santa Maria. The extent of the city comprehends better than a mile in breadth and a mile and a half in length. The houses for the most part are three stories high. It is well walled round about with two gates belonging

thereto, excepting only where a creek comes into the city, the which, at high water, lets in barks, to furnish the inhabitants with all sorts of necessities. . . . Round about the city for the space of seven leagues, more or less, all the country is savanna. Only here and there is to be seen a spot of woody land.

There the similarity of Ringrose's description to the present city ceases, for he goes on to say:

The ground whereon the city stands is very damp and moist, which renders the place of bad repute for the concern of health. The water is also very full of worms. Here, one night after our arrival, we found worms three quarters of an inch in length both in our bed clothes and other apparel.

Of very "bad repute" for the "concern of health" was Panama, not only in the buccaneers' days, but up to the time when Yankee engineers and Yankee energy and brains took charge and transformed the place from a pest-hole into a clean and sanitary city, wherein the death-rate is now as low as in the best of Northern cities. But no one except Ringrose has ever called attention to the "worms," though no doubt even to-day he or any one else would find numerous other detestable creatures both in his "bed clothes and other apparel" after a night spent in a native Panamanian hotel or on a Panamanian ship in the offing.

Unquestionably, could Ringrose and his comrades look upon Panama from the sea to-day they would recognize it, and could point out many a familiar landmark, for outwardly the town has altered little. The walls "round about" have disappeared in places, the "creek" is now dry land, and where it was are buildings and streets; and the eight churches, and more, have been finished, and many of them have crumbled to ruin in the long years since Sharp's literary pilot wrote his description. But the town is still "round" except where it "runs along the sea side." Its houses are still mainly of brick and stone and tiles, and are mostly two or three stories in height, and about it still stretch the savannas with their spots of "woody land."

But if the meticulous Ringrose could but step into Panama to-day he would find it a very different city from the one he knew. Along the smooth asphalt streets pass scores of jitneys, motor-cars, and rumbling trolley-cars. Busy shops and great stores line the narrow sidewalks, electric lights blaze everywhere at night, people of every color and nationality throng the thoroughfares; motor-driven fire-engines, glorious in red and gold, dash clangingly to infrequent fires. There are ice-plants and breweries, great power-plants and sawmills, cabarets and motion-picture theaters; a splendid, white concrete railway station and even electric signs. In other words, Panama to-day is thoroughly up-to-date, a modern, clean, busy, and attractive town, externally unaltered but internally completely transformed, while even more modern and typically American, in sharp contrast to the typically Spanish Panama, Ancon and Balboa rise upon the slopes of the hills behind the old city that Ringrose and Sharp looked upon. But despite its modernity in innumerable ways, Panama is still a bit of the Old World, a bit of old Spain, a city of Spanish architecture and Spanish plazas, with many a narrow, quaintly steep, and out-of-the-way street, where the jutting balconies and grilled windows almost meet above one's head; with many a spot where time seems to have stood still while the rest of the city went on, and with many a relic, many a survival of the Panama of three centuries ago.

At the tip-end of the city is the old fortress of Chiriqui and the Bovedas,—now used as a prison but still reminiscent of buccaneer days,—a rambling structure partly above and partly under ground, with low, broad walls and outstanding sentry-boxes, mellow with age and unchanged from the day when it was built for the purpose of keeping the dreaded and hated pirates from this treasure-house of Spain.

Along Avenue A, at the corner of Ninth Street, is the Herera Plaza, now a children's playground, the spot where the creek came into the city which at high water let in barks. And a few steps up the hill on Ninth Street, at the corner of Avenida Central, is the Piza Piza store, which was once the Hotel Aspinwall, and which, not so long ago, was at the waterfront of the same creek which Ringrose mentioned. Farther along Avenue A, fragments of that massive wall "round about the city with two gates" may be seen half concealed by houses and shops and partly in ruins but still frowning and grim wherever it stands, while on Eleventh Street it borders one side of the thoroughfare for nearly an entire block. This, in the days of Ringrose, was the limit of the city to the west, for Panama was by no means as large as he thought, but as it has grown it has overflowed the old walls and has left them isolated in the heart of the town like forgotten tombstones.

Some of the churches of which the pirate historian wrote are still to be seen, though mostly in ruins, for in the fire which swept the city in 1756 many of them were destroyed, and few were re-

PANAMA The ruins of the cathedral, and bit of wall, Old Panama

PANAMA All that is left of the ancient fort, Old Panama

PANAMA Ruins left from Morgan's raid, Old Panama

PANAMA Ruins of the governor's house, Old Panama

built. Santa Maria, the "chief" one mentioned by Ringrose, has been superseded by the cathedral with its pearl-shell-studded towers. San Francisco, on Bolivar Plaza, has been modernized, externally at least, until it is no longer recognizable, although its massive iron-studded portals with their gigantic knockers a dozen feet above the street are still there. Las Mercedes, at Avenida Central and occupying the block from Eighth to Ninth Street, and Santa Ana on Santa Ana Plaza have been kept in repair and remodeled. San Domingo, on Avenue A at Third Street, with its celebrated flat arch, is scarcely more than a ruin, and crumbling walls and falling masonry mark many another, while San Felipe de Neri, at Avenue B and Fourth Street, remains as it was in Ringrose's day. Doubtless the chronicler often looked upon its great walls, with stagings and ladders against them, and artisans at work, for San Felipe was being built at the time of the buccaneers' visit and was completed in 1688.

These old churches are very interesting, even those in ruins; veritable architectural curiosities, marvelous in their construction, for they were built of the wreckage salvaged from the ruins of Old Panama. Brick, cut stone, rubble, bits of ornately carved stone, odds and ends—a hodgepodge of material forms their walls, and often, amid the crumbling heterogeneous masonry, one may see some beautifully decorated niche with its carven saint still intact and with its paint-work and colored plaster as fresh and bright as though the rains and storms of centuries had not beaten upon it.

But the most interesting church of all, the most interesting spot in the whole of Panama City, is modest little San José at Eighth Street and Avenue A, a plain white building, bare-walled and unimpressive externally, but containing within the most gloriously dazzling sight in all the republic—the golden altar of San José, whose history reads like a romance and links the time of Morgan with the present. When the pirates took old San Lorenzo, at the mouth of the Chagres, and word was carried to Panama that the dreaded freebooters were on Panamanian soil and making for the city, the terrified inhabitants rushed madly to secrete and safeguard what treasures they possessed. The churches were filled with a wealth of gold and silver vessels, jeweled chalices and crucifixes, vestments heavy with gems and gold: and in San José, richest of all the houses of God in the treasure-filled town, was the famous, priceless altar of solid gold. Formed from the tithe of all gold that came to Panama which was paid the church, this marvelous structure was of plates of beaten metal beautifully chased, delicately fashioned—a masterpiece of art worth a fabulous sum for the metal alone.

Hastily the priests and monks gathered together their treasures, and the Fathers of San José dismantled their altar and, stripping their church, loaded their precious cargo on a waiting ship and put to sea, along with many another craft bearing wealth untold. When the pirates arrived, they found little in the way of ecclesiastical riches, and ships were seized and sent in chase of the vessels, for by means of torture Morgan had learned of their departure. But, though some were overhauled and their treasures looted, the craft bearing the golden altar of San José was never found.

Many of the ships that fled from the threatened city were never heard from; no one knows their fate. Some no doubt were wrecked on uninhabited parts of the coast, as befell on the shores of Darien. On others, perchance, the crews mutinied and, killing their officers, made off with the cargo, while rumor has it that much of the salvaged treasure was buried on outlying islets and cays to keep it secure from future pirate raids. But at any rate, chaos reigned after the destruction of the city, and when the Spaniards moved from the scene of slaughter and pillage and founded the new town the priests of San José builded themselves a church on Avenue A, a severely plain little building close to the city walls and near that creek that Ringrose mentions. And within their church, in place of the wondrous thing of gleaming gold, the priests erected an insignificant white altar. Through fire and flood, through lean and prosperous years, the little church and its modest altar passed in safety. Dread of pirates troubled the Fathers of San José not at all. They had nothing to tempt robbers, and gradually, as the years passed, the famous altar and its story were forgotten. But at last came a time when there was no longer fear of buccaneers, when the despotic rule of Spain was ended, when revolutions were no more, and when, under the protection of Uncle Sam, the new republic was sure of a peaceful and stable future.

Then, for a time, the Fathers of San José worked quietly and in secret; the little white altar was scraped and cleaned; and lo, the covering of paint removed, the golden altar once more blazed forth in all its long-forgotten glory!

There in the unimposing little church it stands, beneath a great window of rich stained-glass through which the sun beats down in dazzling radiance upon the burnished surface of the mass of gold. Unchanged in all its delicate chasing and engraving, as beautiful and wonderful as when it shone in its brilliancy in old Panama, the altar of San José has endured through the centuries, unsuspected, a secret known only to the Fathers of the church, to burst from its chrysalis of white paint when the time was ripe. Probably it is the only treasure that survived the pirates' raid and still exists, the only remnant of that stupendous store of priceless treasure which made Old Panama famous as the richest city of New Spain.

But aside from this altar, so strangely and romantically saved from the pillage and destruction of Panama, there is much to be seen of the old city laid low by Morgan and his men. By motor-car one may travel easily and quickly to the spot, a scant five miles along the shore from the present city.

First of the ruins to be seen is the low, arched bridge of stone, partly fallen but still spanning a little tidal stream—the very bridge across which Morgan and his pirates swarmed on that fateful day in 1671. Beyond and to the left is the still massive ruin of a great building; to the right are others; and standing, still majestic, above all, is the tower of the old cathedral, all that remains of St. Anastasio. In its roofless aisles great trees have grown; from crevices and chinks in the masonry, plants, bushes, and vines have sprung; but still the tower stands intact, the same "beautiful building whereof makes a fair show at a distance like that of St. Paul's in London," as Ringrose described it.

But it took a homesick seaman who had been long absent from London Town, and had, perchance, dim memories of St. Paul's, to see the similarity between that mighty pile and St. Anastasio's lonely tower. Still, it is impressive as it stands there, a vivid reminder of the pirates' ruthlessness, a fitting monument to the countless innocent people who died within its shadow and whose bones have long since crumbled to dust among the undergrowth of this forsaken spot.

Close to the old church and at the very edge of the sea, still stands a remnant of the city wall and the forts at the harbor mouth, and scattered about among the underbrush are many other walls and ruins.

Unappreciative of such matters, though ever boastful of the ruins, the Panamanians have allowed the site of Old Panama to be defiled by a disreputable cantina or drinking- and dance-hall; and they have neglected the place until, for the most part, it is a mere tangle, a miniature jungle of weeds, bushes, and trees.

Dr. Dexter, while superintendent of the schools of Panama, devoted a great deal of time to a thorough investigation of the ruins; and with the aid of natives, supplied by the Government, the place was cleaned of brush, and careful measurements and plans were made. From these Dr. Dexter modeled a reproduction of the ruins of accurate scale, and then secured from the archives of Seville copies of the original reports and descriptions of Panama as it was in Morgan's day.

From these data we know that the city was very different from the generally accepted ideas of that "goode and statelye city" which Esquemelling described as having "two thousand houses of magnificent and prodigeous building, being all or the greatest part inhabited by merchants of that country, who are vastly rich. For the rest of the inhabitants of lesser quality and tradesmen, this city contained five thousand houses more." If by "magnificent and prodigeous building" the chronicler of the raid meant stone or brick buildings, then he was utterly at fault, for the official records show that there were few buildings of stone or of note, and that the majority of the houses, as well as some of the public buildings, were of wattled cane, wood, and adobe thatched with palm. Moreover, the bulk of these were little more than huts, and in the official description of the town the dwellings were divided into two classes,—those with floors and those without,—and those minus flooring were greatly in the majority.

But there is no reason to think that Esquemelling meant that the "magnificent and prodigeous building" or the lesser houses were of stone. Indeed, he specifically says: "All the houses of this city were built with cedar, being of a very curious and magnificent structure." Had the town been of solid stone and masonry, as has been assumed (although the buccaneers' accounts do not state this), it would have been a difficult matter to burn it to the ground, whereas we can readily understand how the conflagration swept the hundreds of flimsy wooden and cane structures before it and left only the indestructible stone walls and buildings standing.

Unquestionably, in comparison with other cities of its day Panama was a "goode and statelye" town, for it contained the massive St. Anastasio Cathedral, seven monasteries, and two nunneries; at least four churches, a hospital, a great number of stables wherein were kept the horses and mules used in transporting treasure and merchandise over the Gold Road; a huge public market; a "statelye and magnificent house belonging to the Genoese for their trade and commerce in negroes"; a number of big warehouses; barracks; a governor's house; a vault wherein were stored the treasures to be transported; and several forts, most of which were of massive stone construction. The ruins of all of these may still be traced, although the greater portion of the ruined churches, monasteries, and other buildings were torn down and the material carried to the new city of Panama, where it was used in constructing the buildings.

In clearing up the ruins, Dr. Dexter also secured an enormous collection of odds and ends, many of which were of great historical interest. There were bottles and glassware; crockery; buttons; coins; remains of daggers, guns, and pistols; sword hilts; locks; household utensils, et cetera. Some of them were in a good state of preservation, but most of them had been partly melted by the flames and illustrated graphically the terrific heat of the fire which Esquemelling tells us "continued for four weeks after the day it began."

Never in the history of piracy has there been such wanton destruction. Not only was the city burned, but, out of pure villainy, Morgan set the torch to two hundred warehouses in which the pirate chief had placed "great numbers of slaves together with an infinite number of sacks of meal."

There has been much confusion as to the origin of the fire, and it has been contended that it was accidental, or that the residents started the blaze in order to keep the pirates from occupying the town. But there is not the least question that it was the deliberate act of Morgan, who was in a frenzy of demoniacal rage when he found that after his hard battle and heavy losses the bulk of the valuables had been "transported to remote and occult places." Esquemelling, who was present at the sack of the town and who should know the truth, states particularly:

> The same day about noon [the day the town was taken] he caused certain men privately to set fire to several great edifices of the city, nobody knowing whence the fire proceeded nor who were the authors thereof, much less what motives persuaded Captain Morgan thereto, which are as yet unknown to this day.

But he goes on to say:

> Captain Morgan endeavored to make the public believe the Spaniards had been the cause thereof, which suspicions he surmised among his own people, perceiving they reflected upon him for that action.

That the houses were, as I have said, of flimsy construction is evident from Esquemelling's statement that "in less than half an hour the fire consumed a whole street"; and later he says, speaking of the Genoese slave market: "This building likewise was commanded by Captain Morgan to be set on fire; whereby it was burnt to the ground."

Doubtless the villainous Morgan, finding his own men demurred at thus destroying a city without cause (and perhaps realizing that by so doing he could not demand the usual ransom), endeavored to put the blame on the unfortunate inhabitants, as Esquemelling says, but he was a ready liar, an utterly unprincipled scoundrel, and time and again betrayed the trust his men placed in him. So there is no use in trying to lessen the blackness of his character by endeavoring to absolve him of the crime of burning old Panama or of cremating the helpless slaves.

The taking of the city was the most noteworthy exploit cvcr performed by the buccaneers; in accomplishing it they displayed unparalleled bravery; they endured untold hardships and sufferings; they conquered against overwhelming odds, and with a scant one thousand men Morgan achieved what many a general with an army at his back would have hesitated to undertake. But he spoiled all by his execrable cruelty and by wanton, ruthless destruction, and to the end of time the sack of Panama will remain as the most utterly disgraceful and detestable crime of the British buccaneers. As long as the crumbling stones of Old Panama stand they will remain mute testimonials of the most despicable act of that most despicable rascal, Sir Henry Morgan.

CHAPTER XX

HOW MORGAN KEPT HIS PROMISE

WHEN Morgan sent his pistol and his bullets to the viceroy of Panama with word that he would call for them in person within the twelvemonth, it is doubtful if he dreamed of doing so. But there is many a true word spoken in jest, and Harry Morgan was ever fond of jesting—in earnest. While pressing matters delayed him elsewhere and the twelve months passed without his appearance at Panama (for which, no doubt, the viceroy gave fervid thanks to his saints), yet all too soon for the Dons he kept his half-joking promise to the letter.

Having established his reputation as a buccaneer leader by the successful if not very remunerative attack on Puerto Principe, Morgan proceeded to equip a fleet and recruit men for a still greater coup, which was nothing less than a descent upon Maracaibo. Never in the history of this unfortunate town, which had been repeatedly ravished by pirates, were such cruelties and inhumanities practised as by Morgan and his ruffians. Even Lolonais, who had been there, could not invent atrocities so fiendish as those devised and put into execution by the British buccaneer, and when at last he sailed away he left the place fairly heaped with burned, racked, broken, and dying men and women.

But so successful had he been, so cleverly had he outwitted the Spanish fleet sent to block his exit from the Lake of Maracaibo, and so complete had been his victory over the Spanish ships of war that his prestige was enormously increased, and he at once began to plan greater deeds.

Compared with the plan Morgan now had in mind, his former exploits had been mere bagatelles, for his intention was to gather together the most tremendous pirate fleet ever assembled and with it attack Vera Cruz, Cartagena, or Panama. All three were marvelously rich towns, and all three were heavily fortified. While Panama promised by far the greatest loot, yet the difficulties to be overcome in taking it seemed well-nigh insurmountable.

Although, as Esquemelling mentions, Morgan's name and fame were enough to bring him more men and ships than he could employ, still, to make sure of gathering a large enough force, Morgan sent letters to "all the ancient and expert pirates inhabiting Tortuga," to the half-wild hunters and planters of Haiti, and to the rascals on Trade Wind Cay. In ships, canoes, and boats the buccaneers came, responding to his summons from far and near, even traversing the forests of Hispaniola on foot, until on October 24, 1670, the army of cutthroats was assembled.

To provision his expedition, Morgan despatched four ships to Rio de la Hacha, where the crews sacked the town, tortured the inhabitants, and secured four thousand bushels of maize. In the meantime, his men had been busy hunting, and thus thoroughly provisioned, with bucanned meat and corn, the fleet set sail from La Vaca Island, and at Cape Tiburon, Haiti, met those who were coming from Jamaica.

The fleet now numbered thirty-seven ships, the largest of which was Morgan's, mounting twenty-two large and six small guns, while the smallest vessel carried four. Never in the annals of piracy had such a fleet been seen, and with two thousand fighting fiends, in addition to the sailors, Morgan felt confident that he could take any city of the Spanish Main.

When the other captains were summoned to a council and lots were drawn to decide their objective, the choice fell upon Panama. So dangerous did the pirates consider this adventure that the usual accident insurance to be paid for loss of limbs, eyes, et cetera, was greatly increased, fifteen hundred pieces of eight being adjudged right for the loss of both legs, eighteen hundred for the loss of both hands, six hundred for either leg, the same for a hand, and one hundred pieces of eight for an eye. In addition, heavy rewards were offered for special acts of bravery, and the usual bonuses of the officers were increased.

All this being arranged, the flotilla set sail, but Morgan had no mind to leave an enemy in his rear and decided first to attack and conquer Old Providence (St. Catherine). Not only would this leave a way clear for his retreat, but, in addition, he well knew that countless outlaws and bandits were deported to this island from Panama and that these scoundrels would serve him well as guides.

So great was Morgan's fame by now that the governor of Old Providence made no show of resistance,—although the place was heavily fortified and well garrisoned,—and offered to surrender provided Morgan would enter into a scheme by which his Excellency might save his face, and his neck as well. This was nothing more nor less than for Morgan to make a sham attack which the governor would pretend to resist. The scheme was carried out; the island fell into the buccaneers' hands without a real blow being struck, and the pirates at once proceeded to rob the people. They destroyed the forts, spiked the guns, and secured thirty thousand pounds of powder, vast amounts of ammunition, and several hundred muskets.

As Morgan had foreseen, there were outlawed bandits on the island, and three of these gladly offered to join his ranks. The next step in the game was in a way the most difficult of all, for in order to reach Panama or to ascend the Chagres River it was necessary to silence Fort San Lorenzo at the river's mouth, a fortification which was considered absolutely impregnable and had been strengthened and more heavily armed since the capture of Porto Bello two years previously.

Making the excuse that if he sent his entire fleet the Dons would suspect his designs upon Panama, but unquestionably in reality preferring not to risk his own precious life in the taking of a place which would yield no loot, Morgan sent four ships with four hundred men under charge of Captain Brodely (one of the "ancient and expert pirates" referred to by Esquemelling), with orders to take San Lorenzo.

Although all the credit for this spectacularly daring and almost hopeless task is always given to Morgan, he actually had no hand in it, but waited in safety at St. Catherine, enjoying good wine and excellent food while Brodely took all the risks and paved the way for the descent upon Panama.

Never in all their savage conflicts did the pirates do harder and more desperate fighting than that at San Lorenzo. We are so accustomed to hearing of the buccaneers' uninterrupted victories that we have come to think that the Spaniards were cravens, and that they offered little resistance to their enemies. But this is a great mistake. Even the buccaneers freely acknowledged the courage, the determination, and the valor of the Spanish troops. In every case, with the exception of the treacherous surrender of Old Providence by its governor, the Spaniards fought like furies, and in nearly every battle they performed feats of bravery that won the greatest admiration and praise from the pirates. But they were always taken by surprise, were always at a disadvantage, and they were not the adepts at hand-to-hand fighting that the buccaneers were.

Never before had the pirates been so hard put to it as in the taking of the massive fort that guarded the entrance to the Chagres. For an entire night and the following day the battle raged, and when at last the fort was in the hands of the buccaneers they found but thirty men remaining of the three hundred and fourteen who had formed its garrison, and *not one officer was left alive.* Indeed, many of the Spaniards, finding the place was about to fall, cast themselves from the parapets into the river, or upon the rocks at the base of the cliffs, rather than surrender to the hated English.

And had it not been for a mere accident it is questionable if the pirates could have won the day. For hours they had made not the least headway, for outside of the fortress proper were heavy palisades of stakes set in double rows and filled between with earth, and so galling was the fire from the soldiers that, try as they might, the attacking force could not approach these to set them afire or pull them down. But during an assault an arrow from the fort struck one of the pirates in the back and passed completely through his body.

With a curse the fellow dragged the arrow from the wound, wrapped a bit of rag about it, rammed it down his musket, and fired it at the Spaniards. Mad with pain as he was, his only thought was to use the first missile that came to hand, but his act won the day for the buccaneers. The cotton cloth, catching fire from the powder, dropped upon the tinder-like thatch of a house within the fort, and in an instant it was in flames. Close at hand was a great quantity of powder, and ere the Dons realized what had occurred there was a terrific explosion which killed many of the soldiers, dismounted several cannon, and caused consternation and confusion among the defenders of the fort. Taking advantage of this, the pirates rushed the works. fired and pulled down the palisades, and clambering across the moat, which was filled with the earth falling from between the palisades, gained the interior of the fortress.

But the fight was by no means over. Inch by inch the Spaniards contested the pirates' advance, fighting furiously with swords, pistols, and even sticks and stones, while others sought desperately to extinguish the fire now raging within the castle. Although the buccaneers had made the breach and had entered the inner fortifications soon after midnight, yet they had gained not a dozen yards at noon on the following day, and back and forth the battle raged, first one side, then the other, gaining an advantage, while dead and wounded fell on every hand, and Dons and Britons were piled deep in bloody heaps. Soon after noon, however, the pirates gained a breach where the Spanish governor himself with a company of picked *corps de garde* was stationed, and after desperate hand-to-hand fighting the brave governor fell with a musket ball through his brain.

Demoralized by the death of their leader, the *corps de garde* surrendered, when, to their amazement, the pirates found that, besides these twenty-five picked men, only *five* Spaniards remained alive and that of the thirty survivors more than twenty were seriously wounded.

The pirates also had lost heavily; in fact, their losses were the greatest they had ever suffered in an attack, for over one hundred men had been killed, and more than seventy were seriously wounded.

Forcing the captured Spaniards to cast the dead bodies over the walls into the river, the victorious pirates then shut the wounded men and the few women into the stone church above the fort and proceeded to repair the damages, after sending word of the victory to Morgan.

But the leader's plans had in a way fallen through, for he had thought to take San Lorenzo quickly and to annihilate the Dons, so that no warning of the pirates' approach would reach Panama. Despite the ferocity of the assault, the desperate fighting, and the fact that the fortress was constantly surrounded by the buccaneers, a party of eight daring Spaniards volunteered to attempt to get through the pirates' lines, make their way to the capital, and give warning of the enemy's approach. It seemed an all but hopeless undertaking, but the men succeeded. They reached Panama in safety, and ere Morgan started up the river on his way across the isthmus the inhabitants knew of his coming and were preparing to meet him.

Before leaving Old Providence, en route to San Lorenzo and Panama, Morgan sacked the island, put the town and all the houses to the torch, and, leaving only the one fortress of Santa Teresa, which he garrisoned with his own men, he made prisoners of the people, placed them aboard his ships, and set sail for the Chagres. At the mouth of the river four of his ships went on the bar and were lost, among them the flag-ship, but by heroic efforts all lives were saved—with the exception of a few score of Spanish captives, who were of course of no account whatsoever in the pirates' estimation!

Reaching captured San Lorenzo, Morgan hoisted the British colors over it (the rascal invariably committed his villainies under the British ensign), and, chaining his prisoners in gangs, he forced them to labor from dawn till dark at repairing the fortress, setting up a new palisade, and remounting the guns. He had no intention of leaving the Chagres unguarded so that a Spanish fleet could enter and bottle him up on the isthmus. Having reconditioned the fortress and garrisoned it with five hundred men, in addition to one hundred and fifty men on the ships anchored in the stream, he felt quite secure and with twelve hundred desperate pirates he and his fellows embarked in five large boats and thirty-two canoes and started up the Chagres.

At the spot called Cruz de Juan Gallego, which they reached on the second day, the company were compelled to desert their boats, for it was the middle of the dry season (January) and the river was so low that farther navigation was impossible.

Then began a journey of hardship, suffering, and dogged perseverence which is almost unparalleled. The pirates had carried few provisions, expecting to supply themselves from settlements and Indian camps on the way, but word had gone ahead of their coming, every village and camp was deserted, fields had been destroyed, and provisions taken away. Day after day they tramped on, ever rushing madly toward some clearing or group of huts, only to curse and rave when they found them deserted, surrounded by smoking, blackened gardens, and without a morsel of anything that could be eaten.

On the fourth day so ravenous had the men grown that they actually devoured their leathern wallets, in order, as Esquemelling informs us, "to afford something to the ferment of their stomachs, which was now grown so sharp that it did gnaw their very bowels, having nothing else to prey upon." Maddened with hunger, they even fought over the scraps of leather, and their chronicler continues: "Thus they made a huge banquet upon those bags of leather, which doubtless had been more grateful unto them if divers quarrels had not arisen as to who should have the greatest share." Indeed, they were ready for cannibalism, and Esquemelling, referring to the Spaniards they hoped to meet, says, "Whom they would certainly in that occasion have roasted or boiled to satisfy their famine."

But neither Dons nor foodstuffs were forthcoming, and with hunger somewhat assuaged by their meal of leather they plodded wearily on, most of them bereft even of the leathern equipment to devour, while a few, who were more fortunate, had reserved a portion of their former rations. "Here again he was happy," says their historian, "that had reserved since noon any small piece of leather whereof to make his supper."

Furthermore, Esquemelling goes into details regarding the culinary phase of this leathern diet, evidently thinking that some future traveler on the isthmus might find it of value in preparing an evening meal. He says:

> Some persons who were never out of their mothers' kitchens may ask how these Pyrates could eat, swallow and digest these pieces of leather so hard and dry. To whom I only answer: That could they once experiment with hunger, or rather famine, is that they would certainly find the manner, by their own necessity as the Pyrates did. For these first took the leather and sliced it in pieces. Then did they beat it between two stones and rub it, often dipping it in the water of the river to render it by these means supple and tender. Lastly they scraped off the hair and roasted or broiled it upon the fire. And being thus cooked they cut it into small morsels and eat it, helping it down with frequent gulps of water, which by good fortune they had near at hand.

Evidently there was some sustenance in the dried hides, for there is no mention of any one having died of starvation, but hunger was not the only trouble with which the company met. At every turn they were beset by ambuscades; they were harassed by Indian allies of the Dons, who shot poisoned arrows from the woods and hurled down rocks in narrow defiles, until on the sixth day they discovered a cave containing two sacks of meal, a few plantains, and two jars of wine. This providential find was distributed by Morgan among the weakest men, who were put into canoes; and, heartened and encouraged, the great troop pressed on and on the following day found a store of maize in an Indian camp. On the seventh day they also captured some emaciated cats and dogs which had been deserted by the fleeing natives, and these they instantly killed and devoured. On the same day they found sixteen jars of wine which they gulped down, only to fall deathly sick as a result.

And yet not one man complained, not one thought of turning back. Ahead lay Panama and its vast treasure; and subsisting on stray dogs and cats and half-burnt corn, or going hungry, the company stumbled ever onward, until, on the ninth day after leaving San Lorenzo, they ascended a hill and saw the vast Pacific stretching to the horizon.

Filled with joy, shouting and laughing and cursing by turns, the pirates hurried down the hill and reached a vale where a herd of donkeys and horses and a few cattle were grazing. Falling upon these beasts, the pirates slaughtered them, half roasted the still quivering flesh over fires, and had their first full meal in more than a week. Esquemelling says of them:

"Such was their hunger that they more resembled cannibals than Europeans at this banquet, the blood many times running down from their beards to the middle of their bodies."

Having finished the meal and satisfied themselves with "these delicious morsels," the men resumed the march, and a little later they came within sight of the tower of the cathedral—that same stone tower that to-day stands alone and in ruins beside the sea. Here they pitched camp for the night and, "sounding their trumpets and drums" (which are not usually associated with pirates), prepared to attack the city at break of day. That same evening a troop of fifty cavalry approached almost within musket shot, taunted the pirates with derisive shouts, and retired to the city, leaving a few scouts to watch the enemy's movements. Soon after this the big guns of the city began to thunder, the shots falling about the pirates' camp but doing no damage.

The following morning the buccaneers formed in columns, sounded their trumpets, and with drums beating marched toward the doomed town, choosing a trail through the woods to avoid attacks by the cavalry. In the meantime the governor of Panama had gathered two squadrons of cavalry, four regiments of infantry, a huge herd of wild bulls, and a number of Indians and negroes to resist the invaders. Coming from the woods and looking down upon the plain, the pirates were amazed at the forces arrayed against them, and for the first time became doubtful of their success.

Indeed, as their chronicler puts it: "Yea few or none there were but wished themselves at home, or at least free from the obligation of that engagement, wherein they perceived their lives must be narrowly concerned."

But needs must when the devil drives, and the devil himself was there in the person of Morgan. Being ordered to advance, the company marched against the Dons. Fortunately for the pirates, heavy rains had rendered the ground soft and soggy, the cavalry could not manœuver, and the first squadron of two hundred pirates fired such a well-aimed volley of musketry that "the battle was instantly kindled very hot." Although the fire was returned with vigor, and despite the Spaniards' "valiant attempts," the pirates succeeded in separating the various groups of soldiery and fell upon them tooth and nail. Thinking to demoralize the enemy, the Spaniards drove herds of bulls against them, but the cattle, frightened at the firing and the drums, scattered and ran away, while the few that broke through the pirates' ranks were quickly killed and did no damage.

For two hours the battle raged, the Spanish cavalry suffering almost total annihilation. The infantry, seeing the tide of battle turning in favor of the enemy, threw down their arms and took to their heels. But the exhausted pirates, after days of suffering and hours of fierce fighting, could not follow up the advantage. They contented themselves with hunting the wounded Spaniards down, murdering them in cold blood, and capturing some priests and taking them before Morgan, who had them instantly pistoled.

From one captive captain Morgan learned by means of torture that the entire force in the city was less than three thousand, and, also discovering how the forts and guns were disposed, he planned to change his route to the city. But the pirates had not won the day without loss, though their three hundred men killed or wounded were far less than the six hundred dead and several hundred wounded among the Dons.

With their captives in the van, the pirates rushed on the town, fighting doggedly at every turn, cut down by volleys of musketry and cannon shot, mutilated by scrap-iron with which the Spaniards had charged their howitzers, and after three hours of desperate fighting and heavy loss won the low-arched bridge and poured, shouting and yelling, into the town.

Then hell broke loose in earnest. The buccaneers, mad with fighting, frenzied at the losses inflicted upon them, drunk with lust of blood, ran hither and thither, shooting, cutting, stabbing all they met; looting right and left, yelling like fiends, and ripping and tearing tapestries, hangings, and paintings from the houses.

With difficulty, and only after shooting down several of his men, Morgan succeeded in gathering them together and commanded them under threat of the most severe punishment to refrain from touching wines or liquor,—not that he had any scruples against drinking, but because he feared poison. Also, no doubt he wished to prevent his men from becoming so befuddled with drink that the Spaniards could retake the city.

This matter being settled, Morgan turned his men loose once more, and from building to building, from house to house they ran, slashing priceless furnishings, battering down doors, trampling silks and velvets underfoot, destroying, murdering, looting. From their hiding-places they dragged cowering, trembling women, and in a stream the captives and the loot were carried to Morgan.

But, as we have seen, the most valuable treasures, the gold and silver and jewels of the churches, the bulk of plate and bullion from the treasury, the greatest private fortunes, had been carried to sea, and Morgan, in a towering rage, sent vessels in chase and in his fury burned the town. In addition, he sent searching parties into the woods and these returning brought prisoners from far and near about the country-side, who were "presently put to the most exquisite tortures imaginable to make them confess both other people's goods and their own."

One man happened to be garbed in "taffety breeches" belonging to his master, and the pirates assumed from his raiment that he was a person of position. Moreover, he had a small silver key hanging at his belt. Questioned as to where the cabinet to which the key belonged was secreted, the poor trembling fellow declared he was a servant and knew not where his master had taken the cabinet. Instantly, Morgan had the terrified, babbling serving-man placed upon the rack and disjointed. This failed to wring from his tortured lips the secret he was supposed to know, and the pirates twisted a cord about his forehead until, as Esquemelling assures us, "his eyes appeared as big as eggs and were ready to fall from his skull." Finding that even this had not the desired result, Morgan had him hung up, beat him almost to death, cut off his ears and nose, singed his face with burning straw, and finally had a negro run him through with a lance and put an end to his agonies.

"After this execrable manner did many others

of those miserable prisoners finish their days," says Esquemelling, and adds: "The common sport and recreation of these Pyrates being these and other tragedies not inferior."

Sex or age made no difference. Children and women were tortured, ravished, and murdered, although when those of evident high standing and wealth were taken, they were usually put aside and kept in safety for ransom.

For three long weeks the pirates wrought their will in Panama; and then, having scraped it bare, having desolated the country about, and having secured every man and woman within reach, Morgan prepared to leave. On February 24, 1671, he evacuated the ruined town and with one hundred and seventy-five mules laden with gold, silver, and precious stones, silks and velvets, satins and brocades, and accompanied by over six hundred prisoners began his return march toward San Lorenzo and the Atlantic.

With fiendish cruelty Morgan ordered that the poor captives, most of whom were women and children, should be given barely enough food and water to keep them alive, his idea being, as our old friend Esquemelling explains, that "it would excite them more earnestly to seek money wherewith to ransom themselves according to the tax which had been set upon every one."

Never had the great forest trees and the smiling plains looked upon a more pitiful, a more harrowing scene than that of those starved and thirsty prisoners marching under the broiling sun, urged on with curses, coarse jests, and blows; wading rivers, stumbling through muck, clad in laces and silks and high-heeled, flimsy shoes, and bareheaded. Bereft of homes and loved ones, unaccustomed to hardship, unused to walking a dozen rods, these delicate, carefully nurtured ladies were flogged like beasts, and subjected to every insult and indignity. If they dropped from hunger or exhaustion, a blow from a pirate followed; if they stumbled and fell, they were jerked to their feet by their disheveled hair. "Nothing else was heard but lamentations, cries, shrieks and doleful sighs," said Esquemelling, and many fell by the wayside and were ruthlessly trampled underfoot or more mercifully run through with a cutlass still stained with the blood of those cut down in the city. Many of the women fell upon their knees, begging Morgan to put an end to their sufferings with death, or to let them return to the bodies of those they loved; but to all the callous brute, who was later honored by the King of England, replied that "he came not thither to hear lamentations and cries but rather to seek money."

Though the villain was unmoved by the sights and scenes which should have melted a heart of stone, yet on that dreadful march he showed a streak of gallantry which he was known occasionally to exhibit. Among the prisoners taken at Panama was one "beautiful and virtuous lady," a woman of wealth and refinement whom Morgan had selected for himself. But she being, as Esquemelling says, "in all respects like unto Susannah for constancy," and having refused Morgan's offers of pearls, gold, and money, and likewise having repulsed his amorous advances, Morgan stripped the rich garments from her back and cast her into a dungeon on a scant diet of bread and water. But so beautiful was the captive, and so brave and virtuous, that even the rough buccaneers took pity upon her, and Morgan, realizing that he had overstepped the bounds of even pirate propriety, released her and held her for ransom.

On the second day of the march this abused lady's lamentations "now did pierce the skies," and she declared to the two ruffians who guarded her that she had given orders to two priests to go to a certain spot and bring her ransom, that they had promised to do so, but, having secured the cash, had made use of it to ransom one of their own brotherhood. The pirate guards carried the story to Morgan, who at once halted his march, interviewed a slave who had brought the lady word of the friars' duplicity, and even apprehended the priests and wrung a confession from them. Thereupon he placed his hand on his heart, swept the ground with his plumed hat, begged a thousand pardons of his captive beauty, set her at liberty, provided her with an armed escort to accompany her to her home, and —wonder of wonders!—presented her with the ransom money as a gift! Not content with this, he hanged the two deceitful priests from the nearest tree, and calmly proceeded on his way.

It is needless to dwell upon that terrible march across the isthmus, the sack of towns en route, the sufferings of the captives, or the voyage down the Chagres. On March 9th the buccaneers and all their prisoners and loot arrived at San Lorenzo, and at once complaints arose that Morgan had retained more than his share of the loot. For when the vast treasure was divided as Morgan saw fit, it was found that the pirates received but a paltry two hundred pieces of eight each for their share. But though his followers accused him openly of cheating, none dared offer personal violence, and he ordered the fort demolished, the guns taken aboard the buccaneers' ships, and the buildings burned. Then, while the men were busy at these tasks, the detestable scoundrel sneaked off, boarded his own ship, and having secretly seized all the available provisions, sailed away, leaving his followers to fare as best they might—which was ill indeed.

Never in the history of the pirates had any captain been disloyal to his men in this way, and had the buccaneers been able to lay hands upon him Morgan's career would have come to an abrupt as well as unpleasant end, then and there. Realizing that to go to Tortuga would mean falling into the wronged men's hands, Morgan sailed boldly to Port Royal, where he was promptly arrested and, in company with the governor, was sent a prisoner to England. The rest of his story I have told. Knighted and honored, he came back to Jamaica as lieutenant-governor, a pirate Judas, to betray and hang his own men. He died in obscurity, but his deeds, nefarious as they were, will live forever. For years to come the ruins of old Panama will stand beside the Pacific, everlasting monuments to his ruthless villainy, and upon its bluff old San Lorenzo still stands, grim, frowning, but deserted! Its moat is dry and choked with weeds, its guns lie dismounted and thick with rust; its vast underground passages and rooms are empty; its parapets are crumbling away. But within its dungeons may still be seen the manacles that held the few survivors of that bloody battle; beneath the massive walls the Chagres still ripples gently on its way to the sea; upon the bar the waves still break and roar where Morgan's ships went down.

Standing here to-day, it is hard to realize that once the peaceful spot rang to the clash of steel, the crash of musketry, and the roar of cannon; that curses and shots, cries of St. Jago and St. George, shrieks of dying men, and the groans of wounded echoed from the hills; that these ancient, weather-beaten stones once ran with blood; that the weed-grown slopes were dotted with dead and dying men; that bodies lay piled in heaps about the sally-ports and guns, and that Don and buccaneer struggled in mortal combat where now georgeous butterflies flit from flower to flower in the sun and swallows nest beneath the parapets.

For centuries old San Lorenzo has thus stood. For centuries it will stand. It is almost as enduring as the living rock on which it rests. Fire and shot have scarcely left a scar upon it. The pirates' greatest efforts at destruction made hardly an impression. The elements affect it little, and until its last age-gray stone has crumbled to dust it will bind the present with the past, and the past with Morgan—the greatest pirate of them all, the most daring, most famous, and most villainous of the buccaneers.